Business Communication
Process and Product
Fourth Edition

Mary Ellen Guffey

Professor of Business, Emeritus

Los Angeles Pierce College

THOMSON

SOUTH-WESTERN

Australia · Canada · Mexico · Singapore · Spain · United Kingdom · United States

THOMSON

SOUTH-WESTERN

Study Guide to accompany *Business Communication: Process and Product*, 4e
by Mary Ellen Guffey

Vice President/Team Leader:
Melissa Acuna

Acquisitions Editor:
Pamela M. Person

Developmental Editor:
Mary Draper

Marketing Manager:
Marc Callahan

Production Editor:
Kelly Keeler

Manufacturing Coordinator:
Diane Lohman

Production House/Compositor:
Word Crafters Editorial Services, Inc./
GGS, Inc.

Printer:
Patterson Printing, Benton Harbor, MI

Cover Designer:
Tin Box Studio, Inc.

Cover Photographer/Illustrator:
Heidi Stevens

ISBN: 0-324-11454-0

Preface

This Study Guide will be an important resource to you for many reasons. Its exercises supplement and reinforce the concepts presented in Guffey's *Business Communication: Process and Product, 4e.* With the help of this guide, you can try out your knowledge of the chapter concepts and practice its principles. You'll also be able to preview sample test questions.

Employment Interview Kit. In this edition of the Study Guide we've included an Employment Interview Kit to supplement Chapter 16, Employment Communication. In this kit you'll learn how to ace a job interview. The kit includes tips for fighting fear and for sending positive nonverbal messages. Most important are the lists of commonly asked interview questions (and some answers!) as well as questions for you to ask.

Each Study Guide chapter contains similar elements to help you master course content and expand your communication skills.

- **Chapter review of key concepts**. A variety of questions (including fill-in, multiple-choice, true-false, and matching) outline key chapter concepts. These questions include page references in the textbook so that you can easily confirm answers and review your responses.

- **Career track spelling**. Because in any career you will be judged by your communication skills—including your ability to spell—you have an opportunity to hone those skills in regular exercises. Chapter 1 reviews useful spelling guidelines, and each subsequent chapter includes a self-checked exercise. The complete list of spelling words, from which most of the words are taken, appears in Appendix A.

- **Career track vocabulary**. A wide vocabulary enables you to express your ideas clearly. To expand your word power, each chapter includes 15 challenging vocabulary words, along with 5 or 6 confusing words for you to master. Appendix A contains the complete list and definitions of confusing words.

- **Competent Language Usage Essentials (C.L.U.E.).** Each chapter concentrates on a few guidelines that review English grammar, punctuation, and usage. Particular attention is given to troublesome concepts on which business communicators sometimes stumble. C.L.U.E. review exercises and Super C.L.U.E. (cumulative) reviews help you master these guidelines.

- **Career track application and critical thinking.** In chapters that teach letter-, memo-, and report-writing, you will be given a realistic assignment that applies your learning. Critical thinking questions help you analyze the assignment and organize your response. After preparing a document, you can turn to the solutions in Appendix B and compare your response with the key to see how you stack up. Naturally, you'll want to complete your application exercise before examining the key.

We designed this self-checked Study Guide to help you master chapter concepts and to expand your communication skills. Like the textbook, it contains many visual elements to enhance its readability and interest.

Begin by reading and studying the textbook chapter. Then complete the study guide chapter review questions and check your answers. Reread any sections in the textbook that caused you trouble. Finally, complete the remaining study guide exercises and check those responses. I am convinced that your careful efforts will be rewarded with skills that will pay big dividends for you and your career.

Mary Ellen Guffey

Acknowledgments

Personal Thanks

The author wishes to thank Lorraine Korkosz for her contribution of insightful and challenging sentences in the Career Track Spelling and Vocabulary exercises.

References

Page 74   Claire Kehrwald Cook, *Line by Line* (Modern Language Association and Houghton Mifflin, Boston: 1985), 137.

Page 114   Claire Kehrwald Cook, 17.

Page 91   Andrew S. Grove, *Quotable Business*, Louis E. Boone, ed. (New York: Random House, 1992), 61.

Page 198   "A talk is ..." Dale Carnegie, *Quotable Business*, 64.

Page 202   "A résumé is ..." Robert Half, *Quotable Business*, 100.

Page 211   "Knock long ..." "Pep Talks," *Cosmopolitan*, 138.

Art

Art Maker, *The Office I*, Volume 31.

Bob Censoni, *Humorous Office Spot Illustrations* (Mineola, NY: Dover Publications, 1987).

Bob Censoni, *Humorous Spot Illustrations* (Mineola, NY: Dover Publications, 1984).

ClickArt Business Cartoons (Mountain View, CA: T/Maker).

Steve Hornback, *SoftScene* (Orrville, OH).

Key ClipMaster Professional Image Library (Boca Raton, FL: SoftKey Software Products of Florida).

Fred Marvin, *Humorous Attention-Getters* (Mineola, NY: Dover Publications, 1990).

Priceless People (Cross, SC: BCM Graphics).

Ron Soule, *Soule Clip Art Disks* (Uniontown, MD: Public Brand Software).

Tom Tierney, *Office and Business Illustrations* (Mineola, NY: Dover Publications, 1988).

Contents

Unit One • Communication Foundations

Unit Two • The Writing Process

Unit Three • Business Correspondence

Unit Four • Reports and Proposals

Unit Five • Presentations

Chapter 1

Communicating at Work

CHAPTER REVIEW

Understanding key concepts and terms from each chapter is an important part of your success in this course. Each chapter of this study guide will include one or more exercises (matching, true-false, fill-in) giving you the chance to review what you learned and **discover** what you didn't. Read and study each chapter carefully before attempting these exercises.

DISCOVER!

Discover what you know . . .
and what you don't . . .

From Chapter 1 identify the meanings of the following key terms. Some of the terms are common words, but their meanings may be special in this context. Select a term from Column B to match its definition in Column A. The first answer is provided for you! Each term is used only once.

Column A		Column B
__b__	1. Transmission of information and meaning	a. noise
_____	2. Converting an idea into words or gestures	b. communication
_____	3. Miscommunication resulting when individuals have different meanings for words	c. encoding
_____	4. Translating a message from symbols into meaning	d. grapevine
_____	5. Verbal or nonverbal response flowing back to sender	e. sender
_____	6. Combination of your experiences, education, culture, expectations, attitudes, and personality through which messages are filtered	f. filtering
		g. decoding
		h. channel
_____	7. Person originating a message	i. frame of reference
_____	8. Medium that physically transmits a message (letter, telephone, fax, etc.)	j. feedback
		k. bypassing
_____	9. Anything that disrupts the communication process	l. horizontal communication
_____	10. Informal communication channel within organizations	

Indicate whether the following statements are true or false by using T or F.

_____11. To survive in a competitive global economy, businesses have been expanding their management hierarchies and adding layers of management. (Obj. 1, p. 5)

_____ 12. Close to 50 percent of employers in all industries have adopted some form of quality circles or self-directed teams. (Obj. 1, p. 5)

_____ 13. Through teleconferencing and videoconferencing, businesspeople can conduct meetings with associates around the world. (Obj. 1, p. 6)

_____ 14. Thanks to the practice of "hotelling," many employees can now work at home and tele-commute. (Obj. 1, p. 6)

_____ 15. Planning for feedback is an effective way to overcome some communication barriers. (Obj. 2, p. 13)

_____ 16. Successfully decoding a message is impossible because no two people share the same life experiences. (Obj. 2, p. 13)

_____ 17. Organizations communicate externally with customers, suppliers, government agencies, and the public. (Obj. 4, p. 15)

_____ 18. A report describing progress that has been made converting to new equipment on a company's assembly line would flow downward. (Obj. 5, p. 20)

_____ 19. Messages that enable individuals to coordinate tasks, share information, solve problems, and resolve conflict usually flow upward in the organization. (Obj. 5, p. 23)

_____ 20. Many businesses know that they face less litigation, less resentment, and less government regulation if they are ethical. (Obj. 6, p. 26)

21. The key ingredient needed by business to create wealth in the future will be
    a. capital.
    b. raw materials.
    c. knowledge.
    d. physical labor. (Obj. 1, p. 9)

22. Flattened management hierarchies mean that

    a. managers have been beaten into submission.
    b. information must flow through many levels of managers.
    c. lines of communication are longer and decisions are made more quickly.
    d. fewer layers of managers separate decision makers from line workers. (Obj. 1, p. 5)

23. As a knowledge worker, you can expect to
    a. work with upper-level managers only.
    b. work with words, figures, and data.
    c. benefit from physical labor, raw materials, and capital.
    d. work at home and telecommute. (Obj. 1, p. 9)

24. The most useful feedback is
    a. evaluative.
    b. critical.
    c. descriptive.
    d. judgmental. (Obj. 2, p. 13)

25. The three basic functions of business communication are to
    a. inform, entertain, and/or explain.
    b. inform, persuade, and/or promote goodwill.
    c. inform, persuade, and/or explain.
    d. inform, instruct, and/or entertain. (Obj. 4, p. 15)

26. List five steps in the communication process. (Obj. 2, pp. 11–13)

27. Name four obstacles to interpersonal communication. (Obj. 3, pp. 13–14)

28. Describe five ways to overcome interpersonal communication obstacles. (Obj. 3, pp. 14–15)

29. List the advantages of forms of oral communication and written communication.
    (Obj. 4, pp. 17–19)

30. What five questions can you ask yourself when you are facing an ethical dilemma?
    (Obj. 6, pp. 29–30)

Now that you've reviewed the chapter concepts, check your responses at the end of this chapter. For any items that you miss, reread the relevant material in the chapter to be sure you understand the basic concept.

Check your answers now!

CAREER TRACK SPELLING

In any professional or business career you will be judged by your communication skills, including your spelling. Business managers in one study revealed that they had significantly less confidence in employees who could not spell. One executive explained, "Poor spelling . . . can be a reflection of poor basic habits, training, intelligence, and diligence."

To reflect well on yourself and to possess the best communication skills possible, you'll probably need to strengthen your spelling. Although spellcheck programs solve many spelling problems at the computer, such software cannot be with you every moment of your life. Away from your computer you must spell correctly also. Even at the computer such programs do not detect all errors. The wrong word spelled correctly (such as: their for there) will not be detected by a spellcheck program.

Here's a brief spelling pretest to help you assess your present skills. Write the correct spelling for each word and then check your answers at the end of this chapter.

1.	calandar	_____	5.	endispensable _____
2.	concensis	_____	6.	knowlegjible _____
3.	defandent	_____	7.	pirmenant _____
4.	eksagerate	_____	8.	rekemendation _____

Three Approaches to Improving Spelling

If your spelling pretest was disappointing, you are certainly not alone. Luckily, spelling is a skill that can be developed, just as adding, subtracting, typing, and other skills can be developed. Most of us, though, need to work at it to improve. Good spellers are not born with those skills. They must study. Here are three techniques that have met with varying degrees of success:

- **Rules or guidelines.** The spelling of English words is consistent enough to justify the formulation of a few spelling rules, perhaps more appropriately called guidelines, since the generalizations in questions are not invariably applicable. Such guidelines are, in other words, helpful but do not always hold true.

- **Mnemonics.** Another approach to improving one's ability to spell involves the use of mnemonics or memory devices. For example, the word *principle* might be associated with the word *rule*, to form in the mind of the speller a link between meaning and the spelling of *principle*. To spell *capitol*, one might think of the *dome* of the capitol building and focus on the *o*'s in both words. The use of mnemonics can be an effective device for the improvement of spelling only if the speller makes a real effort to develop the necessary memory hooks.

- **Rote learning.** A third approach to the improvement of spelling centers on memorization. The word is studied by the speller until it can be readily reproduced in the mind's eye.

The 1-2-3 Spelling Plan

Proficiency in spelling, of course, is not attained without concentrated effort. Here's a plan to follow in studying a list of spelling words:

- Is a spelling guideline applicable? If so, select the appropriate guidelines and study the word in relation to that guideline.

- If no guideline applies, can a memory device be created to aid in the recall of the word?

- If neither a guideline nor a memory device will work, the word must be memorized. Look at the word carefully. Pronounce it. Write it or repeat it until you can visualize all its letters in your mind's eye.

Spelling Guides

Guide 1: Write *i* before *e* except after *c* and when it sounds like *a*, as in *neighbor* and *weigh*.

i before *e*		Except after *c*	Sounds like *a*
achieve	grief	ceiling	beige
belief	ingredient	conceive	eight
believe	mischief	deceive	freight
convenient	piece	perceive	reign

Exceptions: caffeine, either, height, neither, seize

Guide 2: For most words ending in an *e*, the final *e* is dropped when the word is joined to a suffix beginning with a vowel (such as *ing*, *able*, or *al*). The final *e* is retained when a suffix beginning with a consonant (such as *ment*, *less*, *ly*, or *ful*) is joined to such a word.

Final *e* dropped	Final *e* retained
believe, believing	arrange, arrangement
care, caring	require, requirement
hope, hoping	hope, hopeless
desire, desirable	like, likely
move, movable	definite, definitely

Exceptions: acknowledgment, argument, judgment, ninth, truly, wholly

Guide 3: When *able* or *ous* is added to words ending in *ce* or *ge*, the final *e* is retained if the *c* or *g* is pronounced softly (as in *change* or *peace*).

advantage, advantageous	change, changeable
courage, courageous	service, serviceable
outrage, outrageous	manage, manageable

Guide 4: Words ending in a *y* that is preceded by a consonant normally change the *y* to *i* before all suffixes except those beginning with an *i*.

Y preceded by consonant; change *y* to *i*	*Y* preceded by vowel; do not change *y* to *i*
accompany, accompaniment	annoy, annoying, annoyance
company, companies	attorney, attorneys
industry, industrious	
secretary, secretaries	**Do not change *y* to *i* when adding *ing***
carry, carriage	accompany, accompanying
try, tried	apply, applying
empty, emptiness	study, studying

Guide 5: If one-syllable words or two-syllable words accented on the second syllable end in a single consonant preceded by a single vowel, the final consonant is doubled before the addition of a suffix beginning with a vowel.

One-syllable words	Two-syllable words
can, canned	acquit, acquitting, acquittal
drop, dropped	admit, admitted, admitting
get, getting	commit, committed, committing
plan, planned	occur, occurrence, occurred
slip, slipped	prefer, preferring (BUT *preference* has no double *r* because the accent shifts to the first syllable)

Guide 6: In adding prefixes or suffixes, retain all the letters in the root word. For example, when the prefix *mis* is added to the word *spell*, a double letter results (*misspell*). Don't be tempted to drop it.

Prefix	+	Root word		Root word	+	Suffix
dis		satisfied = dissatisfied		accidental		ly = accidentally
ir		relevant = irrelevant		incidental		ly = incidentally
il		literate = illiterate		clean		ness = cleanness
un		necessary = unnecessary		even		ness = evenness

On the other hand, do not supply additional letters when adding prefixes to root words.

Prefix	+	Root word
dis		appoint = disappoint
dis		satisfied = dissatisfied
mis		take = mistake

Guide 7: Pronounce words carefully so that all their syllables can be heard. Note the following words and letters that are sometimes omitted.

Feb<u>r</u>uary	quan<u>t</u>ity
congra<u>t</u>ulation	represen<u>t</u>ative
gover<u>n</u>ment	su<u>r</u>prise

Spelling Challenge

Every study guide chapter will include a spelling challenge. Many of the words come from the list of 160 frequently misspelled words in Appendix A of this study guide. The pretest words were from this same list. Make it your goal to master those words (and more) by the end of this course. In the following groups identify misspelled words and write correct versions in the spaces provided. More than one misspelled word may appear in a group. Write *C* if all are correct.

1.	achieve	decieve	definitly	courageous	_____
2.	attornies	likely	manageable	applying	_____
3.	unnecessary	suprise	freight	represeative	_____
4.	accidently	writting	preference	slipped	_____
5.	piece	height	advantagous	desireable	_____
6.	companys	seize	ingredient	hopeless	_____
7.	convenient	changeable	industrous	applying	_____
8.	February	congradulation	irelevant	occurrence	_____
9.	planned	occured	goverment	requirement	_____
10.	biege	believing	servicable	valleys	_____

Now check your answers with the solutions at the end of this chapter. If you're like most business writers, some words cause you more trouble than others. A good way to conquer your own spelling monsters is to make a special list of them and practice frequently.

My Spelling Monsters

List each troublesome word. Be sure to spell it correctly. Then, write it four or more times. Review this page often to help you vanquish these spelling demons.

_____

_____

_____

_____

_____

_____

CAREER TRACK VOCABULARY

Expressing ideas clearly requires an extensive and precise vocabulary. To help you expand your career vocabulary, every study guide chapter presents carefully selected words. Some of these words will become part of your reading vocabulary; others will become part of your speaking and writing vocabulary. Use your dictionary to define the following words. Then select the best definition in Column B to match the word in Column A.

Column A		Column B
_____ 1. abut	a.	pardon, vindicate
_____ 2. accrue	b.	pacify, calm
_____ 3. acquit	c.	clever, skillful
_____ 4. adroit	d.	touch, adjoin
_____ 5. allay	e.	deposition, written avowal
_____ 6. affidavit	f.	accumulate, amass

Choose the best meaning for the following underlined words.

_____ 7. Good business <u>acumen</u>, a superior product, and efficient service all contribute to an entrepreneur's success.

    a. partners   b. accountants   c. knowledge

_____ 8. Boxer George Foreman is popular in TV commercials because of his <u>affable</u> nature.

    a. unfriendly   b. pleasant   c. acrimonious

_____ 9. Tabloid headlines <u>allude</u> to sensational news, but their stories are more bizarre than newsworthy.

    a. refer   b. inflate   c. repudiate

_____ 10. Working conditions will <u>ameliorate</u> when we move from these cramped quarters into a suite of offices.

    a. brighten   b. decline   c. improve

_____ 11. In a clever <u>analogy</u>, the Canadian prime minister said that living next to the United States was like sleeping with an elephant: when it rolls over you know it.

    a. distinction   b. comparison   c. divergence

_____ 12. His will specified that each of his grandchildren would receive an <u>annuity</u>.

    a. bond   b. stock certificate   c. annual payment

_____ 13. Real estate has traditionally been a good investment; the recent slump is an <u>anomaly</u>.

    a. exception   b. surprise   c. interlude

_____ 14. Voter <u>apathy</u> caused a low turnout at the polls.

    a. anger   b. indifference   c. despair

Confusing Words

Because words like *accede* and *exceed* sound or look alike, they create much confusion. In each chapter you will be reviewing a small group of these confusing words. The complete list is located in Appendix A of this study guide. Study the confusing words below and then insert your choices in the following exercise.

accede:	to agree or consent	*advice:*	suggestion, opinion
exceed:	over a limit	*advise:*	to counsel or recommend

adverse: unfavorable, antagonistic
averse: unwilling, opposed to

15. Because of _____ economic circumstances, profits are slipping.

16. Please take my _____ and reduce your investment in gold.

17. If the union will _____ to the demands of management, production may resume.

18. Although she was generally _____ to buying anything on credit, she had to borrow to purchase a home.

19. The realtor found it difficult to _____ the quiet client.

20. These last two transactions will cause you to _____ your credit account limit.

Now look back over the 20 vocabulary words in this chapter. Select 5 new words that you would like to own. To "own" a word, you must be able to use it correctly in a sentence. Double-check the meanings of your selections in a dictionary. Then write a sentence for each of your words.

_____

_____

_____

_____

_____

_____

_____

_____

SOLUTIONS

Chapter Review

1. b
2. c
3. k
4. g
5. j
6. i
7. e
8. h
9. a
10. d
11. F   Businesses are flattening management hierarchies and delayering.
12. F   Nearly 80 percent are team based.
13. T
14. F   Thanks to mobile technologies, many workers telecommute.

15. T
16. F   Decoding may be difficult, but it is not impossible.
17. T
18. F   Such a report would flow upward from employees to management.
19. F   Horizontal flow achieves these results.
20. T
21. c
22. d
23. b
24. c
25. b

26. Five steps in the communication process
    a. Sender has idea.
    b. Sender encodes idea in message.
    c. Message travels over channel.
    d. Receiver decodes message.
    e. Feedback travels to sender.

27. Four obstacles to interpersonal communication
    a. Bypassing
    b. Frame of reference
    c. Lack of language skill
    d. Distractions

28. Five ways to overcome interpersonal communication obstacles
    a. Realizing that the communication process is imperfect
    b. Adapting your message to the receiver
    c. Improving your language and listening skills
    d. Questioning your preconceptions
    e. Planning for feedback

29. Advantages of oral and written communication

Oral communication	*Written communication*
Immediate feedback	Permanent record
Nonverbal clues	Convenience
Warm feeling	Economy
Forceful impact	Careful message
Multiple input	Easy distribution

30. Five questions to ask when facing an ethical dilemma
    1. Is the action you are considering legal?
    2. How would you see the problem if you were on the opposite side?
    3. What are alternate solutions?
    4. Can you discuss the problem with someone whose advice you trust?
    5. How would you feel if your family, friends, employer, or coworkers learned of your action?

Spelling Pretest
1. calendar
2. consensus
3. defendant
4. exaggerate
5. indispensable
6. knowledgeable
7. permanent
8. recommendation

Career Track Spelling Challenge
 1. deceive, definitely
 2. attorneys
 3. surprise, representative
 4. accidentally, writing
 5. advantageous, desirable
 6. companies
 7. industrious
 8. congratulation, irrelevant
 9. occurred, government
10. beige, serviceable

Career Track Vocabulary

1. d		11. b
2. f		12. c
3. a		13. a
4. c		14. b
5. b		15. adverse
6. e		16. advice
7. c		17. accede
8. b		18. averse
9. a		19. advise
10. c		20. exceed

Chapter 2

Communicating in Small Groups and Teams

CHAPTER REVIEW

Team Skills

Use the listed words to complete the following sentences. Each word is used only once.

autonomy	deadlines	groupthink	leadership
averaging	ground rules	individuals	norming
consensus	group	issues	team

1. In most models of future organizations, teams, not _____, function as the primary performance unit. (Obj. 1, p. 41)

2. A team is a group of individuals who interact over time to achieve a purpose. A _____ is a collection of three or more individuals who think of themselves as a unit but who may work independently. (Obj. 1, pp. 41–42)

3. Self-directed teams are most successful when they have clearly stated goals, decision-making authority, frequent communication, ongoing training, and _____. That is, they can hire, fire, and discipline their own members. (Obj. 1, p. 43)

4. Most teams struggle through disruptive, although ultimately constructive, team-building stages. These stages include forming, storming, _____, and performing. (Obj. 2, pp. 43–45)

5. Most teams experience some conflict. Cognitive conflict centers on _____ and is considered healthy and functional. (Obj. 2, p. 47)

6. When teams fall victim to _____, they tend to make faulty decisions because they are overly eager to agree with one another. (Obj. 2, p. 47)

7. The way teams reach decisions affects the morale and commitment of a team. In American culture the majority usually rules. But another method produces creative, high-quality discussion and generally elicits commitment by all members to implement the decision. This preferred method for reaching decisions is called _____. (Obj. 2, p. 47)

8. The most successful teams are generally small and have a diverse makeup. They agree on their purpose and procedures. They are able to confront conflict, collaborate rather than compete, use good communication techniques, and accept ethical responsibilities. They also share _____. (Obj. 3, p. 49)

9. Team projects can be harmonious and productive when members establish _____ related to preparing, planning, collecting information for, organizing, rehearsing, and evaluating their activities. (Obj. 4, p. 51)

10. In planning a group document or presentation, you should establish the purpose, decide on the final format, discuss the audience, and develop a work plan. If time is short, work backward from the due date and then set _____. (Obj. 4, p. 52)

Meetings and Groupware

accomplished	consensus	ideas	support
agenda	dysfunctional	participatory	understanding
career	groupware	productive	Web

11. Because businesses are becoming more team oriented and management is becoming more _____, workers are attending more meetings than ever before. (Obj. 5, p. 53)

12. Meetings consist of three or more individuals who gather to pool information, solicit feedback, clarify policy, seek consensus, and solve problems. Meetings are also important in helping you advance your _____. (Obj. 5, pp. 53–54)

13. No meeting should be called unless the topic is important, can't wait, or requires an exchange of _____. (Obj. 5, p. 54)

14. At least two days in advance of a meeting, a list of topics to be discussed should be distributed. It should include the date and place of the meeting, the start time and end time, and a brief description of each topic and its time allotment. This list is called a(n) _____. (Obj. 5, pp. 55–56)

15. When a group seems to have reached a(n) _____, the leader should summarize the group's position and check to see whether everyone agrees. (Obj. 5, p. 57)

16. At meetings some members may play the roles of blocker, attacker, joker, and withdrawer. To control this _____ behavior, team leaders should establish rules, seat members strategically, and use a number of other techniques to encourage harmonious participation. (Obj. 5, pp. 57–58)

17. At the end of a meeting, the leader should summarize what was decided, name who is going to do what, and establish deadlines. No one should leave a meeting without a full _____ of what was accomplished. (Obj. 5, p. 58)

18. Software designed to facilitate group activities is called _____. This software relates to a number of constantly evolving technologies that help groups exchange information, collaborate in project management, and reach consensus. (Obj. 5, p. 59)

19. Completing a group project often requires unrestricted sharing of information. Project management software can allow remote team members, suppliers, partners, and others with an interest in the project's successful completion to view the project and modify their own tasks via the _____. (Obj. 5, p. 60)

20. When large groups want to solve problems quickly, they may decide to use group decision _____ software (GDSS). This software involves participants, seated at networked computers, who offer ideas anonymously, vote on responses, and make recommendations. (Obj. 5, p. 61)

Indicate whether the following statements are true or false by using T or F.

_____ 21. As companies were restructured and reengineered, they were expected to meet higher standards and increase profits, but they could do so because they had more people and more resources. (Obj. 1, p. 41)

_____ 22. Self-directed teams are most useful to solve problems that require people with different skills to work together. (Obj. 1, p. 42)

_____ 23. During the storming phase of team development, a good leader should avoid setting limits or controlling the chaos since teams must work out the conflict on their own. (Obj. 2, p. 44)

_____ 24. Task roles are those that help a group meet its goals; relationship roles facilitate the smooth functioning of the group. (Obj. 2, p. 45)

_____ 25. Cognitive conflict stimulates discussion and creative thinking; it also promotes acceptance of a team decision. (Obj. 2, p. 47)

_____ 26. The best way for a team to make decisions is by averaging; members bargain and negotiate to reach a middle position, which often requires compromise. (Obj. 2, p. 48)

_____ 27. In developing the ground rules for a team project, it's a good idea to discuss how you will deal with team members who are not pulling their share of the load. (Obj. 3, p. 51)

_____ 28. Because meetings are a necessary part of team-based operations, you should learn to make them efficient, satisfying, and productive. (Obj. 5, p. 53)

_____ 29. If a meeting requires intensive problem solving, no more than ten people should participate. (Obj. 5, p. 55)

_____ 30. An effective meeting leader is one who controls the meeting, follows the agenda, and does most of the talking. (Obj. 5, p. 57)

Matching

Select a term from Column B to match to its definition in Column A. The first answer is provided for you. Each term is used only once.

Column A	Column B
__f__ 31. One who defines problems, sets rules, and contributes ideas	a. blocker
_____ 32. One who compares the group's ideas with feasibility of real-world implementation	b. consensus
_____ 33. One who distracts the group with excessive humor, inappropriate comments, and disruptive comments	c. forming
_____ 34. One who constantly puts down the ideas and suggestions of others	d. groupware
_____ 35. A form of decision making that requires all team members to agree	e. groupthink
_____ 36. The stage in team development in which members are getting to know each other and attempting to bond	f. initiator
_____ 37. Software designed to facilitate group activities	g. joker
_____ 38. A technology that combines audio, video, and communication devices to enable real-time team collaboration	h. norming
_____ 39. A group of individuals who interact over time to achieve a purpose	i. reality tester
_____ 40. Faulty decision-making processes by team members who are overly eager to agree with each other	j. team
	k. videoconferencing

41. List seven reasons that organizations are forming company groups and teams.

42. Name nine kinds of positive group task roles. Which of these roles do you think you have played or would play in a team?

43. Name five kinds of positive group relationship roles. Which of these roles do you think you have played or would play in a team?

Check your answers now!

CAREER TRACK SPELLING

Underline misspelled words. Write correct forms in the spaces provided. Some sentences may have more than one misspelled word. If a sentence is correct, write *C*. Then check your answers with those at the end of the chapter.

_____ 1. Her absense made it difficult to accommodate all the customers.
_____ 2. Mark's business prospered because of his excellent judgement.
_____ 3. He was a key manufacture for the government.
_____ 4. On his reccommendation we invested in stocks and bonds.
_____ 5. A valuable element in his business was his highly trained personnal.
_____ 6. With suficient training you, too, will be offered many opportunities.
_____ 7. On the opposite corner is a fine resterant I plan to visit.
_____ 8. As an independent manufacturer, Mark relied on key suppliers.
_____ 9. Lisa must occassionally call freight companies to check deliveries.
_____ 10. You can acheive higher grades if you emphasize your studies.

My Spelling Monsters

List any words that you missed or that were troublesome to you. Be sure to spell them correctly. Then, write each one four or more times. Review this page often to help you vanquish these spelling demons.

_____
_____
_____
_____
_____
_____

CAREER TRACK VOCABULARY

Use your dictionary to define the words in Column A. Then select the best definition in Column B to match the word in Column A.

Column A	Column B
_____ 1. apex	a. overdue debt
_____ 2. arbitrate	b. examine, review
_____ 3. arrears	c. top, summit
_____ 4. articulate (adj)	d. hobby, pastime
_____ 5. audit (v)	e. intelligible, well-spoken
_____ 6. avocation	f. judge, settle

Choose the best meaning for the following underlined words.

_____ 7. Donna Karan's <u>bailiwick</u> is designing clothes, not sewing them.

    a. associate   b. field of knowledge   c. deputy

_____ 8. The division of Yugoslavia into three ethnic states will further <u>balkanize</u> the region.

    a. break up   b. benefit   c. isolate

_____ 9. That attorney sometimes <u>barters</u> her services for car repair and child care.

    a. employs   b. contracts   c. trades

_____ 10. Cautious investors will not let salespeople <u>beguile</u> them into risking their life savings on junk bonds.

    a. coerce   b. flatter   c. mislead

_____ 11. When the response to a proposal is overwhelming, the <u>beleaguered</u> congressional staff disconnects the phones.

    a. set upon   b. fortunate   c. hot-headed

_____ 12. Because of his <u>benign</u> nature, Edmond is reluctant to fire anyone.

    a. kind-hearted   b. wimpy   c. fiendish

_____ 13. Although a glass partition <u>bisects</u> the office, it preserves the room's bright, spacious ambience.

    a. illuminates   b. improves   c. cuts in half

_____ 14. Most professional football commentators have a <u>blasé</u> attitude about flying; but John Madden, who travels by bus, is not among them.

    a. casual   b. fearful   c. belligerent

Confusing Words

affect	to influence		*all ready*	prepared
effect	(n) outcome, result		*already*	by this time
	(v) to bring about, to create			
altar	structure for worship			
alter	to change			

15. Will the strike have any _____ on your company?

16. The owners built an _____ at Mile High Stadium for the Pope's mass.

17. Mark and Maria had _____ decided to attend Penn State.

18. A truckers' strike, of course, will _____ my company adversely.

19. The hurricane in Florida caused us to _____ our plans.

20. He wrote the contract yesterday, and it is _____ for your signature.

Look back over the vocabulary words in this chapter. Select five or more new words that you would like to own. Remember, to "own" a word, you must be able to use it correctly in a sentence. Double-check the meanings of your selections in a dictionary. Then write a sentence for each of your words.

_____

_____

_____

_____

_____

_____

COMPETENT LANGUAGE USAGE ESSENTIALS (C.L.U.E.)

Sentence Structure

   In this chapter and the following ones you will concentrate on the most used—and abused—elements of language. These C.L.U.E. exercises are not meant to teach or review **all** the principles of English grammar and punctuation. Instead, they focus on 50 guidelines that cover the majority of problem areas for most business communicators. You will be examining these guides and applying them in exercises that review and reinforce what you are learning. By looking closely at these frequently used language concepts and by applying the clues and tips, you will develop confidence in expressing yourself correctly in writing and speaking.

Guide 1: Express ideas in complete sentences. You can recognize a complete sentence because it (a) includes a subject (a noun or pronoun that interacts with a verb), (b) includes a verb (a word expressing action or describing a condition), and (c) makes sense (comes to a closure). A complete sentence is an independent clause. Punctuating a fragment as if it were a complete sentence is one of the most serious errors a writer can make. A fragment is a broken-off part of a sentence.

Fragment:	Although the candidate spoke well and seemed to communicate confidently.
Improved:	Although the candidate spoke well and seemed to communicate confidently, the recruiter required a writing sample.
Fragment:	Because most recruiters agree that a one-page résumé, is the right length for a recent graduate.
Improved:	Because most recruiters agree that a one-page résumé is the right length for a recent graduate, you should try to fit yours on a single page.

TIP. Fragments often can be identified by the words that introduce them—words like _after, although, as, because, even, except, for example, if, instead of, since, so, such as, that, which,_ and _when._ These words introduce dependent clauses. Make sure such clauses are always connected to independent clauses.

Independent clauses make sense by themselves and can stand alone. Dependent clauses require additional words to be complete.

Independent Clauses	Dependent Clauses
Rick graduated in June.	After Rick graduated in June, ...
Finding a job is tough.	Although finding a job is tough, ...
Her résumé was flawless.	As her résumé was flawless, ...

Guide 2: Avoid run-on (fused) sentences. A sentence with two independent clauses must be joined by a coordinating conjunction (*and, or, nor, but*) or by a semicolon (;). Without a conjunction or a semicolon, a run-on sentence results.

Run-on: Nancy read the classified ads, she also tried a little networking.

Improved: Nancy read the classified ads, and she also tried a little networking.
            Nancy read the classified ads; she also tried a little networking.

Guide 3: Avoid comma-splice sentences. A comma splice results when a writer joins (splices together) two independent clauses—without using a coordinating conjunction (*and, or, nor, but*) or a semicolon.

Comma Splice: He wrote to the hiring manager, she wrote to the personnel department.

Improved: He wrote to the hiring manager, but she wrote to the personnel department.

Improved: He wrote to the hiring manager; she wrote to the personnel department.

Comma Splice: James sent a résumé to GE, however he didn't receive a response.

Improved: James sent a résumé to GE; however, he didn't receive a response.

 TIP. In joining independent clauses, beware of using a comma to precede words like *consequently, furthermore, however, therefore, then,* and *thus.* These conjunctive adverbs are preceded by semicolons. They are followed by commas, unless the adverbs have only one syllable (as *thus, then, hence*).

C.L.U.E. Checkpoint

In the following word groups identify any fragments (FG), comma splices (CS), or run-ons (RO). Write your identifying initials after each group of words. Then revise the group to rectify its fault. If a sentence is correct, write *C*.

1. Some companies are adopting four-day work weeks. Although such schedules can produce grueling days.

    _____

    _____

2. We use toll-free lines and comment cards, however they only supplement our constant customer surveys.

    _____

    _____

3. Give workers defined targets to hit get them involved in their jobs.

_____

_____

4. If an experienced operating manager is given the right guidance. He or she can almost invariably do a better job than someone from corporate headquarters.

_____

_____

5. You don't ask people what new products they want, you ask them what problems they have.

_____

_____

6. The CEO recognized that you can't control employees, however you can enlist their support.

_____

_____

7. Robin visited resorts of the rich and the famous he also dropped in on luxury spas.

_____

_____

8. Disney World operates in Orlando, Euro Disney serves Paris.

_____

_____

9. Visitors expected a resort vacation, however they were disappointed.

_____

_____

10. Managers must set realistic deadlines, then they must go out of their way not to change them.

_____

_____

SOLUTIONS

Chapter Review

1. individuals
2. group
3. autonomy
4. norming
5. issues
6. groupthink
7. consensus
8. leadership
9. ground rules
10. deadlines

11. participatory
12. career
13. ideas
14. agenda
15. consensus
16. dysfunctional
17. understanding
18. groupware
19. Web
20. support

21. F As companies were restructured, they were expected to increase profits with fewer people and fewer resources.
22. T
23. F During the storming phase, a good leader should set limits and control the chaos.
24. T
25. T
26. F The best decisions are reached through consensus.
27. T
28. T
29. F Problem-solving meetings ideally should have fewer than five members.
30. F An effective leader allows participants to talk more than he or she does.

31. f
32. i
33. g
34. a
35. b

36. c
37. d
38. k
39. j
40. e

41. Seven reasons that organizations are forming groups and teams:
   a. Better decisions
   b. Faster response
   c. Increased productivity
   d. Greater "buy-in"
   e. Less resistance to change
   f. Improved employee morale
   g. Reduced risks

42. Nine kinds of positive group task roles:
    a. Initiator
    b. Information seeker/information giver
    c. Opinion giver/opinion seeker
    d. Direction giver
    e. Summarizer
    f. Diagnoser
    g. Energizer
    h. Gatekeeper
    i. Reality tester

43. Five kinds of positive group relationship roles:
    a. Participation encourager
    b. Harmonizer/tension reliever
    c. Evaluator of emotional climate
    d. Praise giver
    e. Empathic listener

Career Track Spelling
1. absence
2. judgment
3. manufacturer
4. recommendation
5. personnel
6. sufficient
7. restaurant
8. C
9. occasionally
10. achieve

Career Track Vocabulary
1. c
2. f
3. a
4. e
5. b
6. d
7. b
8. a
9. c
10. c
11. a
12. a
13. c
14. a
15. effect
16. altar
17. already
18. affect
19. alter
20. all ready

C.L.U.E. Checkpoint
1. The second group of words is a fragment.   . . . weeks, although . . .
2. CS . . . cards; however, they. . .
3. RO . . . to hit; get them. . .   OR . . . to hit, and get . . .
4. FG . . . guidance, he . . .
5. CS . . . want; you ask . . .
6. CS . . . employees; however, . . .
7. RO . . . famous; he . . .
8. CS . . . Orlando; Euro Disney . . .
9. CS . . . vacation; however, . . .
10. CS . . . deadlines; then . . .

Chapter 3

Workplace Listening and Nonverbal Communication

CHAPTER REVIEW

action	distractions	interpretation	perception
assertions	evaluation	notes	reviewing
awareness	explanations	opinions	service

Listening

1. Workers are doing more communicating than ever before largely because of the Internet, team environments, global competition, and an increasing emphasis on customer _____. (Obj. 1, p. 70)

2. On the job one of your most important tasks will be listening to instructions, assignments, and _____ about how to do your work. You will be listening to learn and to comprehend. (Obj. 1, p. 71)

3. Many organizations are learning that listening to customers results in increased sales and profitability as well as improved customer acquisition and retention. The truth is that consumers just feel better about companies that value their _____. (Obj. 1, p. 72)

4. The listening process begins with _____, the moment when you become conscious of and begin to concentrate on sounds around you. (Obj. 2, p. 73)

5. The second stage in the listening process includes _____, when you focus your attention on a sound or message and begin to decode it. (Obj. 2, p. 74)

6. The third stage involves _____, the time when you analyze the merit of a message and draw conclusions about it. (Obj. 2, p. 74)

7. The final stage is _____, when you respond to a message, perhaps storing it in memory for future use or reacting with a physical response or feedback. (Obj. 2, p. 74)

8. Being able to remember something involves three factors: (1) deciding to remember, (2) structuring the incoming information to form relationships, and (3) _____. (Obj. 2, p. 75)

9. Workplace listening is hard because information may be disorganized, unclear, and cluttered with extra facts. You can improve your listening effectiveness by controlling external and internal _____. (Obj. 3. p. 76)

10. Facts are truths known to exist. Opinions are statements of personal judgments or preferences. Good listeners must separate facts from opinions. They don't automatically accept _____ as facts. (Obj. 3, p. 76)

Nonverbal Messages

attitudes	harmony	palm	style
customers	judgments	pride	territory
distress	nonverbal	spoken	verbal

11. All unwritten and unspoken messages, both intentional and unintentional, are considered to be _____ communication. (Obj. 4, 79)

12. Effective communicators must be sure that all of their nonverbal messages reinforce their _____ messages and their professional goals. (Obj. 4, p. 81)

13. Good eye contact helps you determine whether a listener is paying attention, showing respect, responding favorably, or feeling _____. (Obj. 5, p. 81)

14. The expression on a communicator's face can be almost as revealing of emotion as the eyes. In the workplace, maintaining a pleasant expression with frequent smiles promotes _____. (Obj. 5, p. 82)

15. Leaning toward a speaker suggests attraction and interest. Erect posture sends a message of confidence, competence, diligence, and strength. Using an upward _____ gesture can help you immediately establish rapport. (Obj. 5, p. 82)

16. How we structure and use time tells observers about our personality and _____. (Obj. 5, p. 82)

17. North Americans generally allow only intimate friends and family to stand closer than about 1½ feet. If people violate their _____, they feel uncomfortable and defensive and may step back to reestablish their space. (Obj. 5, p. 83)

18. Your clothing, grooming, and posture send instant messages about you. They help viewers make quick _____ about your status, credibility, personality, and potential. (Obj. 5, p. 83)

19. Casual dress at work may change the image you project and may even affect your work
_____. (Obj. 5, p. 84)

20. Business communicators who look the part are likely to be more successful in working with
superiors, colleagues, and _____. (Obj. 5, p. 84)

Indicate whether the following statements are true or false by using T or F.

_____21. To advance more rapidly in organizations, most people need good speaking skills rather
than good listening skills. (Obj. 1, p. 70)

_____22. Experts say that we listen at only 25 percent efficiency; they
say that we ignore, forget, distort, or misunderstand 75 percent of everything we hear. (Obj. 1, p. 70)

_____23. Managers can be more efficient and productive by lowering
their levels of intensity while listening to employees.
(Obj. 1, p. 71)

_____24. Any employee listening to a customer should learn to defer
judgment, pay attention to content rather than surface issues,
and focus on main ideas. (Obj. 1, p. 72)

_____25. One of the most reliable ways to improve your retention is to
take notes of the important ideas to be remembered. (Obj. 2, p. 75)

_____26. Women tend to listen for facts, whereas men tend to perceiving listening as an opportu-
nity to connect with the other person on a personal level. (Obj. 3, p. 78)

_____27. Nonverbal messages can amplify, modify, or provide details for a verbal message.
(Obj. 4, p. 79)

_____28. Nonverbal messages are important regulators in conversation. Shifts in eye contact,
slight head movements, changes in posture, raising of eyebrows—all of these cues tell
speakers when to continue, to repeat, to elaborate, to hurry up, or to finish.
(Obj. 4, p. 80)

_____29. The longer you can sustain eye contact with an individual, the more confidence and
trust you display. (Obj. 5, p. 81)

_____30. In the workplace a simple way to leave a good impression is to make sure your upper
body is aligned with the person to whom you are talking. (Obj. 5, p. 82)

31. What are three types of workplace listening? Which do you think will be most important to
you on the job? (Obj. 1, pp. 70–73)

32. List ten ways in which you can improve your listening skills. Put a check mark next to the five
items that you think would be most helpful to you in becoming a better listener. (Obj. 3, pp.
78–79)

33. List seven techniques you could employ in improving your nonverbal communication skills in the workplace. Place a check mark next to the five items that you think would be most helpful to you in improving your communication skills. (Obj. 6, pp. 85–86)

CAREER TRACK SPELLING

In the space provided write the correct version of the words in parentheses. If the word is correct, write *C*.

1. Statistical tables consist of rows and (colums). _____

2. This computer has a 24-month (guarantee). _____

3. The start-up company came into (exestanse) one year ago. _____

4. Several (promenant) attorneys represented the company. _____

5. Your product will (succede) if promoted appropriately. _____

6. Serving their customers is a (privaledge) for most companies. _____

7. Economic conditions forced the company into (bankrupsy). _____

8. Please give this matter your (emediate) attention. _____

9. Formatting throughout the report must be (consestant). _____

10. We hope to become less (dependant) on our suppliers. _____

 **My Spelling Monsters**

List any words that you missed or that were troublesome to you. Be sure to spell them correctly. Then, write each one four or more times. Review this page often to help you vanquish these spelling demons.

_____

_____

_____

_____

_____

_____

CAREER TRACK VOCABULARY

Use your dictionary to define the words in Column A. Then select the best definition in Column B to match the word in Column A.

	Column A		Column B
_____	1. buoyant	a.	truth
_____	2. burgeoning	b.	light, floating
_____	3. candor	c.	trite expression
_____	4. chronology	d.	cautious, prudent
_____	5. circumspect	e.	growing, enlarging
_____	6. cliché	f.	in order of time

Choose the best meaning for the following underlined words.

_____ 7. Howard Hughes lived a <u>cloistered</u> existence from the 1950s until the time of his death.

    a. secluded   b. neighborly   c. miserable

_____ 8. Mexico, Canada, and the United States have achieved a free-trade <u>coalition</u>.

    a. reunion   b. division   c. alliance

_____ 9. You can rely on Dr. Jackson to bring council discussions to an end with a few <u>cogent</u> comments.

    a. humorous   b. sound   c. devilish

_____ 10. If Robert were less focused on his computer program, he would be more <u>cognizant</u> of the activity around him.

    a. aware   b. sagacious   c. ignorant

_____ 11. To improve efficiency, we are looking for a copier that sorts and <u>collates</u> sheets.

    a. color-codes   b. staples   c. assembles

_____ 12. The Johnsons used their home equity as <u>collateral</u> for a business loan.

    a. deposit   b. security   c. speculation

_____ 13. A federal judge ruled the airlines guilty of <u>collusion</u> in the price-fixing trial.

    a. bookmaking   b. conspiracy   c. ingenuity

_____ 14. Residents chose to <u>commingle</u> their recyclables rather than separate them into different containers.

    a. mix   b. return   c. crush

Confusing Words

appraise   to estimate   *ascent*   rising, going up
apprise   to inform   *assent*   agree or consent

assure   to promise
ensure   to make certain
insure   to protect from loss

15. We watched the shuttle's _____ on television.

16. At the checkout stand Sue scanned the register tape to _____ its accuracy.

17. Some insurance companies will no longer _____ houses in coastal areas prone to hurricanes.

18. The travel agent will _____ you of any changes made in your schedule.

19. When I asked for a day off, the manager nodded his head in _____ .

20. Carole had a certified gemologist _____ her diamond ring.

Now look back over the 20 vocabulary words in this chapter. Select 5 or more that you would like to own. Remember, to "own" a word, you must be able to use it correctly in a sentence. Double-check the meanings of your selections in a dictionary. Then write a sentence for each of your words.

_____

_____

_____

_____

_____

_____

COMPETENT LANGUAGE USAGE ESSENTIALS (C.L.U.E.)

Capitalization

Because capitalization, number usage, and punctuation are so important to business writers, we will present those guidelines *before* discussing grammar guidelines. Therefore, this chapter begins a review of capitalization use.

Guide 39: Capitalize proper nouns and proper adjectives. Capitalize the *specific* names of persons, places, institutions, buildings, religions, holidays, months, organizations, laws, races, languages, and so forth. Don't capitalize common nouns that make *general* references.

Proper Nouns	**Common Nouns**
Stacy Wilson	the account executive
Everglades National Park	the wilderness park
Towson State University	a university
World Trade Center	the downtown building
Environmental Protection Agency	the federal agency
Persian, Armenian, Hindi	modern foreign languages

Proper Adjectives

Hispanic markets	Russian dressing
Xerox copy	Japanese executives
Swiss chocolates	Reagan economics

Guide 40: Capitalize only specific academic courses and degrees.

Professor Jane Williams, Ph.D., will teach Accounting 121 next spring.

Lee Walker, who holds bachelor's and master's degrees, teaches business communications and marketing.

Alicia enrolled in classes in marketing, English, and business communication.

Guide 41: Capitalize courtesy, professional, religious, government, family, and business titles when they precede names.

Mr. Jameson, Mrs. Alvarez, and Ms. Robinson (Courtesy titles)
Professor Andrews, Dr. Lee (Professional titles)
Rabbi Cohen, Pastor Williams, Pope John (Religious titles)
Senator Tom Harrison, Mayor Jackson (Government titles)
Uncle Edward, Mother Teresa, Cousin Vinny (Family titles)
Vice President Morris, Budget Director Lopez (Business titles)

Do not capitalize such titles when they function as appositives (that is, when they rename or explain previously mentioned nouns or pronouns).

Only one professor, Jonathon Marcus, favored a tuition hike.

Local candidates counted on their president, George Bush, to raise funds.

Do not capitalize titles following names unless they are part of an address.

Mark Yoder, president of Yoder Enterprises, hired all employees.

Paula Beech, director of Human Resources, interviewed all candidates.

Send the package to Amanda Harr, Advertising Manager, Cambridge Publishers, 20 Park Plaza, Boston, MA 02116. (Title is part of address)

Generally, do not capitalize a title or office that replaces a person's name.

Only the president, his chief of staff, and one senator made the trip.

The director of marketing and the sales manager will meet at 1 p.m.

Do not capitalize family titles used with possessive pronouns.

my mother, his father, your cousin

C.L.U.E. Checkpoint

Draw three small underlines under any letter(s) that should be capitalized.

Example: The ucla-sponsored survey examined hispanic buying habits.

1. Our finance class took a field trip to see the new york stock exchange in manhattan.

2. The president of data systems, inc., received his bachelor's degree from pepperdine university.

3. When pope john visited denver, president Clinton and he exchanged greetings in english.

4. Daniel Sand, director of research for general electric, delivered the keynote address.

5. Attending the conference were vice president atwood and president wilkerson.

6. Richard enrolled in management 304, computer science 205, and marketing.

7. Our vacation included shenandoah national park in the blue ridge mountains.

8. Send the xerox copies to kimberly gorman, marketing manager, globex incorporated, 769 valencia street, san francisco, CA 94010, as soon as possible.

9. The pacific design center featured french prints, mexican pottery, and asian fabrics.

10. Because uncle frank speaks spanish and italian, he was hired as an interpreter.

SOLUTIONS

1. service
2. explanations
3. opinions
4. perception
5. interpretation
6. evaluation
7. action
8. reviewing
9. distractions
10. assertions

11. nonverbal
12. verbal
13. distress
14. harmony
15. palm
16. attitudes
17. territory
18. judgments
19. style
20. customers

21. F   To advance rapidly, people need good listening skills.

22. T

23. F   Half listening is counterproductive for managers.

24. T

25. T

26. F   Women tend to perceive listening as an opportunity to connect, whereas men tend to listen for facts.

27. T

28. T

29. F   Prolonged eye contact can be intrusive and intimidating.

30. T

31. Three types of workplace listening:
    a. Listening to superiors
    b. Listening to employees
    c. Listening to customers

32. Ways to improve your listening skills:
    a. Stop talking.
    b. Work hard at listening.
    c. Block out competing thoughts.
    d. Control the listening environment.
    e. Maintain an open mind.
    f. Paraphrase the speaker's ideas.
    g. Listen between the lines.
    h. Distinguish between facts and opinions.
    i. Capitalize on lag time.
    j. Use memory devices.
    k. Take selective notes.

33. Techniques to improve your nonverbal communication skills:
    a. Improve your decoding skills.
    b. Probe for more information.
    c. Avoid assigning nonverbal meanings out of context.
    d. Associate with people from diverse cultures.
    e. Appreciate the power of appearance.
    f. Observe yourself on videotape.
    g. Enlist friends and family.

Career Track Spelling

1. columns	6. privilege
2. C	7. bankruptcy
3. existence	8. immediate
4. prominent	9. consistent
5. succeed	10. dependent

Career Track Vocabulary

1. b	11. c
2. e	12. b
3. a	13. b
4. f	14. a
5. d	15. ascent
6. c	16. ensure
7. a	17. insure
8. c	18. apprise
9. b	19. assent
10. a	20. appraise

C.L.U.E. Checkpoint

1. New York Stock Exchange   Manhattan [Do not capitalize the common noun *finance*.]

2. Data Systems, Inc.   Pepperdine University [Do not capitalize business titles standing alone.]

3. Pope John   Denver   President   English

4. General Electric [Do not capitalize the business title *director of research*.]

5. Vice President Atwood   President Wilkerson [Do capitalize business titles when they precede names and act as courtesy titles, such as *Mr.*]

6. Management   Computer Science [Capitalize only specific courses; *marketing* is a common noun. Clue: Numbered academic courses are capitalized.]

7. Shenandoah National Park   Blue Ridge Mountains

8. Xerox   Kimberly Gorman, Marketing Manager, Globex Incorporated, 769 Valencia Street, San Francisco [Do capitalize titles in mailing addresses.]

9. Pacific Design Center   French   Mexican   Asian

10. Uncle Frank   Spanish   Italian

Chapter 4

Communicating Across Cultures

CHAPTER REVIEW

agreements
communication
culture

dreams
generalizations
immigration

the Internet
misunderstanding
prejudice

self-identity
systems
technologies

1. In your future career you may find that your employers, fellow workers, or clients are from other countries. Learning about the powerful effect that culture has on behavior will help you reduce friction and _____. (Obj. 1, p. 94)

2. Major contributors to increased global interconnectivity are the development of new transportation and information _____. (Obj. 1, p. 95)

3. One significant factor in the movement toward globalization of markets and the blurring of national identities is the passage of favorable trade _____. Another important element in the new global market is the explosive growth of the middle class. (Obj. 1, p. 95)

4. Rapid oral and written communication across time zones and continents is now made possible by using _____. (Obj. 1, p. 96)

5. Attracted by the prospects of peace, prosperity, education, or a fresh start, persons from many cultures are migrating to countries promising to fulfill their _____. (Obj. 1, p. 97)

6. Over the next fifty years, the population of the United States is expected to grow by nearly 50 percent. About two thirds of the increase will be due to net _____. (Obj. 1, p. 98)

7. A powerful operating force that conditions the way we think and behave is our _____. (Obj. 2, p. 99)

8. It is impossible to talk about cultures without using mental categories, representations, and _____ to describe groups. (Obj. 2, p. 100)

9. Culture is the basis of our sense of community and the basis of our _____. That is, culture helps us develop who we are and what we believe in. (Obj. 2, p. 100)

10. A stereotype is an oversimplified behavioral pattern applied uncritically to groups. When a stereotype develops into a rigid attitude and when it is based on erroneous beliefs or preconceptions, it should be called a(n) _____. (Obj. 2, p. 101)

Dimensions of Culture and Intercultural Sensitivity

comprehension	face	low	tolerance
differ	grammar	negative	tradition
ethnocentrism	high	social standing	training

11. Communicators in _____ context cultures, such as the United States, depend little on the context of a situation to convey meaning. (Obj. 2, p. 101)

12. Informality is important to North Americans, but in some cultures ceremony, social rules, and _____ are important cultural values. (Obj. 2, p. 103)

13. The natural belief in the superiority of one's own race is known as _____. Things that you do seem natural and "right" to you. (Obj. 3, p. 104)

14. Developing cultural competence often involves changing attitudes. Because culture is learned, beliefs can be changed through exposure to other cultures and through _____. (Obj. 3, p. 105)

15. As global markets expand and as our own society becomes increasingly multiethnic, _____ becomes especially significant. To improve this desirable attitude, a person must practice empathy, which means trying to see the world through another's eyes. (Obj. 3, p. 105)

16. People in low-context cultures, such as those in Germany and North America, value candor and directness. But members of high-context cultures, such as those in Mexico and Asia, are often more concerned with preserving social harmony and saving _____. (Obj. 3, p. 106)

17. Deciphering nonverbal communication is difficult for people who are culturally similar, and it is even more troublesome when cultures _____. (Obj. 4, p. 107)

18. To improve oral communication with someone for whom English is a second language, you should speak slowly, enunciate clearly, observe eye messages, encourage feedback, and check frequently for _____. (Obj. 4, p. 109)

19. To improve written messages when English is a second language, you should adopt local formats, use short sentences and short paragraphs, avoid ambiguous expressions, strive for clarity, and use correct _____. (Obj. 5, p. 111)

20. In cultures where formality and tradition are important, be very polite. Don't try to be funny in written messages because humor translates poorly and can cause misunderstanding and _____ reactions. (Obj. 5, p. 110)

Indicate whether the following statements are true or false by using T or F.

_____21. Early immigrants to this country were thought to be part of a "melting pot" of ethnic groups, but today they are more like a "tossed salad" or "spicy stew." (Obj. 1, p. 98)

_____22. Rules, values, and attitudes of a culture are inborn and are passed down from generation to generation. (Obj. 2, p. 100)

_____23. "The nail that sticks up gets pounded down" is a common saying that indicates American individuality and its group-oriented culture. (Obj. 2, 103)

_____24. Asian languages are based on pictographical characters representing the meanings of words. Thus, Asians are thought to have a higher competence in the discrimination of visual patterns. (Obj. 2, p. 104)

_____25. If a foreigner is struggling to express an idea in English, we should quickly provide the word needed or finish the sentence to help the speaker save face. (Obj. 3, p. 106)

_____26. The meanings of nonverbal communication (facial expression, body language, etc.), regardless of culture, are as easy to learn as language, if one studies hard enough. (Obj. 4, p. 107)

_____27. In doing business around the globe, some U.S. businesses find that they can't compete because they refuse to pay bribes. (Obj. 6, p. 112)

_____28. The United States is the highest on a list of the least corruptible countries. (Obj. 6, p. 114)

_____29. In some countries the "greasing of palms" is considered the cost of doing business. (Obj. 6, p. 113)

_____30. Gifts are not only a sign of gratitude and hospitality, but they also generate a future obligation and trust. (Obj. 6, p. 113)

_____31. Diversity in the American workforce has many dimensions, including race, ethnicity, age, religion, gender, national origin, physical ability, and countless other qualities. (Obj. 7, p. 115)

_____32. Diversity can be a positive force within organizations, but it can also cause divisiveness, discontent, and clashes. (Obj. 7, p. 116)

_____33. Harmony and acceptance do not happen automatically when people who are dissimilar work together. (Obj. 6, p. 117)

34. Name three high-context and three low-context cultures. List four cultural characteristics that distinguish each of these cultures. (Obj. 2, pp. 101–104)

35. Name six or more tips for helping business communicators improve intercultural sensitivity and communication. (Obj. 5, pp. 111–112)

36. Name seven tips for improving communication among diverse workplace audiences. (Obj. 7, pp. 116–118)

CAREER TRACK SPELLING

For each group below identify misspelled words and write corrected versions in the spaces provided. Write *C* if all words are correct.

1. simular	manageable	referred	efficent	_____
2. itinerary	distroy	truely	criticize	_____
3. necessary	deductable	catalog	excellent	_____
4. nineth	yield	ommitted	grammar	_____
5. forty	fascinate	paid	permanent	_____
6. probibly	harass	budjet	equipped	_____
7. exagerate	annually	adequate	representative	_____
8. consensus	irelevant	familiar	committee	_____
9. milage	tenant	undoubtedly	quanity	_____
10. employe	noticeable	control	heigt	_____

My Spelling Monsters

List each word that you missed. Be sure to spell it correctly. Then, write it four or more times. Review this page often to help you vanquish these spelling demons.

_____

_____

_____

_____

CAREER TRACK VOCABULARY

Use your dictionary to define the words in Column A. Then select the best definition in Column B to match the word in Column A.

	Column A		Column B
_____	1. cohere	a.	stock, merchandise
_____	2. commodity	b.	channel, passageway
_____	3. concede	c.	stick, adhere
_____	4. condone	d.	seize, take possession of
_____	5. conduit	e.	admit, acknowledge
_____	6. confiscate	f.	agree to, overlook

Choose the best meaning for the following underlined words.

_____ 7. Predicting the success of any new television show is pure <u>conjecture</u>.

      a. speculation   b. fact   c. reasoning

_____ 8. Because the stock split is <u>contingent</u> on their approval, we must lobby the shareholders.

      a. certain   b. debatable   c. dependent

_____ 9. The government is probing overseas cartels that <u>contrive</u> to restrict markets.

      a. discriminate   b. diverge   c. plan

_____ 10. Mrs. Fields Cookies, saddled with debt, turned to <u>conversion</u> franchising to save itself.

      a. pumpernickel   b. rearrangement   c. unnecessary

_____ 11. All the participants at the water quality management session took <u>copious</u> notes.

      a. infrequent   b. ample   c. furtive

_____ 12. Some researchers see a <u>correlation</u> between the stock market's fluctuations and the length of women's skirts.

      a. interrelation   b. difference   c. incompatibility

_____ 13. We invested in the company because it was highly recommended by <u>credible</u> sources.

      a. dubious   b. believable   c. vexing

_____ 14. A state court ruled the FDA approval of a drug shields the maker from <u>culpability</u>.

      a. prejudice   b. suspicion   c. guilt

Confusing Words

capital   n.: a city in which the official seat of government is located; the wealth of an individual; adj.: foremost in importance; punishable by death

capitol   building that houses state lawmakers

Capitol   building used by U.S. Congress

cite	to quote or to charge	*cereal*	breakfast food
site	a location	*serial*	arranged in sequence
sight	n.: a view; v.: to see		

15. Jason's favorite breakfast _____ is ChocoDyno Bits.

16. In a research paper you may _____ authorities to support your argument.

17. What a _____ awaits visitors to Alaska's glaciers!

18. "This building _____ is unacceptable," said the geologist.

19. U.S. Senators and Representatives were called into session at the _____ building in Washington.

20. "The Ascent of Man," a _____ on PBS, is most informative.

21. Entrepreneurs must invest considerable _____ to start new businesses.

22. State legislators held weekly budget hearings in the _____ building.

Look back over the vocabulary words in this chapter. Select five or more new words that you would like to own. Remember, to "own" a word, you must be able to use it correctly in a sentence. Double-check the meanings of your selections in a dictionary. Then write a sentence for each of your words.

_____

_____

_____

_____

_____

COMPETENT LANGUAGE USAGE ESSENTIALS (C.L.U.E.)

Capitalization (cont.)

Because capitalization, number usage, and punctuation are so important to business writers, we will present those guidelines *before* discussing grammar guidelines. Therefore, this chapter begins a review of capitalization use.

Guide 42: Capitalize the principal words in the titles of books, magazines, newspapers, articles, movies, plays, songs, poems, and reports. Do *not* capitalize articles (*a, an, the*) and prepositions of fewer than four letters (*in, to, by, for*) unless they begin or end the title.

Book: <u>Life After College</u> or *Life After College*

Magazine: <u>Business Week</u>

Newspaper: <u>The Wall Street Journal</u>

Article: "Why Complainers Are Good for Business"

Movies: <u>Ferris Bueller's Day Off</u>,   <u>Life Is Beautiful</u>

Song: "What Dreams Are Made Of "

Report: "The Search for Intelligent Life in the Universe"

Note that the titles of books, magazines, and newspapers are underlined (or italicized), while the titles of articles and shorter publications are enclosed in quotation marks.

Guide 43: Capitalize *north, south, east, west* and their derivatives only when they represent specific geographical regions.

from the East Coast
living in the South
Midwesterners, Southerners

heading east on the highway
the house faced south
western New York, southern Ohio

 TIP. When the word *the* precedes a compass direction (*the East, the West, the South*), you'll almost always capitalize the direction. *The* signals locations instead of directions.

Guide 44: Capitalize the names of departments, divisions, or committees within your own organization. Outside your organization capitalize only *specific* department, division, or committee names.

Counselors in our Human Resources Department help employees choose benefits.

Four accountants in its Telecommunications Division will be transferred.

Two attorneys serve on our Legal Assistance and Services Committee.

Have you sent an application to their personnel department?

Guide 45: Capitalize product names only when they refer to trademarked items. Don't capitalize the common names following manufacturers' names.

Dell Inspiron laptop computer
Skippy peanut butter
Canon copier

Eveready Energizer
Kingsford charcoal briquettes
Levi 501 jeans

Guide 46: Capitalize most nouns followed by numbers or letters (except page, paragraph, line, and verse references).

Room 340
Apartment C
Chapter 4

Flight 28, Gate 4
Form 1040A
Figure 15

C.L.U.E. Checkpoint

Indicate capitalization with proofreading marks (three small underscores).

1. Proceed south on interstate 4 until you see exit 8, which leads to chicago.

2. Ginger Putnam, a systems programmer in our accounting department, drinks diet coke all day.

3. You are scheduled to leave denver international airport on delta flight 32 at 2 p.m.

4. In the east she bought a book called how to buy a house, condo, or co-op.

5. James Dale, president of quaker oats company, discussed its sports drink gatorade.

6. Please complete form 1040 and send it to the internal revenue service before april 15.

7. Our student fees and admissions committee will meet in room 12 on the east side of douglas campus center.

8. Our director of research brought plan no. 3a to discuss with all vice presidents.

9. Easterners and midwesterners often travel south to florida to spend their winters.

10. Did you see the toshiba computer that vice president rose bought for his trip to europe?

SOLUTIONS

1. misunderstanding
2. technologies
3. agreements
4. the Internet
5. dreams
6. immigration
7. culture
8. generalizations
9. self-identity
10. prejudice

11. low
12. tradition
13. ethnocentrism
14. training
15. tolerance
16. face
17. differ
18. comprehension
19. grammar
20. negative

21. T
22. F   Rules, values, and attitudes are not inborn. They are learned and passed down from generation to generation.
23. F   "The nail that sticks up gets pounded down" is a Japanese saying that indicates a group-oriented culture.
24. T
25. F   English speakers should not finish the sentences of people struggling with English as a second language. They should be patient and wait for the speaker to finish.
26. F   Interpreting nonverbal cues is inexact within one's own culture; it becomes even more difficult across cultures.
27. T
28. F   The United States is about 12th on the corruptions index.
29. T
30. T
31. T
32. T
33. T
34. Three high-context cultures:
    Japanese
    Chinese
    Arab

Three low-context cultures:
German
North American
German-Swiss

Characteristics of high-context cultures:
   a. Prefer indirect verbal interaction.
   b. Tend to understand meanings embedded at many sociocultural levels.
   c. Generally are more proficient in reading nonverbal cues.
   d. Value group membership.
   e. Rely more on context and feeling.
   f. Employ spiral logic.
   g. Talk around point; avoid saying no.

Characteristics of low-context cultures:
   a. Tend to prefer direct verbal interaction.
   b. Tend to understand meaning at one level only.
   c. Generally are less proficient in reading nonverbal cues.
   d. Value individualism.
   e. Rely more on logic.
   f. Employ linear logic.
   g. Say no directly.

35. Tips for helping business communicators improve multicultural sensitivity:
    a. Curb ethnocentrism.
    b. Avoid judgmentalism.
    c. Look beyond stereotypes.
    d. Seek common ground.
    e. Observe nonverbal cues in your own culture.
    f. Use plain English.
    g. Encourage accurate feedback.
    h. Adapt to local preferences.

36. Tips for improving communication among diverse workplace audiences:
    a. Seek training.
    b. Understand the value of differences.
    c. Don't expect conformity.
    d. Create zero tolerance for bias and stereotypes.
    e. Learn about your own cultural self.
    f. Make fewer assumptions.
    g. Build on similarities.

Career Track Spelling
1. similar, efficient
2. destroy, truly
3. deductible
4. ninth, omitted
5. C
6. probably, budget
7. exaggerate
8. irrelevant
9. mileage, quantity
10. employee, height

Career Track Vocabulary
1. c
2. a
3. e
4. f
5. b
6. d
7. a
8. c
9. c
10. b
11. b
12. a
13. b
14. c
15. cereal
16. cite
17. sight
18. site
19. Capitol
20. serial
21. capital
22. capitol

C.L.U.E. Checkpoint
1. Interstate 4   Exit 8   Chicago [Do not capitalize the direction *south*.]
2. Accounting Department   Diet Coke [Do not capitalize business titles.]
3. Denver International Airport   Delta Flight 32 [Use lowercase letters for *p.m.* Do not add an extra period at the end of the sentence.]
4. East   How to Buy a House, Condo, or Co-op [Capitalize *East* because it is a specific geographical region; do not capitalize the preposition *to* or conjunction *or* in a title.]
5. Quaker Oats Company   Gatorade [Do not capitalize business titles; do capitalize trademarked names like *Gatorade*.]
6. Form 1040   Internal Revenue Service   April 15
7. Student Fees and Admissions Committee   Room 12   Douglas Campus Center
8. Plan No. 3a [Remember not to capitalize business titles—unless they replace titles like *Mr.* or *Ms.*]
9. Midwesterners Florida [Do not capitalize compass directions or seasons like *fall*.]
10. Toshiba   Vice President Rose   Europe [Do not capitalize common nouns like *computer*, but do capitalize business titles like *Vice President* when such a title acts as a courtesy title replacing *Mr.*]

Find something you love to do, and you'll never have to **work** a day in your life!

Chapter 5

Preparing to Write Business Messages

CHAPTER REVIEW

Applying a Writing Process

Use the following words to complete the sentences below. Each word is used but once.

anticipation	express	inform	profiling	repeated
collaborative	formality	prewriting	reader-oriented	revising

1. Business writing differs from creative and academic writing in at least three ways. Instead of trying to explain feelings, display knowledge, or meet a minimum word count, business writers tend to be purposeful, economical, and _____. (Obj. 1, p. 130)

2. The goal in business writing is to _____ rather than *impress*. This means that senders try to convey meaning instead of displaying knowledge. (Obj. 1, p. 130)

3. The three phases of the writing process include prewriting, writing, and revising. The phase that requires the most time is _____. (Obj. 1, pp. 130–131)

4. Although most writers perform all the tasks in the writing process, the steps may be rearranged, abbreviated, or _____. (Obj. 2, p. 131)

5. Because today's workers are increasingly part of teams, you can logically expect to participate in a _____ writing project on the job. (Obj. 2, p. 132)

6. As part of the first phase in the writing process, you will analyze your task. You must decide whether your message is meant to persuade or merely to _____. (Obj. 3, p. 135)

7. In the first phase of the writing process, you will select the best channel for delivery of your message. You will consider the importance of the message, the amount of feedback required, the necessity for a permanent record, the cost, and the degree of _____ desired. (Obj. 3, p. 135)

8. Visualizing or _____ your audience means spending some time—before you begin to write—considering the makeup of the primary and secondary receivers of your message. Through this process, you are better able to identify the appropriate tone, language, and channel for your message. (Obj. 4, pp. 135–136)

Adapting to the Task and Audience

age	curt	empathy	first	jargon	stereotype
courteous	disability	familiar	gender	second	tone

9. One important aspect of adaptation is _____ . Conveyed largely by the words in a message, it reflects how a receiver feels upon reading or hearing a message. (Obj. 5, p. 137)

10. Adapting your message to the receiver's needs means putting yourself into that person's shoes. Called _____, this ability makes senders think about how receivers will decode a message. (Obj. 5, p. 138)

11. Effective communicators develop the "you" view. That is, they emphasize _____ -person pronouns, but not in a manipulative or critical manner. (Obj. 5, p. 139)

Empathic writers avoid words that might offend receivers.

12. Expressions like "female attorney," "workman," and "executives and their wives" carry _____ bias and should be replaced by neutral expressions. (Obj. 5, pp. 140–142)

13. Expressions like "afflicted with," "suffering from," and "crippled by" carry _____ bias and will be avoided by sensitive communicators. (Obj. 5, p. 142)

14. Even when you are justifiably angry, using _____ language is far more likely to achieve your objectives than impolite or abusive language. (Obj. 5, pp. 143–144)

15. Some communicators show off with big words; they think that inflated language is necessary to impress people. The best communicators, however, try to use _____ words because their goal is to transmit meaning and be understood. (Obj. 5, p. 144)

16. _____ is specialized or technical language that enables insiders to communicate complex ideas briefly. (Obj. 5, p. 144)

Adapting to Legal Responsibilities

administration	e-mail	lawsuit
defamation	human resources	warnings

17. As a business communicator, you should avoid language that may create a _____ for you or your organization. (Obj. 6, p. 146)

18. The information areas that generate the most litigation are investments, safety, marketing, and _____ . (Obj. 6, p. 146)

19. Manufacturers are obligated to tell consumers of any risks in their products. These _____ must do more than suggest danger; they must also clearly tell people how to use the product safely. (Obj. 6, p. 146)

20. Much litigation today involves employment communication. Lawsuits have become so common that some employers refuse to give letters of recommendation for former employees. Employers fear _____ lawsuits. (Obj. 6, p. 147)

Indicate whether the following statements are true or false by using T or F.

_____21. In business writing, quantity enhances quality. That is, the longer a message, the better. (Obj. 1, p. 130)

_____22. Business writing is generally easier than academic writing, but it still is hard work. (Obj. 1, p. 130)

_____23. The major component in the writing process is preparation. (Obj. 1, p. 131)

_____24. Good writers follow the writing process in the same order each time they create a document. (Obj. 2, p. 131)

_____25. Team-written documents and presentations are standard in most organizations because collaboration has many advantages. (Obj. 2, p. 132)

_____26. Computer software programs can help writers in every phase of the writing process except revision. (Obj. 2, p. 132)

_____27. Most business messages have both primary purposes (to inform or persuade) and secondary purposes (to promote goodwill). (Obj. 3, p. 134)

_____28. Profiling the audience for a message is an important step in the revision process. (Obj. 4, pp. 135–136)

_____29. Skilled communicators adapt a message to the needs of the receiver. (Obj. 5, pp. 137–138)

_____30. E-mail is the best communication channel for communicating with a large, dispersed audience, but it is inappropriate for personal, emotional, and private messages. (Obj. 5, p. 136)

31. Name seven ways that computer software can help you create better written messages, oral presentations, and Web pages. (Obj. 2, pp. 133–134)

32. What communication channel is best when you want to be persuasive, deliver bad news, or share a personal message? (Obj. 4, p. 136)

33. What communication channel is best when you wish to leave important or routine information that the receiver can respond to when convenient? (Obj. 4, p. 136)

34. What communication channel is best when group decisions and consensus are important? (Obj. 4, p. 136)

35. Name four kinds of biases that sensitive writers avoid in choosing words. Give an example of each. (Obj. 5, pp. 140–142)

Reader Benefits and "You" View

Revise the following statements to emphasize the reader's perspective and the "you" view.

36. So that we may bring our client records up to date and make sure we get our monthly newsletter to you in a timely manner, we require the enclosed card to be completed.

37. We are proud to announce "Brainstorm," our new software that reduces writer's block.

38. I am convinced that my education and training match the requirements advertised for the assistant buyer position.

39. To enable us to continue our policy of selling name brands at discount prices, we cannot give cash refunds on returned merchandise.

Language Bias

Revise the following sentences to eliminate language stereotypes.

40. Although Jim is confined to a wheelchair, he travels to all functions easily.

41. A competent word processor uses her spell checker on every document.

42. While executives attend meetings, their wives will tour the city.

43. A new subscriber may cancel his subscription within two weeks.

44. Ricky Cortez, a Filipino, is our new sales representative.

Positive Expression

Revise the following sentences to make them more positive.

45. We can't send the VCR you ordered until January 1.

46. In response to your complaint, we are investigating your unhappy experience at our Orlando resort.

47. Because you apparently did not use our correct address, your letter did not arrive in our New York office until May 5.

48. We cannot allow cash refunds for merchandise returned without a sales receipt.

49. You won't be disappointed with your subscription to *The Wall Street Journal.*

Courteous Expression

Revise the following sentences to show greater courtesy.

50. You MUST complete this application and return it IMMEDIATELY if you expect to be enrolled.

51. Does it take a rocket scientist to insert paper in the fax machine? Anyone who can read could see how to do it in the instruction booklet.

52. As I'm sure your agent told you, your policy does not cover drivers under the age of 21.

Familiar Words

Revise the following sentences to use familiar words.

53. Please ascertain what the remuneration will be for this position.

54. Pursuant to our dialogue, I plan to interrogate Kathleen about computer usage.

CAREER TRACK SPELLING

Spelling Challenge
In the space provided write the correct version of the words in parentheses. If the word is spelled correctly, write *C*.

1. Fax messages travel (accross) oceans and continents. _____
2. Have you (payed) all the bills for this month? _____
3. Bond income is (exemt) from the latest tax laws. _____
4. We set up a special file for (miscelanous) items. _____
5. This watch band is made from (jenuwine) leather. _____
6. Second-semester classes begin in early (Febuary). _____
7. Only (perminant) residents were allowed to enter. _____
8. Traffic (volume) increased on holiday weekends. _____
9. The president will (congradulat) each graduate personally. _____
10. All 500 (envelops) will be sent out by Monday. _____

My Spelling Monsters

List each troublesome word. Be sure to spell it correctly. Then, write it four or more times. Review this page often to help you vanquish these spelling demons.

_____

_____

_____

_____

_____

_____

CAREER TRACK VOCABULARY

Use your dictionary to define the words in Column A. Then select the best definition in Column B to match the word in Column A.

Column A	Column B
_____ 1. consignment	a. hidden, invisible
_____ 2. contiguous	b. entrusted goods
_____ 3. corroborate	c. touching, adjacent
_____ 4. coup de grace	d. hasty, perfunctory
_____ 5. covert	e. confirm, validate
_____ 6. cursory	f. death blow

Choose the best meaning for the following underlined words.

_____ 7. In *The Journal of Corporate Law,* Professor Dale <u>denounced</u> the specialist system of the New York Stock Exchange.

    a. praised   b. criticized   c. advocated

_____ 8. The <u>derogatory</u> article argues that the system encourages volatility and performs poorly.

    a. disparaging   b. excellent   c. well-written

_____ 9. <u>Deterred</u> by heavy traffic and rainy weather, the limousine arrived late for the prime minister.

    a. placated   b. impelled   c. thwarted

_____ 10. Choosing a printer presents a big <u>dilemma</u>: laser-print quality or ink-jet price?

    a. puzzle   b. certainty   c. expense

_____ 11. Any discussion of health care plans is sure to produce sharply <u>disparate</u> views.

      a. disjointed   b. disdainful   c. differing

_____ 12. Simply put, the CEO's principle is this: Listen to all the debate before you <u>dissent</u>.

      a. depart   b. disagree   c. consent

_____ 13. This edgy market has analysts <u>divesting</u> stocks on a daily basis.

      a. investing in   b. recommending   c. disposing of

_____ 14. Cadillac's reputation soared when the Seville received the <u>elite</u> Malcolm Balridge award for quality.

      a. golden   b. distinguished   c. tarnished

Confusing Words

coarse	rough	*council*	governing body
course	direction, route	*counsel*	(v) to advise; (n) advice

complement   that which completes
compliment   to praise or flatter

15. Call the EPA for _____ on toxic material storage.

16. The popular vice president makes it a point to _____ all employees personally when their work is exemplary.

17. The FCC fines radio stations that broadcast _____ material.

18. Zoning issues make city _____ meetings interminable.

19. Formal gardens surrounding the ornate library _____ its architecture.

20. Race car drivers followed a winding _____ through the Italian countryside.

Look back over the vocabulary words in this chapter. Select five or more words to make your own. Double-check the meanings of your selections in a dictionary. Then write a sentence for each of your words.

_____

_____

_____

_____

_____

_____

COMPETENT LANGUAGE USAGE ESSENTIALS (C.L.U.E.)

Number Style

Usage and custom determine whether numbers are to be expressed in the form of a figure (for example *5*) or in the form of a word (for example, *five*). Numbers expressed as figures are shorter and more easily comprehended, yet numbers used as words are necessary in certain instances. The following guides are observed in expressing numbers that appear in written *sentences*. Numbers that appear in business communications—such as invoices, statements, purchase orders—are always expressed as figures.

Guide 47: Use word form to express (a) numbers *ten* and under and (b) numbers beginning sentences. General references to numbers *ten* and under should be expressed in word form. Also use word form for numbers that begin sentences. If the resulting number involves more than two words, however, the sentence should be recast so that the number does not fall at the beginning.

> The jury consisted of *nine* regular members and *one* alternate.

> *Eighteen* employees volunteered to tutor students in *three* neighborhood schools.

> A total of 117 applicants responded to five classified ads. (Avoid beginning the sentence with a long number such as *one hundred seventeen*.)

Guide 48: Use words to express general references to ages, small fractions, and periods of time. However, exact ages and specific business terms may be expressed as figures.

> He started college at *eighteen* and graduated at *twenty-two*. (General reference)

> Maritza worried that *one third* of her income went for rent. (Note that fractions are hyphenated only when they function as adjectives, such as *one-third ownership*).

> In the past *twenty* years, TV programming has changed greatly. (General reference)

> Angela Ross, 45, and Eric Ross, 47, were injured. (Specific references)

> The note is payable in 60 days. (Business term)

Guide 49: Use figures to express most references to numbers 11 and over.

> More than *175* people from *86* companies attended the two-day workshop.

> A four-ounce serving of toffee ice cream contains *300* calories and *19* grams of fat.

Guide 50: Use figures to express money, dates, clock time, decimals, and percents. Use a combination of words and figures to express sums of 1 million and over.

> One wrench cost *$2.95*; however, most were between *$10* and *$35*. (Omit the decimals and zeros in even sums of money.)

By *5 p.m.* on *June 2* only a fraction of the residents had not voted. (Notice that *June 2* is not written *June 2nd*, although it may be spoken that way.)

International sales dropped *11.7 percent*, and net income dropped *3.5 percent*. (Always use the word *percent* instead of the % symbol in written material.)

Globex earned *$4.5 million* in the latest fiscal year on revenues of *$235 million*. (Use a combination of words and figures for sums 1 million and over.)

 TIP. To ease your memory load, concentrate on the numbers normally expressed in words: numbers *ten* and under, numbers at the beginning of a sentence, and small fractions. Nearly everything else in business is written with figures.

C.L.U.E. Checkpoint

Correct any inappropriate expression of numbers. Mark *C* if a sentence is correct.

1. 1400 people in 4 different counties have already signed the recall petition.

2. 9 employees have signed up to attend the training session at 1 p.m.

3. On January 15th we will advertise 2 job openings.

4. Although Mike budgeted only twenty dollars, he actually spent 39.95 for the gift.

5. At the age of 21, Gordon started a business with an investment of ten thousand dollars.

6. Within 2 years he offered a 1/2 interest to several friends.

7. Our sales force of 9 representatives serves 900 accounts in 3 countries.

8. The unemployment rate was five point six percent for the six-month period.

9. Your loan is at 9% for sixty days and is payable on March 12th.

10. Our 3 branch offices, with a total of ninety-six workers, need to add six computers and three printers.

"Ho-hum" business writing can be invigorated through revision. Revise to eliminate trite expressions (*Please do not hesitate to . . .*), business clichés (*As per your letter*), and wordy lead-ins (*This is to inform you that . . .*).

Super C.L.U.E. Review

These cumulative exercises review all the C.L.U.E. guides presented and even contain some spelling and confusing word errors for you to correct. See how many errors you can find and correct.

1. whoppers new Double bacon burger contains eight hundred 10 calories and costs three dollars and forty-nine cents.

2. Striving to garantee its sucess, whopper launched a three million dollar ad campaign.

3. The american association for training and development estimates that five percent of the nations employers will annually spend thirty billion dollars on employee training.

4. A rule of thumb for determining office-space needs is one hundred fifty to two hundred square feet per employee, plus fifteen percent for traffic flow.

5. Every cpa on our staff must occassionally travel to europe or asia.

6. In the next two years, government taxing policies will effect many businesses adversely.

7. The Manager received 3 complementary messages from customers about good service.

8. Centron oil company, with headquarters in western texas, hopes to accede it's past record of ten thousand gallons in a day.

9. 110 companys formerly located in the world trade center had to relocate.

10. The absense of our business manager and executive vice president for 5 days created havoc in the office.

SOLUTIONS

1. reader-oriented
2. express
3. revising
4. repeated
5. collaborative
6. inform
7. formality
8. profiling
9. tone
10. empathy

11. second
12. gender
13. disability
14. courteous
15. familiar
16. jargon
17. lawsuit
18. human resources
19. warnings
20. defamation

21. F In business, conciseness counts. Shorter is better.
22. T
23. F The major component in the writing process is revision.
24. F Writers complete each phase, but the order may be altered.
25. T
26. F Computer software programs help writers in all phases, especially in revising.
27. T
28. F Profiling is an important step in the prewriting phase of the process.
29. T
30. T

31. Seven ways that computer software can help you create better messages:
    a. Fight writer's block.
    b. Collect information electronically.
    c. Outline and organize ideas.
    d. Improve correctness and precision.
    e. Add graphics for emphasis.
    f. Design and produce professional-looking documents, presentations, and Web pages.
    g. Use collaborative software for team writing.

32. Face-to-face conversation

33. Voice mail

34. Face-to-face group meeting

35. Four kinds of biases: gender, racial or ethnic, age, and disability

36. So that you may receive your monthly newsletter on time, please complete the enclosed card.

37. You no longer need to suffer from writer's block. Our new software "Brainstorm" . . .

38. Your requirements for the assistant buyer position match my education and training.

39. To enable you to continue purchasing name brands at discount prices, we are unable to give cash refunds on returned merchandise. OR, We offer merchandise exchanges for returned goods.

40. Although Jim uses a wheelchair, . . .

41. uses a spell checker

42. their spouses will

43. New subscribers may cancel their subscriptions...

44. Ricky Cortez is our new sales representative.

45. We can send you your VCR January 1. OR, You will be receiving your VCR about January 1.

46. In response to your message, we are investigating your experience at our Orlando resort.

47. Your letter arrived in our New York office May 5.

48. Cash refunds are given only for merchandise returned with a sales receipt.

49. You'll be pleased with your subscription to...

50. So that you may be enrolled immediately, please complete this application.

51. Let's review the instruction manual and install the fax paper together so that you can learn how to do it.

52. Your policy covers only drivers 21 and over.

53. Please find out what the pay will be for this position.

54. As we discussed, I plan to ask Kathleen about computer use.

Career Track Spelling
1. across
2. paid
3. exempt
4. miscellaneous
5. genuine
6. February
7. permanent
8. C
9. congratulate
10. envelopes

Career Track Vocabulary
1. b
2. c
3. e
4. f
5. a
6. d
7. b
8. a
9. c
10. a
11. c
12. b
13. c
14. b
15. counsel
16. compliment
17. coarse

It isn't aptitude, but attitude that gives you altitude.

18. council
19. complement
20. course

C.L.U.E. Checkpoint
1. Fourteen hundred people in four
2. Nine [Note that only one period ends the sentence.]
3. January 15 [omit the *th*]   two
4. $20 $39.95
5. twenty-one $10,000
6. two   one-half [Note that you hyphenate fractions used as adjectives.]
7. nine   three countries
8. 5.6 percent
9. 9 percent   60 days [Business terms may be expressed as figures.] March 12
10. three   96 workers

Super C.L.U.E. Review
1. Whopper's   Double Bacon Burger 810 calories $3.49
2. guarantee success   Whopper $3 million
3. American Association for Training and Development   5 percent   nation's $30 billion
4. 150 to 200 square feet   15 percent
5. CPA occa<u>s</u>ionally   Europe   Asia
6. <u>a</u>ffect
7. manager   three compl<u>i</u>mentary
8. Centron Oil Company   western Texas   <u>exce</u>ed   its   10,000
9. One hundred ten compan<u>ies</u> [or *A total of 110 companies*] World Trade Center
10. absence   five days

Chapter 6

Organizing and Writing Business Messages

CHAPTER REVIEW

_____ 1. Formal research methods include all but which of the following?
   a. Developing a cluster diagram
   b. Experimenting scientifically
   c. Accessing electronically
   d. Investigating primary sources (Obj. 1, p. 155)

_____ 2. Each major category in an outline should be divided into at least
   a. three subcategories.
   b. four subcategories.
   c. five subcategories.
   d. two subcategories. (Obj. 2, p. 161)

_____ 3. An outline that presents details, explanations, and evidence after the main idea follows the
   a. indirect organizational pattern.
   b. direct organizational pattern.
   c. geographical organizational pattern.
   d. informational organizational pattern. (Obj. 3, p. 163)

_____ 4. The indirect organizational pattern does all but which of the following?
   a. Saves the reader's time.
   b. Ensures a fair hearing.
   c. Minimizes negative reaction.
   d. Respects the feelings of the audience. (Obj. 3, p. 164)

_____ 5. If an audience will be receptive to a message, the most effective organizational pattern to use is the
   a. indirect pattern.
   b. direct pattern.
   c. informational pattern.
   d. geographical pattern. (Obj. 3, p. 163)

_____ 6. *Frontloading* means
   a. presenting the recommendations at the end of the message where they will receive more emphasis.
   b. giving the details at the beginning of the message.
   c. supporting ideas with details.
   d. presenting the main idea at the beginning of the message. (Obj. 3, p. 163)

_____ 7. Ideas that require persuasion should usually be organized
     a. in an indirect pattern.
     b. by geographical area.
     c. in a direct pattern.
     d. in a pivoting pattern. (Obj. 3, p. 164)

_____ 8. Clauses that begin with words like _if, when, because,_ and _as_ are usually
     a. independent.
     b. direct.
     c. indirect.
     d. dependent. (Obj. 4, p. 166)

_____ 9. To be easily understood, sentences should
     a. be no more than 15 words in length.
     b. be about 20 or fewer words.
     c. be no longer than 30 words.
     d. average about 28 words. (Obj. 4, p. 167)

_____ 10. To direct attention away from people and to focus on the action instead, use
     a. dependent clauses.
     b. passive voice.
     c. active voice.
     d. independent clauses. (Obj. 4, p. 168)

_____ 11. A paragraph that describes a new procedure for scheduling a leave of absence would most likely follow the
     a. direct paragraph plan.
     b. indirect paragraph plan.
     c. pivoting paragraph plan.
     d. linked paragraph plan. (Obj. 5, p. 170)

_____ 12. Use the pivoting paragraph plan to
     a. describe an action to be taken.
     b. clarify a new procedure.
     c. build a rationale for an idea.
     d. compare and contrast ideas. (Obj. 5, p. 171)

_____ 13. Which of the following is _not_ a useful technique for linking ideas in a paragraph?
     a. Dovetailing sentences
     b. Pivoting sentences
     c. Sustaining the key idea
     d. Using pronouns (Obj. 5, p. 172)

_____ 14. Research for any writing project should be
     a. conducted before starting to write.
     b. conducted during the writing process so that corrections can easily be made.
     c. done after writing is completed so that facts can be verified.
     d. done with a large brainstorming group. (Obj. 1, p. 154)

_____15. Writers of well-organized messages
   a. always begin with alphanumeric outlines showing ten or more major ideas.
   b. break all subpoints into major components.
   c. strive for overlapping categories so that readers can see relationships.
   d. group similar ideas together. (Obj. 2, p. 160)

Use T or F to indicate whether the following statements are true or false.

_____16. Long reports usually require use of formal research methods. (Obj. 1, p. 155)

_____17. Scientific experiments are usually conducted to gather opinions of a target audience. (Obj. 1, p. 155)

_____18. A cluster diagram can be used to generate and organize ideas. (Obj. 1, p. 158)

_____19. In developing a cluster diagram, you should carefully select ideas, evaluating each to be certain it is appropriate for this topic. (Obj. 1, p. 158)

_____20. Concentrate carefully on punctuation, grammar, and proper wording of a message as you write the first draft of a document. (Obj. 4, pp. 165–166)

_____21. Most routine communication tasks require formal data collection. (Obj. 1, p. 156)

_____22. Passive-voice sentences are generally shorter than active-voice sentences. (Obj. 4, p. 168)

_____23. Organizing an unpleasant message in an indirect pattern guarantees that the reader will react positively. (Obj. 3, p. 164)

_____24. To be most effective, paragraphs should be limited to eight or fewer printed lines. (Obj. 5, p. 173)

_____25. A paragraph is two or more sentences designated as a single thought group. (Obj. 5, p. 169)

_____26. Use transitional expressions to anticipate what's coming, to reduce uncertainty, and to speed up comprehension. (Obj. 5, p. 172)

_____27. Unorganized messages jump from one thought to another. (Obj. 2, p. 160)

_____28. Paragraphs that follow the pivoting plan begin with supporting sentences and conclude with the main sentence. (Obj. 5, p. 171)

_____29. Sentences of fewer than 20 words have the most impact. (Obj. 4, p. 167)

_____30. Organizing one's ideas ahead of time is a good way to prevent writer's block. (Obj. 4, pp. 165–166)

Check your answers now!

Sentence Elements

Indicate whether the following word groups are independent clauses (IC), dependent clauses (DC), or phrases (P). In clauses underline subjects once and verbs twice. (Obj. 4)

_____ 31. you should approach a job interview with lots of self-confidence

_____ 32. when I see someone who is obviously very nervous

_____ 33. if a candidate is well prepared and has done his or her homework

_____ 34. to extend your hand in greeting to the personnel officer

_____ 35. naturally, employers are concerned with employee turnover

Sentence Length

Revise, improve, and shorten the following sentences. Use appropriate transitional expressions. (Obj. 4)

36. Questions about career advancement present a delicate problem because you need this information to make an informed career choice, but you risk alienating an employer who does not want to hire an unrealistically ambitious college graduate for the average entry-level position, so some recruiters warn against asking straight out how soon you can be considered for a promotion.

37. You can tell when an employment interview is winding down because the interviewer will ask if you have any questions, and this is the time for you to ask questions but you also want to accomplish other things, such as recapping your strengths and going over the key points you want to leave the interviewer with, in addition to showing your enthusiasm, dependability, and clarity of focus.

Active and Passive Voice

Business writing is more forceful if it uses active-voice verbs. In the following sentences convert passive-voice verbs to active-voice verbs. Add subjects if necessary. (Obj. 4)

Passive: The accounting report was not turned in on time [by Melissa].
Active: Melissa did not turn in the accounting report on time.

38. A separate bill from AT&T will be sent to customers who continue to lease equipment.

39. Initial figures for the bid were submitted before the June 1 deadline. [Tip: Who submitted the figures?]

40. Substantial sums of money were saved by customers who enrolled early in the plan.

41. A networked system was installed so that company data could be shared more easily.

When you wish to emphasize an action or if you must be tactful, passive-voice verbs may be appropriate. Revise the following sentences so that they are in the passive voice. Notice how the doer of the action may go unmentioned.

Active: Mr. Eaton made three significant errors in the Globex audit.
Passive: Three significant errors were made in the Globex audit.

42. We will notify you immediately if we make any changes in your travel arrangements.

43. We cannot ship your order for 20 printers until May 15.

44. The government first issued a warning about the use of this pesticide 15 months ago.

45. The private laboratory rated products primarily on the basis of their performance.

Misplaced Modifiers

Remedy any dangling or misplaced modifiers in the following sentences. Add subjects as needed, but retain the introductory phrases. Mark *C* if correct. (Obj. 4)

46. When shopping for computers, the best buys are from mail-order houses.

47. As assistant editor, your duties will include interviewing executives.

48. To receive double frequent-flyer miles, reservations must be made before September 1.

49. The computer packs a lot of power into a one-pound package that fits in a man's coat pocket or a midsized woman's purse.

50. Having located the error, the search was halted.

51. Yoko Ono will discuss her husband John Lennon, who was killed in an interview with Barbara Walters.

52. To train employees in flowcharting, simple examples were used for illustrations.

53. Ignoring the warning on the screen, the computer was turned off.

54. The bride was given away by her father wearing a dress with a blue bodice.

55. Speaking before a large audience, butterflies filled my stomach.

56. To enter the drawing for a free trip to Acapulco, fill out the enclosed coupon.

Transitional Expressions

Add transitional expressions to improve the flow of ideas (coherence) of the following sentence groups. (Obj. 5)

57. We tailor our service efforts specifically to individual customer needs. We have seen the volume at our plants grow. Our profitability has increased. We expect even better results in the future.

58. No business can anticipate every customer's needs. We keep our hotel management staff on duty 24 hours a day. Customers always have someone of authority available.

59. Your responsibility is to listen to customers. Your responsibility is to understand what they are saying. Your responsibility is to make them feel that their concerns are your most important concerns. Your responsibility is to take care of their concerns to their satisfaction.

CAREER TRACK SPELLING

Spelling Challenge

Underline misspelled words. Write correct forms in the spaces provided. Some sentences may have more than one misspelled word. If a sentence is correct, write *C*. Then check your answers with those at the end of the chapter. Be sure to add any words that you missed to your Spelling Monsters list.

_____ 1. Only 120 useable questionnaires were returned to the researchers.

_____ 2. The secretery filed all the softwear in separate folders.

_____ 3. To receive a good recomendation, you must make a smart request.

_____ 4. Your checks will be automaticly canceled when they reach the bank.

_____ 5. Parking was becomming unecessarily difficult because of visitors.

_____ 6. Checking references thoroughly is benificial to accurate reporting.

_____ 7. We sincerly believe, therefor, that honesty is the best policy.

_____ 8. I am writing to inform you of an ommission in my application.

_____ 9. We received a pamflet describing a procedure to reduce junk mail.

_____ 10. Our local libary has pleazant surroundings and helpful clerks.

My Spelling Monsters

List each troublesome word. Be sure to spell it correctly. Then, write it four or more times. Review this page often to help you vanquish these spelling demons.

_____

_____

_____

_____

_____

_____

CAREER TRACK VOCABULARY

Use your dictionary to define the words in Column A. Then select the best definition in Column B to match the word in Column A.

	Column A		Column B
_____	1. discretionary	a.	list, agenda
_____	2. disperse	b.	humility, respect
_____	3. deign	c.	scatter, strew
_____	4. deference	d.	positive, assertive
_____	5. docket	e.	optional, voluntary
_____	6. dogmatic	f.	condescend, to see fit

Choose the best meaning for the following underlined words.

_____ 7. Who can resist the smell that <u>emanates</u> from freshly baked bread?

       a. emigrates   b. flows from   c. erupts

_____ 8. The basketball star told his fans not to <u>emulate</u> him; but then, paradoxically, he endorsed products on television.

       a. imitate   b. quote   c. parody

_____ 9. Plants chosen as state flowers are usually <u>endemic</u> to the area.

       a. foreign   b. imported   c. native

_____ 10. From executives, stockholders want performance that is <u>equivalent</u> to their lofty salaries.

       a. transcendent   b. commensurate   c. inferior

_____ 11. Some computer programs are difficult for some users to use because of <u>esoteric</u> keyboard entries.

       a. obscure   b. rapid   c. obvious

_____ 12. This item is needed immediately; please <u>expedite</u> the order.

       a. reserve   b. hand carry   c. rush

_____ 13. Use care when putting paper in the fax; it is difficult to <u>extricate</u> when jammed.

       a. smooth   b. remove   c. photocopy

_____ 14. The organization's glamorous <u>facade</u> was shattered by recent scandals.

       a. artificial appearance   b. prosperous clientele   c. entertainment schedule

Confusing Words

conscience	regard for fairness	*desert*	arid land; abandon
conscious	aware	*dessert*	sweet food
credible	believable or reliable	*device*	invention or mechanism
creditable	bringing honor or praise	*devise*	to design or arrange

15. We rely on *The Wall Street Journal* for _____ financial news.

16. This new document holder is a great _____ for computer users.

17. The bakery's motto is, "Eat _____ first; life's uncertain."

18. Before asking all employees to work overtime, the manager searched his _____.

19. Please _____ an effective, efficient disk-storage system for our office.

20. Sara's academic record was so _____ that she was named winner of the John F. Kennedy award.

21. Most employees are very _____ of an organization's communication climate.

22. In the midst of a huge traffic jam, the driver wished he could _____ his car.

Look back over the 20 vocabulary words in this chapter. Select 5 or more new words to add to your vocabulary. Double-check the meanings of your selections in a dictionary. Then write a sentence for each of your words.

_____

_____

_____

_____

_____

_____

 COMPETENT LANGUAGE USAGE ESSENTIALS (C.L.U.E.)

Commas

Guide 21: Use commas to separate three or more items (words, phrases, or short clauses) in a series.

The president was tanned, rested, and ready to return to work.

Robert designed a questionnaire, collected data, and made recommendations.

From the freezer section she selected corn, broccoli, peas, and carrots.

 TIP. Some writers omit the comma before *and*. However, business writers prefer to retain the comma because it prevents misreading the last two items as one. Notice in the previous example how the final two vegetables (peas and carrots) could be misread if the comma had been omitted.

Guide 22: Use commas to separate introductory clauses and certain phrases from independent clauses. This guideline describes the comma most often omitted by business writers. Sentences that open with dependent clauses (often introduced by words like *since, when, if, as, al-*

though, and *because*) require commas to separate them from the main idea. The comma helps readers recognize where the introduction ends and the main idea begins. Introductory phrases of more than five words or phrases containing verbal elements also require commas.

> Since she does all her writing at her computer, she needed a laptop for traveling. (Introductory dependent clause requires a comma.)

> When you purchase a small truck, you have many models from which to choose. (Introductory dependent clause)

> If necessary, you may have a co-signer help you with the purchase. (You may assume the subject and verb of the introductory clause, *If it is necessary*.)

> In the fall of next year, we plan to hire new representatives. (Introductory phrases of five or more words require a comma.)

> Having studied our competitor's techniques, we see many areas for improvement. (Introductory phrase containing a verbal element requires a comma.)

> To succeed, we must cut costs and improve quality. (Introductory phrase containing a verbal element requires a comma.)

Guide 23: Use a comma before the coordinating conjunction in a compound sentence.

> Interest rates were falling, and homeowners were eager to refinance.

> Some homeowners refinanced immediately, but others waited for even lower rates.

 TIP. Before inserting a comma, test the two clauses. Can each of them stand alone as a complete sentence? If either is incomplete, skip the comma.

> Lenders require a letter from your employer *or* a copy of your W-2 forms from the past two years. (Note that the words following *or* do not form an independent clause; hence, no comma is needed.)

> Judy majored in communications *and* took a job in public relations. (No comma is required because the words following *and* do not form an independent clause.)

C.L.U.E. Checkpoint

Use proofreading marks to insert necessary commas.

1.   When she enrolled at Midwestern University Tina was unsure of a major.

2.   Mike found courses in history marketing and management to be most stimulating.

3.   After writing a dynamite résumé he sent it to 11 companies on his list.

4.   Government in this country is intended to be of the people by the people and for the people.

5. Having considered many companies Mike decided to target those in the West.

6. In the spring of this year Unitech received hundreds of résumés.

7. A cover letter is meant to introduce your résumé and to help you secure a personal interview.

8. She submitted a résumé to eight companies and began thinking about friends relatives and acquaintances to serve as a network in her job search.

9. A few companies send recruiters to college campuses in the fall but many more send representatives and conduct interviews in the spring.

10. When possible Unitech sends campus representatives distributes promotional literature and conducts interviews with promising candidates.

Super C.L.U.E. Review

In this cumulative review, use proofreading marks to correct punctuation, number usage, capitalization, spelling, and confusing word use. Mark *C* if a sentence is correct.

1. Approximatly twenty to thirty percent of all companies must restructure to reduce errors delays and inflexibility.

2. When coca-cola and pepsi compete in asia they will spend hundreds of thousands of dollars in marketing efforts.

3. Employees are encouraged to ask questions and these questions become a valuable source of feedback to management.

4. 34% of the twelve hundred job applicants in one study falsified information on their résumés.

5. The same study reported that only one third of employers use any verification procedures in checking employment applications.

6. Our human resources manager schedules and attends all job interviews but the hiring managers make all final selections.

7. The house was apprised at 125,000 dollars, however we felt its actual worth was at least twenty percent more.

8. We reccommend that fifteen realtors visit the property at ten a.m. and that the remaining twenty-three inspect it between 3:30 and five p.m.

9. When the recruiter visited indiana state university she was conscience of increased campus interest in ethics.

10. Having compared the 2 propertys we plan to offer ninety thousand dollars for the plaza building.

SOLUTIONS

Chapter Review

1. a
2. d
3. b
4. a
5. b
6. d
7. a
8. d
9. b
10. b
11. a
12. d
13. b
14. a
15. d

16. T
17. F   Surveys, not scientific experiments, usually gather opinions of target audiences.
18. T
19. F   Avoid evaluating ideas in the initial stages of cluster diagramming.
20. F   Save careful proofreading for the final draft.
21. F   Most routine communication tasks require only informal data collection.
22. F   Active-voice sentences are generally shorter than passive-voice sentences.
23. F   The indirect pattern *improves* the chance of a positive reader reaction but does not guarantee such a reaction.
24. T
25. F   A paragraph may have only *one* sentence.
26. T
27. T
28. F   A paragraph that follows the pivoting plan begins with limiting sentences followed by the main sentence.
29. T
30. T

31. IC; subject = you, verb = should approach
32. DC; subject = I, verb = see
33. DC; subject = candidate, verb = is prepared and has done
34. P [phrases do not have subjects and verbs]
35. IC; subject = employers, verb = are concerned

36. Questions about career advancement present a delicate problem. On one hand, you need this information to make an informed career choice. On the other hand, you risk alienating an employer who does not want to hire an unrealistically ambitious college graduate for the average entry-level position. As a result, some recruiters warn against asking straight out how soon you can be considered for a promotion.

37. You can tell when an employment interview is winding down; the interviewer will ask if you have any questions. This is the time for you to ask questions. However, you also want to accomplish other things. First, you should recap your strengths. Second, you'll want to go over key points with which to leave the interviewer. Finally, you'll try to show your enthusiasm, dependability, and clarity of focus.

38. AT&T will send separate bills to customers who continue to lease equipment.

39. The company submitted additional figures for the bid before the June 1 deadline.

40. Customers who enrolled early in the plan saved substantial sums of money.

41. We installed a networked system so that we could share company data more easily.

42. You will be notified immediately if any changes are made in your travel arrangements.

43. Your order for 20 printers cannot be shipped until May 15. OR, We can ship your order for 20 printers May 15.

44. A warning about the use of this pesticide was first issued 15 months ago.

45. Products were rated by a private laboratory primarily on the basis of their performance.

46. When shopping for computers, customers [or you] will get the best buys from mail-order houses.

47. As assistant editors, you will be interviewing executives.

48. To receive double frequent-flyer miles, you must make reservations before September 1.

49. The computer packs a lot of power into a one-pound package that fits in a man's coat pocket or a woman's midsized purse.

50. Having located the error, we halted the search.

51. In an interview with Barbara Walters, Yoko Ono will discuss her husband John Lennon.

52. To train employees in flowcharting, trainers [or *we*] used simple examples as illustrations.

53. Ignoring the warning on the screen, the operator turned the computer off.

54. Wearing a dress with a blue bodice, the bride was given away by her father.

55. Speaking before a large audience, I felt butterflies filling my stomach.

56. C [The subject of this command is "you"; therefore, the introductory verbal phrase is followed by its logical subject.]

The following sentences may be correctly revised in many ways other than the revisions shown.

57. We tailor our service efforts specifically to individual customer needs. Consequently, we have seen the volume at our plants grow. Moreover, profitability has increased, and we expect even better results in the future.

58. Because no business can anticipate every customer's needs, we keep our hotel management staff on duty 24 hours a day. In this way, customers always have someone of authority available.

59. Your responsibility is to listen to customers and hear what they are saying. In addition, you are responsible for making them feel that their concerns are your concerns. Your responsibility also includes taking care of their concerns to their satisfaction.

Career Track Spelling

1. usable
2. secretary, software
3. recommendation
4. automatically
5. becoming, unnecessarily
6. beneficial
7. sincerely, therefore
8. omission
9. pamphlet
10. library, pleasant

Career Track Vocabulary

1. e
2. c
3. f
4. b
5. a
6. d
7. b
8. a
9. c
10. b
11. a
12. c
13. b
14. a
15. credible
16. device
17. dessert
18. conscience
19. devise
20. creditable
21. conscious
22. desert

C.L.U.E. Checkpoint

1. University,
2. history, marketing,
3. résumé
4. of the people, by the people,
5. companies,
6. year,
7. No commas [No comma is necessary before *and* because it does not introduce an independent clause.]
8. friends, relatives, [No comma is necessary after *companies* because it is not followed by an independent clause.]
9. fall,
10. possible,   representatives, distributes promotional literature,

Super C.L.U.E. Review

1. Approximately 20 to 30 percent   errors, delays,
2. Coca-Cola   Pepsi   Asia,
3. to ask questions, and
4. Thirty-four percent   1,200
5. C [Do not hyphenate *one third* because it functions as a noun in this sentence.]
6. interviews,
7. appraised $125,000; however,   20 percent
8. recommend   15 realtors   10 a.m.   23   5 p.m. [No comma is needed before *and* because it does not introduce an independent clause.]
9. Indiana State University,   conscious
10. two properties, $90,000   Plaza Building.

Chapter 7

Revising Business Messages

CHAPTER REVIEW

Use the listed words to complete the following sentences. Each word is used but once.

| anticipation | graphic highlighting | parallelism | pompous | redundant |
| boring | heading | perfect | readability | simple |

1. Revision is an important part of the writing process. Only amateurs expect their writing to be _____ on the first effort. (Obj. 1, p. 183)

2. Because the goal of business writing is to *express* rather than *impress*, your writing should be conversational and _____. (Obj. 1, p. 183)

3. Expressions that repeat meaning or include unnecessary words are _____. (Obj. 1, p. 185)

4. Much business writing has been criticized as lifeless, cautious, and "really, really _____." Your writing can avoid this fault by eliminating wordiness and dull, trite expressions. (Obj. 2, p. 187)

5. A writing technique that involves balanced construction is called _____. This technique matches nouns with nouns, verbs with verbs, and phrases with phrases. (Obj. 3, p. 188)

6. The Fog Index is a formula that measures _____. Long sentences and long words (those over two syllables) make writing foggy. (Obj. 3, p. 190)

7. A well-written _____ enables readers to separate major ideas from details. This writing device helps readers skim familiar or less important information. (Obj. 3, p. 189)

8. One of the best ways to improve comprehension is through _____. This technique includes spotlighting ideas with numerals, letters, bullets, lists, headings, capital letters, underscoring, and other graphic techniques. Because of laser printers and desktop-publishing programs, today's business writers are increasingly making use of design techniques to turn out professional-looking documents. (Obj. 3, p. 189)

Proofreading and Evaluating

analysis	feedback	numbers	speed	time
expertise	grammar checker	rough draft	spell checker	words

9. Two items that require special care in proofreading are names and _____ because inaccuracies are not immediately visible. (Obj. 4, p. 193)

10. Although you may proofread routine documents on a computer screen, it's better to print a _____ and read from a printed copy. (Obj. 5, p. 193)

11. Because a common excuse for sloppy proofreading is lack of _____, you should develop and follow a careful schedule for writing projects. (Obj. 5, p. 195)

12. One way to improve your proofreading accuracy is to reduce your reading _____. (Obj. 5, p. 195)

13. Proofreading complex documents requires that you concentrate on individual _____ instead of ideas. (Obj. 5, p. 195)

14. A computer program that analyzes writing characteristics—such as passive voice, trite phrases, split infinitives, and wordy expressions—is called a _____. (Obj. 5, p. 195)

15. Although it's sometimes difficult to avoid being defensive, business writers should welcome _____ and constructive criticism. (Obj. 6, p. 195)

Indicate whether the following statements are true or false by using T or F.

_____ 16. Business writing requires many technical words and third-person constructions. (Obj. 1, p. 183)

_____ 17. Trim sentences, like trim bodies, require far more effort than flabby ones. (Obj. 1, p. 185)

_____ 18. *There is, it is*, and *this is* are usually good conversational openings for sentences. (Obj. 1, p. 185)

_____ 19. The Fog Index accurately detects all words that may be difficult for readers. (Obj. 3, p. 190)

_____ 20. To be most effective, graphic highlighting techniques should be used repeatedly throughout the text of a document. (Obj. 3, p. 189)

_____ 21. Business writers should focus on using noun phrases (*to make an analysis of*) instead of using action verbs (*to analyze*). (Obj. 2, p. 187)

_____22. Proofread an important document immediately after completing the first draft.
(Obj. 5, p. 195)

_____23. A useful technique for proofreading important documents that must be perfect is reading those documents aloud. (Obj. 5, p. 195)

_____24. Encourage feedback from the receiver as part of the process of evaluating your writing efforts. (Obj. 6, p. 195)

_____25. *Advance warning*, *each and every*, *grateful thanks*, and *positively certain* are examples of
a. jargon.
b. parallel construction.
c. redundancies.
d. compound prepositions. (Obj. 1, p. 186)

_____26. Which of the following examples is free of clichés, fillers, and compound prepositions?
a. This is to inform you that the meeting will be held next Thursday.
b. Due to the fact that many people were busy, the meeting was postponed.
c. The meeting has been rescheduled for Thursday.
d. Please do not hesitate to call if you have any questions about the meeting.
(Objs. 1 & 2, pp. 185–187)

_____27. Which of the following expressions is free from redundancy?
a. proposed meeting
b. midway between
c. exactly identical
d. collect together (Obj. 1, p. 186)

_____28. Business expressions that have been used excessively over the years and are no longer original are called
a. noun phrases.
b. parallel construction.
c. trite expressions.
d. noun constructions. (Obj. 2, p. 187)

_____29. Which of the following statements is *incorrect*?
a. Headings can be used effectively for graphic highlighting.
b. Graphic highlighting can be used to achieve parallelism.
c. Graphic highlighting helps improve comprehension.
d. Writers who use graphic highlighting are usually considered efficient and well organized. (Obj. 3, p. 189)

_____30. All but which of the following is important when proofreading complex documents?
a. Proofread the document at least a day after it has been completed.
b. Read the message at least twice.
c. Be sure the document is in WYSIWYG mode.
d. Allow adequate time to proofread carefully. (Obj. 5, p. 195)

_____ 31. Bullets, enumerated lists, headings, boldface, and italics help writers to
  a. improve comprehension.
  b. eliminate redundancies.
  c. reduce trite phrases.
  d. apply the KISS formula. (Obj. 3, p. 189)

_____ 32. Some business writers are unable to produce simple, direct messages because they
  a. worry that plain messages won't sound impressive or important.
  b. fear that plain talk won't impress the boss.
  c. have not learned to communicate clearly.
  d. all of the above. (Obj. 1, p. 183)

33. Name six specific items to check in proofreading. (Obj. 4, pp. 192–193)

34. List seven techniques for proofreading complex documents. (Obj. 5, p. 195)

35. How is revision different from proofreading? (Objs. 1–5, pp. 182–195)

"Many seem to believe that what matters is what you say, not how you say it, and they're half right. Thoughts that are trite or shallow or poorly reasoned do not, when felicitously expressed, turn into penetrating insights. An embroidered sow's ear remains a sow's ear, and style is no substitute for substance. But substance buried in an unreadable presentation isn't worth much either. Polishing can enhance a diamond in the rough, and if you have the right stuff, editing can vastly increase its value."
—Claire Kehrwald Cook, _Line by Line_

Clarity

Revise the following sentences to make them direct, simple, and conversational. (Obj. 1)

36. As you suggested in your verbal instruction, the employees on our staff will initiate and conduct an examination of our credit card policy to determine if it is possible and probable that it needs to be changed.

37. If on our part there is any doubt entertained regarding an optimal solution to the problem of acquisition of new computers, it is my suggestion that we commence an investigation of our usage of our current computer equipment.

38. Please be assured that the undersigned takes pleasure in advising you that your order will be delivered about February 10.

39. It is our considered opinion that you should not attempt to advance or proceed with this project until you seek and receive approval of said project from the department head prior to beginning the project.

40. This organization is honored to have the pleasure of extending a welcome to you as a new customer.

Conciseness

Revise and shorten the following sentences. (Obj. 2)

41. There are three employees who wish to vacation in July.

42. Due to the fact the statement seemed wrong, I sent a check in the amount of $200.

43. In the case of Mattel and Fisher-Price, the two toy companies merged their lines.

44. It is perfectly clear that he was aware of the fact that sales figures were slipping.

45. Until such time as we can locate all addresses that are duplicates, this is to notify you that mass mailings must be avoided.

46. Despite the fact that there is only one van available, response to the program designated for employee van pooling is remarkable.

47. It is important to remember the fact that service is our first and foremost priority.

48. Those who are functioning as vendors may not have a complete and full understanding of our difficulty.

49. This is just to let you know that applications will be accepted at a later date for positions that are at the entry level.

50. There are many words that can be eliminated through revision that is carefully executed.

Vigor

Revise the following sentences to reduce noun conversions, trite expressions, and other wordiness. (Obj. 2)

51. There are three members of our staff who are making every effort to locate your order.

52. Sandy Jones has been asked to make a comparison of health care plans.

53. Please give consideration to our latest proposal, despite the fact that it comes into conflict with our original goals.

54. After we engage in the preparation of a report, we will make a recommendation in regard to an improved parking plan.

55. If you are in need of any further assistance, please do not hesitate to make a call to me at (212) 499-3029.

Parallelism

Revise the following sentences to improve parallelism. (Obj. 3)

56. As a successful entrepreneur, I wrote a business plan and cash flow was analyzed, as well as designed promotional materials and was responsible for the marketing of the business.

57. After reviewing the frequency, duration, and the amount of intensiveness of exercise, researchers classified 58 percent of the people as sedentary.

58. Ensuring equal opportunities and the elimination of age discrimination are our goals.

59. Ms. Cortez reads all incoming résumés, sorts them into categories, and their distribution is completed within five days.

60. In my last job I set up a log of all incoming materials, the contents were inspected and findings documented, after which I reported results to shipping.

Check your answers now!

CAREER TRACK SPELLING

For each group below identify misspelled words and write corrected versions in the spaces provided. Write *C* if all words are correct.

1. analyze	license	embarass	separate	_____
2. supervisor	schedule	profited	refered	_____
3. using	employee	developement	correspondence	_____
4. ocurred	advisable	practicle	remittance	_____
5. emphasis	consecutive	calander	describe	_____
6. especially	fascinate	ninty	division	_____
7. courteous	nevertheless	greatful	excellent	_____
8. maintinance	fiscal	forty	qualify	_____
9. extraordinary	incredible	evidentally	foriegn	_____
10. friend	representative	yield	surprise	_____

My Spelling Monsters

List each word that you missed or had trouble with. Be sure to spell it correctly. Then, write it four or more times. Review this page often to help you vanquish these spelling demons.

_____

_____

_____

_____

_____

CAREER TRACK VOCABULARY

Use your dictionary to define the words in Column A. Then select the best definition in Column B to match the word in Column A.

Column A

_____ 1. efface
_____ 2. egress
_____ 3. equitable
_____ 4. escrow
_____ 5. fluent
_____ 6. formidable

Column B

a. emergence, exit
b. obliterate, wipe out
c. arduous, difficult
d. eloquent, well-spoken
e. equal or identical in value
f. money put in trust, deposit

Choose the best meaning for the following underlined words.

_____ 7. Dr. Loy's neat desk illustrates his <u>fastidious</u> personality.

a. indifferent   b. meticulous   c. creative

_____ 8. As a result of the Republican <u>filibuster</u>, the budget failed to pass.

a. delaying speeches   b. investment   c. support

_____ 9. Demonstrators worked hard to <u>foment</u> a riot, but their words were ignored.

a. delay   b. incite   c. avoid

_____ 10. California leads the nation in <u>fraudulent</u> auto accident claims.

a. honest   b. expensive   c. deceitful

_____ 11. Pictures can't impart the <u>grandeur</u> of Niagara Falls.

a. majesty   b. tranquility   c. ferocity

_____ 12. Jim received a <u>gratuity</u> from the company for his cost-cutting suggestion.

      a. compliment   b. tip   c. salary

_____ 13. In the hotel business a <u>gregarious</u> personality is an asset.

      a. defiant   b. placid   c. sociable

_____ 14. Unfamiliar with the storeroom, the secretary <u>groped</u> for the light switch.

      a. looked   b. fumbled   c. lunged

Confusing Words

disburse	to pay out	*elicit*	to draw out
disperse	to scatter wildly	*illicit*	unlawful

envelop	to wrap, surround, or conceal
envelope	a container for a letter

15. Our treasurer promised to _____ all funds in accordance with the by-laws.

16. Use a Priority Mail _____ for two-day delivery.

17. David's humorous comments are sure to _____ laughter from his audience.

18. The executive was charged with _____ behavior for attempting to bribe a congressman.

19. Because clouds often _____ Mount McKinley, photographers have difficulty getting a clear picture.

20. When planting wildflowers, lightly rake the soil before you _____ the seeds.

Now look back over the 20 vocabulary words in this chapter. Select 5 new words to add to your vocabulary. Double-check the meanings of your selections in a dictionary. Then write a sentence for each of your words.

_____

_____

_____

_____

_____

_____

_____

_____

_____

_____

_____

COMPETENT LANGUAGE USAGE ESSENTIALS (C.L.U.E.)

Commas (cont.)

Guide 24: Use commas appropriately in dates, addresses, geographical names, degrees, and long numbers.

November 3, 1976, is his birthday. (For dates use commas before and after the year.)

Send the announcement to Rob Silver, 1901 NW 23 Avenue, Portland, OR 97210, as soon as possible. (For addresses use commas to separate all units except the two-letter state abbreviation and the zip code.)

The Lees plan to move from Naperville, Illinois, to Waterloo, Iowa, in June. (For geographical areas use commas to enclose the second element.)

Mark Hendricks, Ph.D., and Davonne Williams, C.P.A., were the speakers. (For professional designations and academic degrees following names, use commas to enclose each item.)

We have budgeted $135,000 for new equipment. (In figures use commas to separate every three digits, counting from the right.)

Guide 25: Use commas to set off internal sentence interrupters. Sentence interrupters may be verbal phrases, dependent clauses, contrasting elements, or parenthetical expressions (also called transitional phrases). These interrupters often provide information that is not grammatically essential.

Globex International, having registered its name in Washington, started business. (Use commas to set off an interrupting verbal phrase.)

The new company, which planned to ship cargo only, was headquartered in Juneau. (Use commas to set off nonessential dependent clauses.)

Joe Franklin, who helped organize the new company, invested energy and capital. (Use commas to set off nonessential dependent clauses.)

It was Sam Williams, not Mike Thomas, who became the company attorney. (Use commas to set off a contrasting element.)

Several investors, on the contrary, were eager to meet the organizers. (Use commas to set off a parenthetical expression.)

Parenthetical (transitional) expressions are helpful words that guide the reader from one thought to the next. Here are representative parenthetical expressions that require commas:

as a matter of fact	consequently	in addition	nevertheless	on the other hand
as a result	for example	in the meantime	of course	therefore

TIP. Always use *two* commas to set off an interrupter, unless it begins or ends a sentence.

C.L.U.E. Checkpoint

Insert necessary commas.

1. Send the material to Scott M. Gallagher 20 Farrell Road Boston MA 02114 as soon as possible.

2. Our manager by the way is from Raleigh North Carolina.

3. Joan Winkoff who is one of the executives attending the conference plans to leave Thursday June 5.

4. The Family and Medical Leave Act which went into effect January 1 introduced new regulations about leaves of absence.

5. In the meantime please list David Smith as a contract not a permanent employee.

Super C.L.U.E. Review

In this cumulative review, use proofreading marks to correct punctuation, number usage, capitalization, spelling, and confusing word use. Mark *C* if a sentence is correct.

1. Start-up costs which should average about three thousand five hundred dollars include phones and advertising.

2. Eric Sims one of the four company founders invested capitol of just under thirty thousand dollars.

3. Companys now include disclaimers saying that the employee policy manual is not a contract that policies may be changed or withdrawn and that the individual and the company may seperate at any time for any reason.

4. Our new policy manual which was adapted from an industry publication is twenty-six pages long.

5. We advice that you call mrs. johnson not mr. andrew when you have accounting questions.

6. In today's fast-paced global marketplace companies that can move products through the development process fastest enjoy a cost advantage through increased efficeincy.

7. He wrote the book called How to align purpose strategy and structure.

8. Our goal should be a 20% not a 10% reduction in overhead costs.

CAREER APPLICATION

Using the proofreading marks shown in Chapter 7 or in Appendix D of Guffey's *Business Communication: Process and Product*, revise the following letter. Rectify wordy and trite phrases, sexist language, spelling, capitalization, number expression, and other faults. When you finish, compare your revision with that shown in the solutions at the end of this study guide (Appendix B).

October 5, 200x

Ms. Sharon Taylor
Title Guaranty Company
3401 Providence Avenue
Anchorage, AK, 99508

Dear Sharron:

Pursuant to our telephone conversation of October 4, this is to advise you that two (2) agent's packages will be sent to you October 6th. Due to the fact that you need these immediatly; we are using federal express.

Although we cannot offer a 50/50 commission split, we are able to offer new agents a 60/40 commission split. There are two new agreement forms that show this commission ratio. When you get ready to sign up a new agent have her fill in both forms.

When you send me an executed agency agreement, please make every effort to tell me what agency package was assigned to the agent. On the last form that you sent, you overlooked this information. We need this information to distribute commissions in an expeditious manner.

If you have any questions, don't hesitate to call on me.

Very truly yours,

SOLUTIONS

Chapter Review

1. perfect
2. simple
3. redundant
4. boring
5. parallelism
6. readability
7. heading
8. graphic highlighting

9. numbers
10. rough draft
11. time
12. speed
13. words
14. grammar checker
15. feedback

16. F Good writers strive for simple, conversational language.
17. T
18. F These are wordy fillers and should be avoided.
19. F The Fog Index merely reflects sentence and word length.
20. F Overuse of graphic highlighting reduces its effectiveness.
21. F Verbs are always preferable to noun phrases.
22. F It's better to put a document away and read it after a breather.
23. T
24. T

25. c
26. c
27. a
28. c
29. b
30. c WYSIWYG ("What you see is what you get") is a mode used to proofread on a computer screen. Instead, you should proofread complex documents from printed copy.
31. a
32. d

33. Spelling, grammar, punctuation, names, numbers, and format.

34. a. Proofread from a double-spaced printed copy.
    b. Set copy aside for a day and proofread after a breather.
    c. Be prepared to find errors.
    d. Read once for word meanings and once for grammar/mechanics. For long documents, read again for format consistency.
    e. Reduce your reading speed.
    f. Have someone read the message aloud. Verify names, difficult words, capitalization, and punctuation.
    g. Use standard proofreading marks to indicate changes.

35. Revision involves changing wording to improve clarity, tone, conciseness, vigor, and readability. Proofreading involves verifying spelling, grammar, punctuation, and format.

Clarity

36. As you suggested, we will examine our credit card policy to see whether it should be changed.

37. If we have doubts about purchasing new computers, we should investigate our current computer use.

38. Your order will be delivered about February 10.

39. We suggest that you gain the department head's approval before beginning the project.

40. We are pleased to welcome you as a new customer.

Conciseness

41. Three employees wish to vacation in July.

42. Because the statement seemed wrong, I sent a $200 check.

43. Mattel and Fisher-Price merged their toy lines.

44. Clearly, he knew that sales figures were slipping.

45. Until we can locate all duplicate addresses, avoid mass mailings.

46. Although only one van is available, response to the employee van pooling program is remarkable.

47. Please remember that service is our first priority.

48. Vendors may not fully [or *completely*] understand our difficulty.

49. Applications for entry-level positions will be accepted later.

50. Careful revision eliminates many words.

Vigor

51. Three staff members are trying to locate your order.

52. Sandy Jones has been asked to compare health care plans.

53. Please consider our latest proposal, even though it conflicts with our original goals.

54. After we prepare a report, we will recommend an improved parking plan.

55. If I may help, please call me at (212) 499-3029.

Parallelism

56. As a successful entrepreneur, I wrote a business plan, analyzed cash flow, designed promotional materials, and marketed the business.

57. After reviewing the frequency, duration, and intensity of exercise, researchers classified 58 percent of the people as sedentary.

58. Ensuring equal opportunities and eliminating age discrimination are our goals.

59. Ms. Cortez reads all incoming résumés, sorts them into categories, and distributes them within five days.

60. In my last job I set up a log of all incoming materials, inspected the contents, documented the findings, and reported the results to shipping.

Career Track Spelling

1. embarrass
2. referred
3. development
4. occurred, practical
5. calendar

6. ninety
7. grateful
8. maintenance
9. evidently, foreign
10. C

Career Track Vocabulary

1. b
2. a
3. e
4. f
5. d
6. c
7. b
8. a
9. b
10. c

11. a
12. b
13. c
14. b
15. disburse
16. envelope
17. elicit
18. illicit
19. envelop
20. disperse

C.L.U.E. Checkpoint

1. Gallagher, 20 Farrell Road, Boston, MA 02114,
2. manager, by the way,   Raleigh,
3. Winkoff,   conference,   Thursday,
4. Act,   January 1,
5. meantime,   contract,   permanent,

Super C.L.U.E. Review

1. costs, $3,500,
2. Sims, founders, capital $30,000
3. Companies   contract,   withdrawn,   separate   [Don't add any other commas than those shown here.]
4. manual,   publication,   26
5. advise   Mrs. Johnson,   Mr. Andrew,
6. marketplace,   efficiency   [Don't be tempted to add commas after *fastest* or *through*. They are unnecessary.]
7. How to Align Purpose, Strategy, and Structure
8. 20 percent,   10 percent,
9. costs,   analyze   strategies
10. way,   [This comma is necessary to join independent clauses.]

Career Application—Critical Thinking Questions

1.   The format of the letter should be either block or modified block rather than the combination shown. For block style avoid indenting the paragraphs. For modified block style, move the closing lines to the center.

2. A negative tone is created by such expressions as *you complain*, *misunderstanding*, *you claim*, *you must be aware*, and *we can't prevent you*.

3. The letter should be organized directly because the reader will be pleased with its message. It is now organized indirectly with explanations preceding the good news.

4. In adjustment letters the writer's three goals are to (a) rectify the wrong, if one exists, (b) regain the confidence of the customer, and (c) promote further business.

5. The good news is that the problem has been solved and that the double mailing will cease.

6. In this instance the writer should explain why the double mailing occurred, since little liability exists. However, if an explanation might place an organization at risk, that explanation should be avoided.

7. This letter should end with a forward-looking, pleasant statement.

"Trim sentences, like trim bodies, require far more effort than flabby ones. But though striving toward a lean and graceful style involves hard work, it can also be fun—like swimming or running. Shaping an attractive sentence from a formless mass of words is a [writer's] high."

—Claire Kehrwald Cook, *Line by Line*

Chapter 8

Routine E-Mail Messages and Memos

CHAPTER REVIEW

Writing Memos and E-Mail Messages

abilities	conversational	identification	lists	summary
confrontational	e-mail	letter	nonsensitive	word

1. Memos were always a favorite means of internal communication, but _____ is rapidly becoming the communication channel of choice. (Obj. 1, p. 207)

2. Since memos and e-mail messages are generally sent to familiar individuals, these messages are sometimes written informally. They contain only what's necessary to convey meaning and be courteous. Effective memos include headings, focus on one topic, are _____ in tone, and use graphic highlighting. (Obj. 1, p. 208)

3. A surprising result of the information revolution is that momentum has turned back to the written _____. Businesspeople are writing more messages than ever before, and many of them are electronic. (Obj. 1, p. 209)

4. Careful writing always takes time, especially for inexperienced writers. Following a systematic plan like the 3-x-3 writing process enables communicators to work at maximum speed while producing a good product. Remember that your speaking and writing _____ can determine how much influence you'll have in your organization. (Obj. 1, p. 210)

Catching a wave to success can depend greatly on your communication skills.

5. A subject line is a mandatory part of every memo because it summarizes the central idea of a message and provides quick _____ for the reader and for filing. (Obj. 2, p. 211)

6. Most memos and e-mail messages carry _____ information that can be revealed in a straightforward manner in the opening sentence. (Obj. 2, p. 212)

7. The body of a memo often includes numbered or bulleted _____, headings, or other graphic techniques that facilitate comprehension. (Obj. 2, p. 212)

8. Memos may conclude with (a) action information such as dates and order deadlines, (b) a _____ of the message, or (c) a closing thought. (Obj. 2, p. 212)

bounce	delete	permission	recipient
closings	embarrassing	personal	spam
correctness	humor	professional	thread

9. The first e-mail users considered their messages "words on the fly," and they gave little thought to editing or proofreading. But as this communication channel matures, messages are becoming more proper and more _____ . (Obj. 2, p. 213)

10. E-mail messages may travel farther than their writers intend. Quickly written notes may end up in the boss's mailbox. E-mail messages are also difficult to _____, yet many people treat them as if they were telephone calls. (Obj. 2, p. 214)

11. E-mail addresses can be complex, illogical, and unforgiving. If you omit one character or mis-read the letter "l," your message will _____. (Obj. 2, p. 216)

12. Messages with misleading subject lines may not be opened or read because receivers think they are junk e-mail called _____. (Obj. 2, p. 216)

13. You should never use e-mail to send sensitive, confidential, inflammatory, or potentially _____ messages. (Obj. 2, p. 215)

14. People are still judged by their writing, whether electronic or paper-based. Sloppy e-mail—with missing apostrophes, haphazard spelling, and confused writing—makes readers work too hard. That's why writers should care about _____. (Obj. 2, p. 216)

15. Unless your company specifically allows it, never use your employer's computers for _____ messages, personal shopping, or entertainment. (Obj. 2, p. 217)

16. When replying to incoming e-mail messages, don't return the entire _____ (sequence of messages) on a topic. Instead, cut and paste the relevant parts. (Obj. 2, p. 217)

17. Many e-mail users are not sure about including a salutation. Some skip it, while others use the name of the _____ in the first sentence. (Obj. 3, p. 218)

18. Be sure to announce a lengthy attachment before sending it, and avoid forwarding any message without _____. (Obj. 3, p. 217)

19. Writers of e-mail messages sent within organizations may omit _____ and even skip their names at the end of messages. They can omit these items because receivers recognize them from the opening lines. But for messages going to outsiders, it's better to identify yourself. (Obj. 3, p. 220)

20. Generally, memos may be grouped by function into all but which of the following categories?
    a. Procedure and information memos
    b. Claim adjustment memos
    c. Confirmation memos
    d. Request and reply memos (Objs. 4–6, pp. 221–226)

21. Which of the following would *not* be considered either a procedure or information memo?
    a. A memo about the upcoming company picnic
    b. A memo stating the specific holidays employees will have off
    c. A memo confirming responsibilities of members of the budget committee
    d. A memo stating guidelines for using company e-mail (Obj. 4, p. 221)

22. An effective opening for a request memo is
    a. *Please send me your answers to the following questions by December 1.*
    b. *Thank you in advance for answering the following questions.*
    c. *Here are the answers to the questions you had about our new software product called "Personal Assistant."*
    d. Please answer the following questions about your new software product called *"Personal Assistant."* (Obj. 5, p. 223)

23. In the body of a request or reply memo, you should
    a. explain and justify your request or reply.
    b. include action information and deadlines.
    c. begin with a polite command.
    d. ask the most important question first. (Obj. 5, p. 223)

24. Because individuals may forget, alter, or retract oral commitments, we sometimes must write a _____ memo.
    a. procedure
    b. information
    c. reply
    d. confirmation (Obj. 6, p. 224)

25. Confirmation memos are often written to
    a. provide a new point of view.
    b. confirm telephone or other oral conversations.
    c. ensure that a permanent e-mail message is destroyed.
    d. conclude a series of e-mails. (Obj. 6, p. 224)

Indicate whether the following statements are true or false by using T or F.

_____ 26. Because organizations are downsizing, flattening chains of command, forming work teams, and empowering rank-and-file employees, managers and employees have less need to exchange information in the form of e-mail messages and memos. (Obj. 1, p. 207)

_____ 27. E-mail messages and memos will probably be your most common business communication medium. (Obj. 1, p. 208)

_____ 28. E-mail is so fast and so easy to use that some writers have been "seduced" into an astonishing lack of professionalism. (Obj. 1, pp. 208–209)

_____ 29. Although e-mail messages are very popular, users are less and less patient with unattractive, unintelligible, and "impenetrable data dumps." (Obj. 1, p. 209)

_____30. Although you might be able to solve a problem with a nearby coworker by telephoning or making a quick visit, it is better to send an e-mail message to avoid the personal contact. (Obj. 1, p. 210)

_____31. Whether electronic or hard-copy, routine memos generally contain three parts: opening, body, and closing. (Obj. 2, p. 211)

_____32. Wise e-mail writers know that thoughtless messages can cause irreparable harm; they also know that erased messages can remain on company computers for years. (Obj. 2, pp. 213–214)

_____33. When sending an e-mail, never use labels such as FYI (For your information) or RE because receivers may not recognize them. (Obj. 3, p. 217)

_____34. Employers do not have the legal right to monitor e-mail messages you may send while working. (Obj. 3, p. 217)

_____35. E-mail messages that travel to outsiders may seem cold and unfriendly if they have no salutation. (Obj. 3, p. 218)

36. What kind of graphic highlighting can e-mail writers use to improve readability? (Obj. 1, p. 209)

37. List what you consider to be ten of the most important do's and don'ts regarding e-mail practices. (Obj. 3, pp. 215–218)

38. Most internal messages describe procedures and distribute information. In what direction do they generally flow? (Obj. 4, p. 221)

Many e-mail receivers feel overwhelmed by the number of messages they receive.

39. Name three items to be included in a confirmation memo or e-mail message. (Obj. 6, p. 224)

40. What does it mean to send "blanket" copies? (Obj. 3, p. 216)

CAREER TRACK SPELLING

In the space provided write the correct version of the words in parentheses. If the word is spelled correctly, write *C*.

1. On the (forth) call Lisa was able to reach the director. _____
2. She wondered, (never the less), why he was never in. _____
3. Gary considered his spell checker (indespensible). _____
4. An (encreadible) drop in stock prices worried investors. _____
5. The friends refused to be drawn into an (arguement). _____
6. My (calender) is free for the week of April 15. _____
7. The third (colume) of figures appears to have an error. _____
8. Jeff saw an (extrodinery) opportunity in computer sales. _____
9. A memo (reguarding) computer passwords is coming. _____
10. Without (suficint) capital, a new business will fail. _____

My Spelling Monsters

List each word that you missed or had trouble with. Be sure to spell it correctly. Then, write it four or more times. Review this page often to help you vanquish these spelling demons.

_____

_____

_____

_____

_____

_____

_____

_____

CAREER TRACK VOCABULARY

Use your dictionary to define the words in Column A. Then select the best definition in Column B to match the word in Column A.

	Column A		Column B
_____	1. franchise	a.	smooth-talking, fluent
_____	2. genesis	b.	break, disruption
_____	3. glib	c.	beginning, origin
_____	4. grotesque	d.	fantastic, bizarre
_____	5. gratis	e.	free, without charge
_____	6. hiatus	f.	right to vote, permission

Choose the best meaning for the following underlined words.

_____ 7. Weak response in consumer trials is a sure <u>harbinger</u> of product failure.

  a. interpretation   b. signal   c. conduit

_____ 8. Visitors to the museum are greeted by <u>hospitable</u> docents who are trained to answer questions and make guests feel comfortable.

  a. attractive   b. predictable   c. gracious

_____ 9. Many companies during the 1990s were victims of <u>hostile</u> takeovers.

  a. unfriendly   b. happy   c. inexpensive

_____ 10. Price and quality determine consumer spending, not advertising <u>hyperbole</u>.

  a. exaggeration   b. restraint   c. jingles

_____ 11. Because <u>icons</u> simplify computer use, many software programs now feature them.

  a. documentation   b. guides   c. images

_____ 12. The misguided CEO was astonished to learn that five quarters of profits were an <u>illusion</u>.

  a. reality   b. actuality   c. fallacy

_____ 13. A showdown over control of the family's corporate holdings is <u>imminent</u>.

  a. impending   b. completed   c. doubtful

_____ 14. The <u>indigenous</u> people of the North wish to be called Inuit and Aleut, not Eskimo.

  a. angry   b. Alaskan   c. native

Confusing Words

every day	each single day	*flair*	natural talent, aptitude
everyday	ordinary	*flare*	to blaze up or spread out

farther	a greater distance
further	additional

15. Paula's _____ for decorating shows in her well-appointed office.

16. David starts _____ with an exercise routine.

17. A dry Christmas tree will ignite and _____ quickly.

18. Although it's _____ from Tucson than Phoenix, Sedona is worth the trip.

19. In this company, emergencies are a(n) _____ occurrence.

20. Do you have any _____ sales information to report?

Now look over the 20 vocabulary words in this chapter. Select 5 words to add to your working vocabulary. Double-check the meanings of your selections in a dictionary. Then write a sentence for each of your words.

_____

_____

_____

_____

_____

_____

_____

COMPETENT LANGUAGE USAGE ESSENTIALS (C.L.U.E.)

Semicolons and Colons

Guide 27: Use a semicolon to join closely related independent clauses. Mature writers use semicolons to show readers that two thoughts are closely associated. If the ideas are not related, they should be expressed as separate sentences. Often, but not always, the second independent clause contains a conjunctive adverb (such as *however, consequently, therefore,* or *furthermore*) to show the relation between the two clauses.

Good visual aids need no explanation; they speak for themselves.

He invested wisely; consequently, he became a wealthy man.

Some stores were open on the holiday; however, most were closed.

TIP. Don't use a semicolon unless each clause is truly independent. Try the sentence test. Omit the semicolon if each clause is not independent.

Faulty: Although some employees work on weekends; the main office is closed. (The initial clause here is dependent, not independent. It fails the sentence test. It can't stand alone; therefore, a comma instead of a semicolon should be used.)

Guide 28: Use a semicolon to separate items in a series when one or more of the items contain internal commas.

> Attending the conference were Roberta Carrera, president, Carrera Industries; William Franker, CPA, General Systems; and Gail Gomez, vice president, Sun Company.

> Production sites being considered include Canton, Ohio; Mesa, Arizona; and Waterford, Connecticut.

Guide 29: Use a colon after a complete thought that introduces a list of items. Words such as *these, the following*, and *as follows* may introduce the list or they may be implied.

> At the top of our list are the following cities: Portland, San Diego, and Virginia City.

> An alternate list includes cities in the South: New Orleans, Miami, and Atlanta.

 TIP. Be sure that the statement before the colon is grammatically complete. An introductory statement that ends with a preposition (such as *by, for, at*, or *to*) or a verb (such as *is, are,* or *were*) is incomplete. The list following a preposition or a verb actually functions as an object or as a complement to finish the sentence.

Faulty: Send invitations to: Jim, Pat, and Tim. (Omit the colon because the introductory statement is incomplete.)

Faulty: Some of the best colors are: salmon, red, and green. (Do not use a colon after an incomplete statement.)

Guide 30: Use a colon after business letter salutations and to introduce long quotations.

> Ladies and Gentlemen: Dear Ms. Lee: Dear Lisa:

> The advertising executive said: "As opposed to nations in the West, Asia is a growing market. By the year 2000, two-thirds of the world's consumers will live around the edge of the Pacific Rim."

C.L.U.E. Checkpoint

Use proofreading marks to add or delete semicolons and colons.

1. Studying history is easy, learning its lessons is almost impossible.

2. John was determined to become a CPA consequently he majored in accounting.

3. Although hotel managers say that customers' needs are met nearly all the time; only 40 percent of travelers agree.

4. General Electric interviewed marketing candidates from: Eastern Michigan University, Ohio University, and Texas Tech.

5. Nominees for president included: Jacki Ames, Miami, Thomas Hart, Atlanta, and Tamala Wilson, Tampa.

Super C.L.U.E. Review

In this cumulative review, use proofreading marks to correct punctuation, number usage, capitalization, spelling, and confusing word use. Mark *C* if a sentence is correct.

1. Some information is tabulated in columes, other information is shown in rows.

2. Underinflation reduces the life of a tire, however overinflation may cause a blowout.

3. As I sighted in my september report, your present insurance program is inadequate; and needs to be reviewed.

4. The recruiter was looking for three principle qualitys; initiative, reliability, and enthusiasm.

5. The american bar association elected dennis r. radiman, president, harriet lee-thomas, vice president, and e. m. miles, secretary.

6. After studying the matter farther we decided on three cities; akron, toledo, and columbus.

7. We are greatful that twenty-four companies submitted bids, unfortunately only three will be selected.

8. Reports from: ms sampson, mr tomas, and mrs jay are overdo.

9. All employees will persenally recieve copies of their Performance Evaluations; which the President said would be the primary basis for promotion.

10. Our manager gives many oral complements to deserving workers, however the praise would be more lasting if written in notes or reports.

CAREER APPLICATION

Your boss, Pauline M. Wu, director, Human Resources, asks you to draft a memo for her signature. It announces the open enrollment period for employees to change their benefit coverage. This is an important announcement because employees may make changes to their benefits only during this period. The cutoff date is November 29; all applications must be in by that time.

Pauline is very concerned about the attitude of employees in the past. They don't seem to realize that changes to health, dental, and life insurance programs can be made only once a year, during the month of November. She wants you to get this announcement out by November 3. Emphasize that the decisions employees make are important—to themselves and to their families as well. You will want to caution employees that voluntary changes can be made only in November, although qualified changes in family status, of course, may be made during the year.

She wants you to tell employees that most of the benefit program is unchanged. However, dental coverage is a little different; two carriers now offer dental coverage. Family members are also eligible for increased coverage in life insurance, and medical coverage now offers a basic plan plus a prudent buyer plan. You don't have to describe these improvements; just encourage employees to read about them in the enrollment package you will enclose.

She asks you to select times on three days when representatives from Human Resources will be available to answer employee questions. When you push her for more details, she says that you will be one of the representatives. Therefore, consult with another representative to work out a schedule. But do choose two-hour blocks of time. She suggests that these question-and-answer sessions be held in the East Lounge.

You know that Pauline appreciates concise, straightforward expression. Before drafting your memo, answer the following questions.

Critical Thinking Questions

1. In the first phase of the writing process, you'll want to analyze the audience for your message. Who is the audience for this memo?

2. In analyzing your employee audience, what assumptions can you make about these readers?

3. What assumptions can you make about your boss's reaction to your memo?

4. What is the purpose of this memo? What do you want employees to do?

5. What research will you have to do to collect information for this memo?

6. Should the memo be developed directly or indirectly? Why?

7. The opening sentence should tell the main idea for writing. Prepare a rough draft of your opening here.

8. What three benefit programs have changes?

9. What two sets of information could be itemized for improved readability?

10. What action information should be contained in the closing?

Check your responses with the solutions for this chapter. Then write your memo on a separate sheet of paper or at your computer. Use proper formatting techniques. When you finish, compare your version with that in Appendix B. How does yours measure up? Did you include enough information? Too much?

SOLUTIONS

1. e-mail
2. conversational
3. word
4. abilities
5. identification
6. nonsensitive
7. lists
8. summary
9. professional
10. delete

11. bounce
12. spam
13. embarrassing
14. correctness
15. personal
16. thread
17. recipient
18. permission
19. closings

20. b
21. c
22. d
23. a
24. d
25. b

26. F   Because of downsizing, flattened chains of command, work teams, and empowered rank-and-file employees, everyone needs to exchange more information, thus resulting in more e-mail and memos.

27. T
28. T
29. T
30. F   It's better to make a quick telephone call or conduct a conversation than to take the time to write an e-mail message.

31. F   Routine memos contain four parts: subject line, opening, body, and closing.

32. T
33. F   Using such labels can save time for readers.
34. F   Employers may monitor all e-mail messages sent on company equipment.
35. T

36. E-mail users can use asterisks, headings, and all caps as graphic highlighting devices. Some systems also recognize bullets.

37. Answers will vary, but here are some important do's and don'ts:
   a. Do get the address right.
   b. Avoid misleading subject lines.
   c. Be concise.
   d. Don't send anything you wouldn't want published.
   e. Don't respond when you are angry.
   f. Be careful about correctness (grammar, spelling, punctuation, etc.)
   g. Don't make jokes.
   h. Don't send blanket copies.
   i. Never send spam.

    j.   Avoid using all capitals except for emphasis.

    k.   Don't forward without permission.

    l.   Don't use company computers for personal matters.

    m. Remember that employers have the right to monitor all e-mail.

38. Most internal messages describing procedures and distributing information flow downward.

39. Three items to be included in a confirmation memo:
    a.   Names and titles of involved individuals
    b.   Concise statement of major issues or points
    c.   Request for feedback regarding unclear or inaccurate points

40. Blanket copies are those sent to a large number of people.

Career Track Spelling

1. fourth
2. nevertheless
3. indispensable
4. incredible
5. argument
6. calendar
7. column
8. extraordinary
9. regarding
10. sufficient

Career Track Vocabulary

1. f
2. c
3. a
4. d
5. e
6. b
7. b
8. c
9. a
10. a
11. c
12. c
13. a
14. c
15. flair
16. every day
17. flare
18. farther
19. everyday
20. further

C.L.U.E. Checkpoint

1. easy;
2. CPA; consequently,
3. time, [Don't use a semicolon after a dependent clause.]
4. from Eastern Michigan [No colon is necessary because the list is not preceded by a complete statement.]
5. included Jackie Ames, Miami; Thomas Hart, Atlanta; [Note the lack of a colon after *included*.]

Super C.L.U.E. Review

1. colum̲n̲s;
2. tire; however,
3. cited   September   inadequate [Omit semicolon. No punctuation is required after *inadequate*.]
4. principal qualiti̲e̲s:
5. American Bar Association   Dennis R. Radiman, president; Harriet Lee-Thomas, vice president; and E. M. Miles,
6. further, we   cities: Akron, Toledo, and Columbus.

7. grateful   24   bids; unfortunately,   3 [Use the figure *3* instead of *three* because it relates to the previous figure, *24*.]

8. from Ms. Sampson, Mr. Tomas, and Mrs. Jay are over<u>due</u>.

9. person<u>ally</u> rec<u>ei</u>ve   performance evaluations, which   president [Note that a comma, not a semicolon, is used to introduce a nonessential dependent clause.]

10. compl<u>i</u>ments   workers; however,

Career Application—Critical Thinking Questions

1. Although all employees are the primary audience, you should be aware that anything you write for your boss will become part of her evaluation of your skills.

2. Because you know that employees tend to undervalue this information, you'll want to emphasize its importance—particularly the limited open enrollment period.

3. Your boss will be most interested in how clearly you cover all the main points.

4. The purpose of the memo is to announce the open enrollment period. You want employees to read the enrollment package, decide if they want to make changes, and return the application by November 29.

5. You will have to check with other representatives to set up a schedule of times for counseling employees. You would probably also read all of the enrollment package carefully so that you could anticipate areas that might need clarification.

6. This memo delivers important, yet nonsensitive, routine information. Hence, develop it directly. Employees will not be upset by this information.

7. A possible opening sentence: Please examine the enclosed open enrollment package so that you may make any changes before November 29.

8. Dental coverage, life insurance options, and medical coverage.

9. Use itemization techniques to improve readability of the three changes in coverage, as well as the times for answering questions.

10. The closing should tell employees what to turn in, where to do it, and when to do so.

Words, of course, are the most powerful drug used by mankind.
—Rudyard Kipling

Chapter 9

Routine Letters and Goodwill Messages

CHAPTER REVIEW

Strategies for Routine Letters

action	correct form	inside	paragraph
anticipating	detailed	main	questions
block	frontloading	outside	sentence

1. Letters usually deliver messages _____ an organization. (Obj. 1, p. 240)

2. Three characteristics of good letters include clear content, a tone of goodwill, and _____ . (Obj. 1, p. 241)

3. Clearly written letters answer all the reader's _____ or concerns so that no further correspondence is necessary. (Obj. 1, p. 241)

4. In a(n) _____ letter all the parts are set flush left on the page. This means that all parts begin at the left margin. (Obj. 1, p. 242)

5. In routine letters you should avoid starting with introductory material, history, justifications, or old-fashioned "business" language. Instead, you should start directly with the action desired or the _____ idea. (Obj. 1, p. 242)

6. Beginning routine messages in a straightforward manner with the central idea at the beginning so that the reader can anticipate and comprehend what follows is called _____ . (Obj. 1, p. 242)

7. For letters with considerable information, you should develop each idea in a separate _____ . (Obj. 1, p. 243)

8. The three key goals in the first step of the 3-x-3 writing process for routine letters are (a) determining your purpose, (b) _____ the reaction of your audience, and (c) visualizing the audience. (Obj. 1, p. 244)

9. In the last paragraph of a routine letter, the reader looks for _____ information: schedules, deadlines, and activities to be completed. (Obj. 1, p. 244)

Direct Request Letters

appreciation	details	justify	promptly
claims	four	order	relations
costs	information	problem statement	three

10. The majority of business letters are written to request _____ or action. For these direct messages put the main idea first. (Obj. 2, p. 245)

11. The body of a direct request letter should explain your purpose for writing and provide _____ to explain the request. (Obj. 2, p. 245)

12. _____ letters should open directly with an authorization for purchase, method of delivery, and, if appropriate, a catalog source. (Obj. 3, p. 248)

13. In direct request letters, it's always appropriate to show _____. Try to do it, though, in a fresh way. Avoid "Thank you for your cooperation." (Obj. 2, p. 246)

14. Claim letters should open with a clear _____, support the claim with specifics, and close with a statement of goodwill. (Obj. 4, p. 248)

15. Because it costs _____ times as much to win a new customer as it does to retain a current one, businesses especially want to hear what customers have to say. (Obj. 4, pp. 248–249)

16. The body of a claim letter should explain the problem and _____ the request. (Obj. 4, p. 249)

17. By delaying the writing of a claim letter, you make the claim more difficult to verify. Delay also makes the claim appear less important. Therefore, act _____ to indicate your seriousness. (Obj. 4, p. 249)

18. Claim letters should conclude with a courteous statement promoting goodwill and expressing a desire for continued _____. (Obj. 4, p. 249)

19. Before writing any letter, consider its _____ in terms of your time and work load. Whenever possible, don't write! Perhaps a telephone call or an e-mail message would accomplish your goal as effectively. (Obj. 2, p. 245)

The paper-free workplace is one of the great unfulfilled promises of the Information Age. One insurance company executive said, "Paper in a service business is like cholesterol in the blood stream . . . . It clogs up the arteries." Many companies are retaining paper for letters and other essential outside communications, but they are replacing memos with e-mail.

Direct Reply Letters

20. Name three circumstances when direct reply letters are used in business. (Obj. 5, p. 251)

21. List three characteristics of a subject line. (Obj. 5, p. 252)

22. Briefly discuss what information is included in the opening, body, and conclusion of a direct reply letter. (Obj. 5, pp. 251–252)

23. List six cautions that writers of recommendations should heed. (Obj. 6, p. 256)

24. What are three goals when granting claims and making adjustments? (Obj. 7, p. 259)

25. List the five Ss in writing goodwill messages. (Obj. 8, p. 264)

26. List four *don'ts* to consider when writing adjustment letters. (Obj. 7, p. 261)

Businesses today often bring in experts to help employees improve their writing skills. One topic that's always discussed is the tone conveyed in letters to customers.

Multiple Choice

_____27. The body of a routine letter should
  a. have at least two paragraphs.
  b. announce the purpose immediately.
  c. provide details that explain the purpose of the letter.
  d. state an end date for action from the reader. (Obj. 1, p. 243)

_____28. For short messages responding to routine inquiries, you might
  a. use a cluster diagram to generate ideas for the letter's content.
  b. outline the letter's content on a separate page.
  c. organize the letter by presenting the desired action in the first paragraph.
  d. jot down notes on the document being answered. (Obj. 1, p. 245)

_____29. To elicit the most information from the receiver of a request letter, ask
  a. yes-or-no questions.
  b. open-ended questions.
  c. multiple-choice questions.
  d. limited-choice questions. (Obj. 2, p. 245)

_____30. A written claim
  a. starts a record of the problem.
  b. gives the writer a chance to vent frustrations.
  c. guarantees the problem will be solved.
  d. needs to state clearly the blame for the problem. (Obj. 4, p. 248)

_____31. Which of the following is the best closing for a routine claim letter?
  a. Thank you for your cooperation.
  b. We would appreciate receiving the additional items by July 23, since our current suppy is low and your cassettes are popular with our customers.
  c. We will expect to receive the rest of our order by July 23.
  d. We look forward to receiving the corrected order soon. (Obj. 4, p. 249)

_____32. The final paragraph of a letter of recommendation should
  a. present traits of the candidate, supported by evidence.
  b. offer global, nonspecific statements.
  c. offer an overall evaluation of the candidate.
  d. encourage the receiver to hire the candidate. (Obj. 6, p. 257)

_____33. When granting a claim,
  a. always apologize if an error has been made.
  b. include only a brief apology in the closing paragraph of the letter.
  c. focus on how you are complying with the customer's claim.
  d. be sure to indicate who or what is to blame for the error. (Obj. 7, p. 260)

_____34. Goodwill letters
  a. should demonstrate the sender's creative writing ability.
  b. should not use pretentious or overly formal language.
  c. should focus on the sender as much as possible.
  d. are longer than most other business messages. (Obj. 8, p. 264)

_____ 35. When you receive a congratulatory note or a written pat on the back, you should
   a. respond but show proper humility by minimizing your achievements.
   b. respond by saying that you appreciate the kindness you were shown.
   c. be appreciative but not overly so.
   d. say that you don't really deserve the praise. (Obj. 8, p. 265)

_____ 36. Which of the following should you avoid in a message of sympathy?
   a. Mention the loss tactfully.
   b. Recognize good qualities of the deceased (in the case of a death).
   c. Assure the receiver that you know exactly how he or she feels and describe similar situations you have experienced.
   d. Offer assistance. (Obj. 8, p. 267)

_____ 37. Most international business letters should be written
   a. in an informal, conversational manner.
   b. following generally accepted principles for American business letters.
   c. using only active-voice verbs.
   d. to conform to the conventions of the receiver's country. (Obj. 9, p. 268)

Check your answers now!

CAREER TRACK SPELLING

For each sentence below write a correct version of any misspelled words. Write _C_ if no words are misspelled.

1. We do not ordinarilly make cash refunds. _____
2. Occassionaly, however, we make exceptions to our rule. _____
3. You must interupt your lunch to take this important call. _____
4. Most correspondence with Asia and Europe is in English. _____
5. We are making a conscience effort to improve service. _____
6. Management thought the divesion of duties was fair. _____
7. Not one of the three proposals is feasable at this time. _____
8. One office tennant refused to pay the rent increase. _____
9. A 30-year morgage offers the lowest interest rate. _____
10. Investors profitted when international sales soared. _____

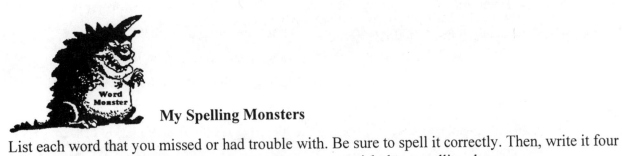

My Spelling Monsters

List each word that you missed or had trouble with. Be sure to spell it correctly. Then, write it four or more times. Review this page often to help you vanquish these spelling demons.

_____

_____

_____

_____

_____

_____

CAREER TRACK VOCABULARY

Use your dictionary to define the words in Column A. Then select the best definition in Column B to match the word in Column A.

Column A	Column B
_____ 1. impede	a. start, get going
_____ 2. impel	b. push, influence
_____ 3. inaugurate	c. hamper, prevent
_____ 4. indiscernible	d. harmless, inoffensive
_____ 5. indolent	e. unclear, vague
_____ 6. innocuous	f. lazy, shiftless

Choose the best meaning for the following underlined words.

_____ 7. Large real estate empires, in danger of becoming <u>insolvent</u>, are trying to go public.

    a. dangerous   b. bankrupt   c. prosperous

_____ 8. Former President Harry Truman wouldn't compromise his <u>integrity</u> for political purposes.

    a. interests   b. intellect   c. ethical values

_____ 9. The dispute between the FCC chairman and the cable companies seems <u>irreconcilable</u>.

    a. unsolvable   b. compatible   c. compulsive

_____ 10. Through the <u>largess</u> of a wealthy graduate, Stanford received a new computer lab.

    a. wrath   b. displeasure   c. generosity

_____ 11. Chuck will act as <u>liaison</u> between the employees' union and management.

      a. arbitrator   b. link   c. informer

_____ 12. Tenants submitted a <u>litany</u> of complaints about the aging apartment building.

      a. list   b. letter   c. tirade

_____ 13. The statistics textbook was easy to read because of the author's <u>lucid</u> writing style.

      a. clear   b. cryptic   c. demented

_____ 14. Small-car manufacturers are targeting the <u>lucrative</u> Generation X market (18- to 30-year-olds).

      a. wasteful   b. troublesome   c. profitable

Confusing Words

formally	in a formal manner		_hole_	an opening
formerly	in the past		_whole_	entire

grate	n.: lattice; v.: to rub on a rough surface, irk, or irritate
great	adj.: large, numerous, distinguished

15. "Managing at IBM is like sandbagging a levy," said a _____ employed executive.

16. To make the right decision, you must read the _____ report.

17. The metal _____ covering the air-conditioning duct must be repainted.

18. The promotion of Margaret Rose to president has yet to be announced _____.

19. Please bore a _____ large enough for this cable to fit through.

20. The undersea tunnel linking England and France is a _____ engineering feat.

Now look over the 20 vocabulary words in this chapter. Select 5 or more to add to your working vocabulary. Double-check the meanings of your selections in a dictionary. Then write a sentence for each of your words.

_____

_____

_____

_____

_____

_____

_____

_____

COMPETENT LANGUAGE USAGE ESSENTIALS (C.L.U.E.)

Apostrophes

Guide 31: Add an apostrophe plus _s_ to an ownership word that does not end in an _s_ sound.

Today's economy is brighter than in the past. (Add _'s_ because the ownership word _today_ does not end in an _s_.)

Put the folder on Bryan's desk. (Add _'s_ because the ownership word _Bryan_ does not end in an _s_.)

All the women's organizations sent representatives. (Add _'s_ because the ownership word _women_ does not end in _s_.)

TIP. To determine whether an ownership word ends in an _s_, use it in an _of_ phrase. For example, _today's economy_ becomes _economy of today_. By isolating the ownership word without its apostrophe, you can decide whether it ends in an _s_ and where to place the apostrophe.

Guide 32: Add only an apostrophe to an ownership word that ends in an _s_ sound—unless an extra syllable can be pronounced easily.

All employees' health benefits will be examined. (Add only an apostrophe because the ownership word _employees_ ends in an _s_.)

Several years' profits were reinvested. (Add only an apostrophe because the ownership word _years_ ends in an _s_.)

We need the boss's signature. (Add _'s_ because an extra syllable can be pronounced easily.)

TIP. Only a few words ending in an _s_ sound require an extra syllable formed with _'s_. Some of these words are _actress, boss, class, fox_, and names like _Ross, Betz_, and _Davis_. Examples: the actress's voice, the fox's den, Ross's car, Mr. Betz's house, Mrs. Davis's office. For all these words we would pronounce an extra syllable in forming the possessive; therefore, we add _'s_.

Guide 33: Use _'s_ to make a word possessive when it precedes a gerund, a verb form used as a noun.

Fellow workers protested _Beth's_ smoking in the office.

We appreciate _your_ (not _you_) writing the final report.

His (not _Him_) talking interfered with the video.

TIP. When words provide description or identification only, the possessive form is _not_ used. Writers have most problems with descriptive nouns ending in _s_, such as _Claims_ Department. No apostrophe is needed; _Department_ is not possessed by _Claims_. Note the lack of apostrophe in these examples: _sales staff, electronics division, Los Angeles Dodgers._

C.L.U.E. Checkpoint

Correct all possessive constructions in the following sentences. *Tip: Don't be tempted to add apostrophes to all nouns ending in* s. *Some are merely plurals, not possessives.*

1. In one years time we should be able to correct all members names and addresses.

2. Some members of the sales staff were very successful with childrens books.

3. John would appreciate you answering his telephone while he is gone.

4. Three months interest on the two notes will be due February 1.

5. After a months delay, Ms. Johnson car registration finally arrived.

Super C.L.U.E. Review

In this cumulative review, use proofreading marks to correct punctuation, number usage, capitalization, spelling, and confusing word use. Mark *C* if a sentence is correct.

1. Although I refered to figure 12 on page 4 I was dissappointed when I could not find Mr. Rivera sales figures.

2. The superviser sincerly hopes that employees will exceed to managements latest wage proposals.

3. A key factor to be observed in our hiring program, is that all candidates references must be checked thoroughly.

4. Everyone has noticed Lorraines flare for words, therefore she is being promoted to our editorial department.

5. Because of her recent accident Mrs. Wilson insurance premium will be increased one hundred twelve dollars for every six-month billing period.

6. Todays weather is much better than yesterdays consequently, we'll work outside.

7. Ted Bowman the new marketing manager offerred 9 different suggestions for targeting potential customers.

8. We are hoping that Teds suggestions are feasable, and that they will succede in turning around our sales decline.

9. Both companys offices will open at eight a.m. however only the atlantic branch will offer full counter service until five PM.

10. Jims spring schedule includes the following courses english, history, and business law.

Check your answers now!

CAREER APPLICATION

As a student intern in the office of a magazine publisher, you are given a group of sample letters to evaluate. Read the letter below and then answer the following critical thinking questions.

April 14, 2000

Mrs. Thomas Dobbin
2950 King Street
Alexandria, VA 22313

Dear Mrs. Dobbin:

We appreciate your letter of April 4 in which you complain that you are receiving two issues of *Home Computing* every month.

My staff has looked into the matter and ascertained that the misunderstanding resulted when you placed an order under the name of Patricia R. Dobbin. You claim that this new subscription was made as part of your son's magazine fund-raising program at his school. You must be aware that the entire circulation operation of a large magazine is computerized. Obviously, a computer cannot distinguish between your current subscription for Mrs. Thomas Dobbin and a new one for another name.

But we think we've straightened the problem out. We're extending your subscription for 14 months. That's a bonus of two issues to make up for the double ones you've received. However, we can't prevent you from receiving one or two more double issues.

Sincerely,

Roger W. Hobart
Circulation Manager

Critical Thinking Questions

1. Is the format of this letter satisfactory?

2. What expressions create a negative tone for this letter?

3. Should this letter be organized directly or indirectly? Why? How is it now organized?

4. In an adjustment letter, what three goals should the writer seek to achieve? Is the writer successful in this letter?

5. What good news does the writer have to offer?

6. In this instance, should the writer explain why the double mailing took place? When must a writer be careful in offering explanations to customers?

7. How should this claim adjustment letter end?

As part of your internship, you are asked to revise the letter (on another sheet of paper or at your computer). Then compare your revision with that shown in Appendix B.

SOLUTIONS

Chapter Review

1. outside
2. correct form
3. questions
4. block
5. main
6. frontloading
7. paragraph
8. anticipating
9. action
10. information
11. details
12. Order
13. appreciation
14. problem statement
15. three
16. justify
17. promptly
18. relations
19. costs

20. Three circumstances when direct reply letters are used in business: (a) complying with requests for information or action, (b) writing letters of recommendation, (c) granting claims and making adjustments

21. Subject lines (a) omit articles, (b) are not complete sentences, and (c) do not end with periods.

22. The opening of a direct reply letter immediately delivers the information the reader wants. The body supplies explanations and additional information. The body might include lists, tables, headings, or other devices to organize information. The conclusion refers to the information provided or to its use. If further action is necessary, the conclusion describes the action to be taken.

23. Writers of recommendations should (a) respond only to written requests, (b) state that their remarks are confidential, (c) provide only job-related information, (d) avoid vague or ambiguous statements, (e) supply specific evidence for any negatives, and (f) stick to the truth.

24. Three goals when granting claims and making adjustments: (a) rectifying the wrong, (b) regaining the customer's confidence, and (c) promoting future business.

25. The five Ss in writing goodwill messages include being (a) selfless, (b) specific, (c) sincere, (d) spontaneous, and (e) short.

26. Four *don'ts* to consider when writing adjustment letters: (a) don't use negative words, (b) don't blame customers, (c) don't blame individuals or departments within your organization, and (d) don't make unrealistic promises.

27. c
28. d
29. b
30. a
31. b
32. c
33. c
34. b
35. b
36. c
37. d

Career Track Spelling

1. ordinarily
2. Occasionally
3. interrupt
4. C
5. conscious
6. division
7. feasible
8. tenant
9. mortgage
10. profited

Career Track Vocabulary

1. c	11. b
2. b	12. a
3. a	13. a
4. e	14. c
5. f	15. formerly
6. d	16. whole
7. b	17. grate
8. c	18. formally
9. a	19. hole
10. c	20. great

C.L.U.E. Checkpoint

1. year's   members' [No apostrophes on the plural words *names* and *addresses*.]
2. children's [No apostrophes on any other nouns.]
3. your
4. months'
5. month's   Ms. Johnson's

Super C.L.U.E. Review

1. referred   Figure 12   page 4,   disappointed   Mr. Rivera's
2. supervis<u>o</u>r sincer<u>e</u>ly   <u>acce</u>de   management's
3. program [omit comma]   candidates'
4. Lorraine's fl<u>ai</u>r   words; therefore,   Editorial Department [Remember to capitalize department names within your organization.]
5. accident,   Wilson's $112
6. Today's,   yesterday's
7. Bowman,   manager,   offered nine
8. Ted's feasible [omit comma]   succeed
9. companies'   8 a.m.; however,   Atlantic   5 p.m.
10. Jim's   courses: English

Career Application—Critical Thinking Questions

1. The format of the letter should be either block or modified block rather than the combination shown. For block style, start each line at the left. For modified block style, move the closing lines to the center and block the paragraphs.

2. A negative tone is created by such expressions as *you complain, misunderstanding, you claim, you must be aware,* and *we can't prevent you.*

3. The letter should be organized directly because the reader will be pleased with its message. It is now organized indirectly with explanations preceding the good news.

4. In adjustment letters the writer's three goals are to (a) rectify the wrong, if one exists, (b) regain the confidence of the customer, and (c) promote further business.

"Trim sentences, like trim bodies, require far more effort than flabby ones. But though striving toward a lean and graceful style involves hard work, it can also be fun—like swimming or running. Shaping an attractive sentence from a formless mass of words is a [writer's] high."

—Claire Kehrwald Cook, *Line by Line*

5. The good news is that the problem has been solved and that the double mailing will cease.

6. In this instance the writer should explain why the double mailing occurred, since little liability exists. However, if an explanation might place an organization at risk, that explanation should be avoided.

7. This letter should end with a forward-looking, pleasant statement.

Chapter 10

Persuasive and Sales Messages

CHAPTER REVIEW

Persuasive Messages

action	documentation	persuasion	relevant	strategy
direct	indirect	purpose	resistance	success

1. Using argument or discussion to change an individual's beliefs or actions is known as _____. Few businesspeople can succeed without developing this valuable skill. (Obj. 1, p. 284)

2. The goal of a persuasive message is to convert the receiver to your ideas or to motivate action. A message without a clear _____ is doomed. (Obj. 1, p. 285)

3. Efficient writers use an organized, systematic procedure—such as the 3-x-3 writing process—to develop messages. Analyzing the purpose of a message helps establish an appropriate _____. (Obj. 1, p. 285)

4. When writing persuasive messages, consider both your purpose and the receivers' needs. How well you convince receivers that your message helps them achieve some of life's major goals (such as money, power, comfort, confidence, importance, and peace of mind) will determine the _____ of your message. (Obj. 1, p. 285)

5. To grab attention, the opening statement in a persuasive request should be brief, _____, and engaging. (Obj. 2, p. 288)

6. One of the biggest mistakes writers make when composing persuasive messages is failure to anticipate and offset audience _____. (Obj. 2, p. 290)

7. Since employees expect to be directed in how to perform their jobs, instructions or directives moving downward from superiors to subordinates usually require little persuasion. However, when employees are asked to perform outside their work roles or to accept changes that are not in their best interests, persuasive memos using the _____ pattern may be most effective. (Obj. 4, p. 296)

8. When sending requests to superiors, employees should appear competent and knowledgeable. The key to obtaining a "yes" answer is for employees to know their needs and have the necessary _____ (facts, figures, and evidence). (Obj. 4, p. 297)

9. Occasionally you will have to write persuasive letters about damaged products, mistaken billing, inaccurate shipments, warranty problems, insurance snafus, faulty merchandise, and so on. When you expect the claim to be granted, the _____ strategy is most efficient. (Obj. 4, p. 298)

10. In the opening of a claim or complaint letter, consider opening with a review of the _____ you have taken to resolve the problem. (Obj. 5, p. 299)

Sales Messages

act	direct-mail	feelings	letter	stimulating
anecdote	dual	illustration	postscript	targeting
competitor	emotional	incentive	rational	testimonial

11. Although e-mail may one day eclipse _____ sales messages, unsolicited e-mail seems to generate enormous ill will at this time. That is one of the reasons that many experts think that traditional mailed sales letters remain one of the most powerful ways to make sales, generate leads, boost retail traffic, and solicit donations. (Obj. 6, p. 301)

12. Sales messages that come in the mail typically contain a brochure, a price list, illustrations of the product, testimonials, and a carefully written _____. (Obj. 6, p. 301)

13. Blanket direct mailings sent "cold" to occupants generally produce low responses—typically only 2 percent. Response rates can be greatly improved by _____ the audience through selected mailing lists. (Obj. 6, p. 302)

14. One of the most critical elements of a sales message is its opening paragraph. To make readers want to continue, the opening should be short (one to five lines), honest, relevant, and _____. (Obj. 6, p. 302)

15. Sales messages center on effective appeals. _____ appeals are generally used when products are inexpensive, short-lived, or nonessential. _____ appeals are associated with reasons and intellect. Some clever sales messages combine both these strategies in _____ appeals. (Obj. 6, p. 303)

16. When price is an obstacle, you can (a) delay mentioning it until after you have created a desire for the product, (b) show the price in small units, (c) demonstrate how the receiver can save money, or (d) compare your prices with those of a(n) _____. (Obj. 6, p. 303)

17. An important technique for building interest in a product involves connecting cold facts with needs and warm _____. (Obj. 6, p. 303)

18. Providing a reply card, a stamped envelope, a toll-free number, an easy Web site, or a promise of a follow-up call are all ways to make sure the reader will _____ on the sales message. (Obj. 6, p. 304)

19. Many sales letters end with an eye-catching _____ describing the strongest motivator to action. (Obj. 6, p. 304)

Indicate whether the following statements are true or false by using T or F.

_____ 20. The first step in planning a persuasive message should be determining the purpose, since it establishes the strategy of the message. (Obj. 1, p. 285)

_____ 21. Persuasive requests are usually somewhat longer than direct requests. (Obj. 2, p. 289)

_____ 22. Increasing the knowledge of an audience is usually an effective way to change attitudes. (Box, p. 287)

_____ 23. Merely exaggerating a point can be considered unethical behavior. (Obj. 2, p. 291)

_____ 24. Appealing to professionalism is a useful technique when requesting favors. (Obj. 3, p. 293)

_____ 25. Although an online sales letter should be conversational and focused, it may be as long as you wish since length is unimportant in sending e-mail messages. (Obj. 6, p. 306)

_____ 26. Although you may never write sales letters, understanding their organization and appeals will make you better able to evaluate them. (Obj. 6, p. 301)

_____ 27. Requests for favors involving time, money, special privileges, or cooperation usually focus on direct reader benefits. (Obj. 3, p. 293)

_____ 28. When only mild persuasion is necessary, the opener can be low-key and factual. (Obj. 2, p. 288)

_____ 29. Because news or press releases are generally self-serving, companies need to apply persuasive techniques to get them published. (Obj. 7, p. 307)

30. Describe the four parts of the indirect pattern in developing a persuasive or sales message. (Obj. 1, p. 288)

31. List four questions that will help you adapt a persuasive request to a receiver. (Obj. 1, p. 286)

32. Identify six techniques that help gain attention in opening a persuasive request. (Obj. 1, pp. 288–289)

33. Name six devices that help a writer build interest in a persuasive request. (Obj. 1, p. 289)

34. Name eight techniques for gaining attention in the opening of a sales message. (Obj. 6, p. 302)

35. List five techniques for overcoming resistance and proving the credibility of a product you are selling. (Obj. 6, p. 304)

Check your answers now!

CAREER TRACK SPELLING

For each group below identify misspelled words and write corrected versions in the space provided. Write *C* if all words are correct.

1. challenge	knowledgible	decision	dropped	_____
2. almost	advertising	deceive	bankrupsy	_____
3. interest	freind	misspell	neighbor	_____
4. critisize	muscle	summary	studying	_____
5. familiar	recognize	forty	fiskal	_____
6. naturally	neccessery	significance	operate	_____
7. adaquate	medicine	financially	safety	_____
8. irresponsible	fulfill	noticible	qualafy	_____
9. physical	opportunaty	restaurant	separation	_____
10. enough	grateful	buziness	suppose	_____

My Spelling Monsters

List each word that you missed or had trouble with. Be sure to spell it correctly. Then, write it four or more times. Review this page often to help you vanquish these spelling demons.

_____

_____

_____

_____

_____

_____

CAREER TRACK VOCABULARY

Use your dictionary to define the words in Column A. Then select the best definition in Column B to match the word in Column A.

	Column A		Column B
_____	1. lenient	a.	slander, defame
_____	2. litigious	b.	kind, merciful
_____	3. lofty	c.	sad, pensive
_____	4. malign	d.	command, requirement
_____	5. mandate	e.	high, exalted
_____	6. melancholy	f.	actionable, disputable

Choose the best meaning for the following underlined words.

_____ 7. To avoid the <u>maelstrom</u> at the entrance, the rock group used an underground passage.

     a. photographers   b. fans   c. frenzy

_____ 8. Bonsai artists shape <u>malleable</u> plants into a dwarf landscape in a dish.

     a. immature   b. pliant   c. vigorous

_____ 9. Avoid strong cologne when job interviewing; recruiters may find it <u>malodorous</u>.

     a. pleasant   b. foul-smelling   c. manly

_____ 10. Two Silicon Valley software companies asked a judge to <u>mediate</u> their trade secret controversy.

     a. ignore   b. inflame   c. reconcile

_____ 11. Intelligence and a <u>mellifluous</u> voice contribute to his success as a talk-show host.

     a. shrewish, harsh   b. loud   c. honeyed, mellow

_____12. Following the war the general wrote a <u>memoir</u> describing his experiences.

        a. biography   b. lecture   c. fantasy

_____13. The <u>mercenary</u> sales representative was interested only in his commission.

        a. ambitious   b. fast-talking   c. greedy

_____14. College students proved their <u>mettle</u> by sandbagging levees and rescuing stranded motorists during the flood.

        a. strength   b. courage   c. brilliance

Confusing Words

imply   to suggest indirectly   *liable*   legally responsible
infer   to reach a conclusion   *libel*   damaging written statement

lean   to rest against; to incline toward; not fat
lien   a legal right or claim to property

15. Newspapers must guard against _____ suits by printing facts, not rumors.

16. Because he wasn't paid, the electrician placed a _____ on the property.

17. The exercise club was held _____ for her injury.

18. Vitamin makers don't promise health benefits, but they often _____ them.

19. If you _____ against the ladder, it will give way.

20. Can we _____ from these test results that our product will sell?

COMPETENT LANGUAGE USAGE ESSENTIALS (C.L.U.E.)

Other Punctuation

Guide 34: Use a period to end a statement, command, indirect question, or polite request.

      Our meeting starts at 2 p.m. (Statement. Note that only one period ends a sentence.)

      Bring the report to our next meeting. (Command.)

      Steven asked if he could attend the meeting. (Indirect question.)

      Will you please send a catalog to Lamps, Inc. (Polite request.)

TIP. Polite requests often sound like questions. To determine the punctuation, apply the action test. If the request prompts an action, use a period. If it prompts a verbal response, use a question mark. *Example: Would you please send me a corrected statement.* Use a period instead of a question mark because this polite request suggests an action rather than an answer.

Guide 35: Use a question mark after a direct question and after statements with questions appended.

Did you send a meeting agenda to each person?

Most departmental members are planning to attend, aren't they?

Guide 36: Use a dash to (a) set off parenthetical elements containing internal commas, (b) emphasize a sentence interruption, or (c) separate an introductory list from a summarizing statement. The dash has legitimate uses. However, some writers use it whenever they know that punctuation is necessary, but they're not sure exactly what. The dash can be very effective, if not misused.

Three outstanding employees—Reba, Thomas, and Erik—were promoted. (Use dashes to set off elements with internal commas.)

Officials at General Motors—despite rampant rumors in the stock market—remained silent about dividend earnings. (Use dashes to emphasize a sentence interruption.)

IBM, Coca-Cola, and Xerox—these were the familiar names always appearing among overseas developers. (Use a dash to separate an introductory list from a summarizing statement.)

Guide 37: Use parentheses to set off nonessential sentence elements, such as explanations, directions, questions, or references.

Prices on framing lumber (see last week's detailed report) have fallen 38 percent.

Only two dates (November 2 and November 17) are acceptable for the meeting.

 TIP. Careful writers use parentheses to *deemphasize* and the *dash* to emphasize parenthetical information. One expert said, "Dashes shout the news; parentheses whisper it."

Guide 38: Use quotation marks to (a) enclose the exact words of a speaker or writer, (b) distinguish words used in a special sense, such as slang, or (c) enclose titles of articles, chapters, or other short works.

"To most of us," said Joe Moore, "the leading economic indicator is our bank account." (Use quotation marks to enclose the exact words of a speaker.)

The recruiter said that she was looking for candidates with good communication skills. (Omit quotation marks because the exact words of the speaker are not quoted.)

Sheila feared that her presentation before management would "bomb." (Use quotation marks for slang.)

In <u>U.S. News & World Report</u>, I saw an article entitled "Trade Show Turn-Offs." (Use quotation marks around article titles; use all caps, underlines, or italics for names of magazines and books.)

 TIP. Never use quotation marks merely for emphasis, such as *Our "summer" sale starts July 15.*

C.L.U.E. Checkpoint

Use proofreading marks to add all necessary punctuation.

1. (Direct quotation) Someone who never asks anything said Malcolm Forbes either knows everything or knows nothing

2. Will you please send me a corrected statement of my account

3. (Deemphasize) Directions for assembly see page 15 are quite simple.

4. (Emphasize) Only three products movie cameras, VCRs, and CD players account for 70 percent of our profits.

5. Learning, earning, and yearning these are natural pursuits for most of us.

6. The meeting is scheduled for Wednesday isn't it

7. In Business Week I saw an article entitled Reengineer—Or Else

8. My computer screen suddenly started showing garbage.

9. (Emphasize) Two of our researchers Emily Smith and José Real resigned yesterday.

10. (Deemphasize) Three employees in our Marketing Department David, Debbie, and Joy were responsible for all product promotional materials.

Super C.L.U.E. Review

In this cumulative review, use proofreading marks to correct punctuation, number usage, capitalization, spelling, and confusing word use. Mark *C* if a sentence is correct.

1. The treasurer will disperse all excess dues collected won't she

2. Regular cleaning of the tape head see chart 2 in your owners manual is nesessary for best performance.

3. The two recruiters remarks seemed to infer that they were most interested in candidates with computer and accounting skills.

4. (Deemphasize) The major functions of a manager planning directing and controling will be covered in management 301.

5. Any letter sent to the banks customers must have a professional appearance, otherwise it's message may be disregarded.

6. 40 people enrolled in the class however only 32 actually appeared at 7 p.m..

7. (Direct quotation) When you are right said Martin Luther King, Jr. you cannot be too radical when you are wrong you cannot be too conservative.

8. (Emphasize) States with the best export assistance programs California, Illinois, Minnesota, and Maryland offer seminars and conferences.

9. When we promote our "inventory reduction sale" in June you'll find the years best prices.

10. (Emphasize) Each of these citys Rochester Albany and Purchase has substantial taxes all ready in affect.

CAREER APPLICATION

The following request for an adjustment needs revision. Read it over and answer the critical thinking questions about it.

Current Date

Mr. James Ferraro
Vice President, Sales
Copy World
2510 East Pine Street
Tulsa, OK 74160-2510

Dear Mr. Ferraro:

Three months ago we purchased four of your CopyMaster Model S-5 photocopiers, and we've had nothing but trouble ever since.

Our salesperson, Kevin Woo, assured us that the S-5 could easily handle our volume of about 3,000 copies a day. This seemed strange since the sales brochure said that the S-5 was meant for 500 copies a day. But we believed Mr. Woo. Big mistake! Our four S-5 copiers are down constantly; we can't go on like this. Because they're still under warranty, they eventually get repaired. But we're losing considerable business in downtime.

Your Mr. Woo has been less than helpful, so I telephoned the district manager, Keith Sumner. I suggested that we trade in our S-5 copiers (which we got for $2,500 each) on two S-55 models ($13,500 each). However, Mr. Sumner said he would have to charge 50 percent depreciation on our S-5 copiers. What a ripoff! I think that 20 percent depreciation is more reasonable since we've had the machines only three months. Mr. Sumner said he would get back to me, and I haven't heard from him since.

I'm writing your headquarters because I have no faith in either Mr. Woo or Mr. Sumner, and I need action on these machines. If you understood anything about business, you would see what a sweet deal I'm offering you. I'm willing to stick with your company and purchase your most expensive model—but I can't take a 30 percent loss on the S-5 copiers. The S-5 copiers are relatively new; you should be able to sell them with no trouble. And think of all the money you'll save by not having your repair technicians making constant trips to service our S-5 copiers! Please let me hear from you immediately.

Sincerely,

Tracy W. Quincy
Manager

Critical Thinking Questions

1. Who is the primary audience for this adjustment request? Do you think this person is responsible for the problem described? Is it necessary to fix the blame for the problem here?

2. What is the specific purpose of this letter? To vent anger? To point fingers? What action does Tracy want taken?

3. Is Copy World likely to resist her request? Why?

4. What three arguments can be used to reduce resistance and encourage Copy World to approve the trade-in of four S-3 copiers with only 20 percent depreciation?

5. Should Tracy also appeal to Copy World's sense of responsibility and pride in its good name? Why?

6. Would Tracy's letter be stronger if she gave a day-by-day account of what happened with the copiers and how angry it made her and the staff? Explain.

7. Should this letter be developed directly (with the request made immediately) or indirectly (with an explanation coming first)? Why?

8. Name four possible openers for a claim letter. Which would be best for this letter?

9. What's wrong with Tracy's closing? What would be better?

10. How can Tracy make it easy for Copy World to approve her request?

Now compare your responses to these questions with those shown at the end of this chapter.

SOLUTIONS

Chapter Review

1. persuasion
2. purpose
3. strategy
4. success
5. relevant
6. resistance
7. indirect
8. documentation
9. direct
10. action
11. direct-mail
12. letter
13. targeting
14. stimulating
15. Emotional, Rational, dual
16. competitor
17. feelings
18. act
19. postscript

20. T
21. T
22. F   Strange as it may seem, research shows that providing more information (knowledge) is not effective in changing attitudes.
23. T
24. T
25. F   Online sales messages should be short since reading on a screen is difficult.
26. T
27. F   These requests generally have to rely on indirect reader benefits or on benefits for other people.
28. T
29. T

30. Four parts of the indirect pattern for sales messages:
    a. Gain attention.
    b. Build interest.
    c. Reduce resistance.
    d. Motivate action.

31. Four questions that help adapt a request to a receiver:
    a. Why should I (the receiver)?
    b. What's in it for me (the receiver)?
    c. What's in it for you (the sender)?
    d. Who cares?

32. Six techniques that gain attention in opening a persuasive request:
    a. Problem description
    b. Unexpected statement
    c. Reader benefit
    d. Compliment
    e. Related fact
    f. Stimulating question

33. Six devices that build interest:
    a. Facts, statistics
    b. Expert opinion
    c. Direct benefits
    d. Examples
    e. Related fact
    f. Indirect benefits

34. Eight techniques for gaining attention in opening a sales message:
    a. Offer
    b. Promise
    c. Question
    d. Quotation or proverb
    e. Product feature
    f. Testimonial
    g. Startling statement
    h. Personalized action setting

35. Five techniques for overcoming resistance and proving the credibility of a product:
    a. Testimonials
    b. Names of satisfied users
    c. Money-back guarantee or warranty
    d. Free trial or sample
    e. Performance tests, pools, awards

Career Track Spelling
1. knowledgeable
2. bankruptcy
3. friend
4. criticize
5. fiscal
6. necessary
7. adequate
8. noticeable, qualify
9. opportunity
10. business

Career Track Vocabulary
1. b
2. f
3. e
4. a
5. d
6. c
7. c
8. b
9. b
10. c
11. c
12. a
13. c
14. b
15. libel
16. lien
17. liable
18. imply
19. lean
20. infer

C.L.U.E. Checkpoint
1. "Someone   anything,"   Forbes, "either   nothing."
2. account. [Don't use a question mark for this polite request.]
3. (see page 15) [Note that you don't capitalize *see*.)
4. products—movie cameras, VCRs, and CD players—
5. yearning—these
6. Wednesday, isn't it?
7. Business Week   "Reengineer—Or Else." [Note that the period goes inside the quotation marks.]
8. "garbage."
9. researchers—Emily Smith and José Real—
10. Department (David, Debbie, and Joy)

Super C.L.U.E. Review
1. disburse   collected, won't she?
2. (see Chart 2   owner's manual)   necessary   [Note that *owner's* is generally considered singular, not plural.]
3. recruiters'   imply [instead of *infer*]
4. manager (planning, directing, and controlling)   Management 301.

5. bank's   appearance; otherwise, it<u>s</u> [Did you catch the *its*? Your spell checker will miss it, too!]
6. Forty   class; however, p.m.
7. "When you are right," said Martin Luther King, Jr., "you   radical;   wrong, conservative."
8. programs—   Maryland—
9. inventory reduction sale [delete quotation marks]   June,   year's
10. cit<u>ie</u>s—Rochester, Albany, and Purchase—   al<u>r</u>eady   <u>e</u>ffect.

Career Application - Critical Thinking Questions

1. The primary audience for this adjustment request is a representative of Copy World, and the chances are that this person has nothing to do with the pain Tracy has suffered. Moreover, this person has feelings and won't like being the target of angry words. In reality, it's probably unnecessary to try to establish who is to blame.

2. The purpose of this letter should not be to vent anger or point fingers. Tracy's letter is so unfocused that it's difficult to tell exactly what she wants done. A better letter would concentrate on an action that would solve the problem. Apparently, she wants to purchase two Model S-55 copiers (at $13,500 each), but she wants Copy World to accept her four CopyMaster Model S-5 copiers (original cost $2,500 each or $10,000) in trade. And she wants $8,000 trade-in on the four returned copiers. At 50 percent depreciation, Copy World would be offering only $5,000 for the returned copiers.

3. Copy World may resist this request, since its representative has already said that Copy World must take 50 percent depreciation on the four used copiers. At 50 percent depreciation, Copy World would be offering only $5,000 for the returned copiers.

4. Three arguments that Tracy could make to reduce resistance are these:
   a. The S-5 machines were used only a short time, and they can be resold easily.
   b. Copy World will be making a sizable profit on the sale of two top-of-the-line Model S-55 copiers.
   c. Copy World service technicians will no longer have to make trips to service the overworked four S-5 models.

5. Tracy would be wise to keep her cool and say something about purchasing these copiers in good faith on the advice of Copy World's salesperson. And she should emphasize that it is Copy World's responsibility to help provide the proper model for a company's needs. Probably one of the most successful appeals to any company is that of maintaining its good reputation.

6. A day-by-day chronology of her copier troubles would bore the reader, causing that person to merely skim over it. Instead, Tracy should use objective language and tell the story briefly. If she has a repair record, she should enclose it.

7. If Tracy opens directly with her request, she risks the chance of an immediate refusal. The reader may never learn what reasons prompted the request. Her letter will be stronger if she starts indirectly with explanations and logical reasoning.

8. Four possible ways to open a claim letter are with (a) sincere praise, (b) an objective statement of the problem, (c) a point of agreement, or (d) a quick review of what has been done to resolve the problem. Probably for this situation a concise statement of the problem would be most effective.

9. Tracy's closing doesn't request any specific action. The reader has to guess what Tracy wants done. A better closing would spell out exactly what would please Tracy.

10. One way to make it easy for Copy World to respond would be to state exactly what action is to be taken and to ask the reader to initial the letter to show approval. Tracy could offer to work out the details with the local salesperson. Enclosing a preaddressed envelope would make the agreement even easier to conclude.

Now that you've done the preparation for writing this adjustment request, write your version on a separate sheet (preferably at your computer). Use your own name or use Tracy's. Then compare it with the version shown in Appendix B. Don't expect yours to look exactly like our version. Yours may be better!

Chapter 11

Negative Messages

CHAPTER REVIEW

1. The bad feelings associated with negative news can sometimes be reduced if
   a. the receiver knows the reasons for the rejection.
   b. an apology is immediately offered.
   c. the writer tells a joke and tries to make the receiver laugh.
   d. the bad news is immediately announced. (Obj. 1, p. 322)

2. In delivering bad news, your goals should include
   a. making sure the reader understands and accepts the bad news.
   b. promoting and maintaining a good image of yourself and your organization.
   c. making sure the message is clear but also avoids creating legal responsibility.
   d. all of the above. (Obj. 1, p. 323)

3. Many bad-news letters are best organized indirectly with the reasons preceding the bad news. However, the direct pattern may be more appropriate when
   a. the receiver may overlook the bad news.
   b. organization policy or the receiver prefers directness.
   c. firmness is necessary or when the bad news is not damaging.
   d. all of the above (Obj. 1, p. 324)

4. In delivering bad news, writers sometimes get into legal difficulties by using abusive language, by using careless language, or by
   a. failing to apologize.
   b. falling into the "bad-guy" syndrome.
   c. falling into the "good-guy" syndrome.
   d. using the direct method to announce the bad news. (Obj. 1, pp. 326-327)

5. Which of the following statements is *not* true of buffers?
   a. A buffer should be relevant and concise.
   b. A buffer should provide a natural transition to the explanation that follows.
   c. An effective buffer might be "Thank you for your letter."
   d. A buffer should include a neutral but meaningful statement that makes the reader continue reading. (Obj. 2, p. 328)

6. In bad-news messages, readers resent
   a. apologies.
   b. policy statements prohibiting something.
   c. any statement that demonstrates that the writer cares about readers and is trying to treat them as important individuals.
   d. efforts to cushion the disappointing news. (Obj. 2, p. 331)

7. Which of the following is generally *not* a goal of messages that must refuse credit to customers?
   a. To avoid negative language that causes hard feelings.
   b. To retain customers on a cash basis.
   c. To prepare for possible future credit.
   d. To provide reasons for the refusal. (Obj. 4, p. 342)

8. References to resale information or promotion may be appropriate in the closing paragraph of a bad-news message when
   a. firmness is necessary.
   b. the bad news is not devastating or personal
   c. you want to maintain goodwill with the reader.
   d. you wish to depersonalize the action. (Obj. 2, p. 332)

Negative and emotional words in a letter make the writer sound grouchy and unreasonable.

9. Which of the following techniques would be least effective in breaking bad news?
   a. Putting the bad news in a subordinate clause.
   b. Using passive-voice verbs to disclose the bad news.
   c. Citing company policy to explain the reasons.
   d. Implying the bad news. (Obj. 2, p. 330)

10. Which of the following statements most effectively implies the refusal?
    a. We are sorry that we cannot contribute at this time, but we may be able to . . .
    b. Although our profits are now being poured back into the firm, we hope . . .
    c. Although we cannot contribute at this time, we may be able to . . .
    d. Unfortunately, we are prevented from contributing at this time, but . . .
       (Obj. 2, p. 330)

11. Bad-news messages should
    a. always use the indirect organizational pattern.
    b. be organized directly when the receiver may overlook the bad news.
    c. be organized directly when the bad news is personal.
    d. be organized indirectly when firmness is necessary. (Obj. 1, p. 324)

12. When writing a letter to a job applicant who has not been selected for a position, a wise communicator
    a. is vague in explaining why the candidate was not selected.
    b. gives specific details as to why the candidate was not selected.
    c. frontloads the bad news, letting the candidate know immediately the details about the refusal.
    d. none of the above. (Obj. 5, p. 346)

Use T or F to indicate whether the following statements are true or false.

_____13. Writing bad-news messages requires less attention to the 3-x-3 writing process than other types of business messages. (Obj. 1, p. 325)

_____14. Good news may be revealed quickly, but bad news should be broken gradually. (Obj. 1, p. 323)

_____15. To keep the reader in a receptive mood, avoid negative expressions like *claim, error, failure, fault, mistaken,* and *violate.* (Obj. 2, p. 330)

_____16. Organizing bad-news messages indirectly helps reduce the bad feelings associated with disappointing news. (Obj. 1, p. 323)

_____17. The following illustrates passive voice: *We cannot give you a cash refund.* (Obj. 2, p. 331)

_____18. The following illustrates passive voice: *Cash refunds cannot be given.* (Obj. 2, p. 331)

_____19. Unlike the active voice, the passive voice highlights the action and is, therefore, a good choice when stating bad news. (Obj. 2, p. 331)

_____20. Letters declining invitations should give explanations and offer a sender's apologies. (Obj. 3, p. 335)

_____21. The most important part of a bad-news letter is the buffer. (Obj. 2, p. 329)

_____22. Offering resale information in a letter that denies a customer's claim is appropriate in many situations. (Obj. 2, p. 332)

_____23. Organizations should strive to communicate bad news openly and honestly. (Obj. 6, p. 346)

_____24. Computerized form letters allow companies to personalize responses to identical requests from a large number of customers. (Box, p. 333)

_____25. Like American writers, British and German writers tend to use an indirect strategy in announcing bad news. (Obj. 7, p. 347)

26. List and describe the four parts of the indirect pattern for revealing bad news. (Obj. 1, pp. 323–324)

27. What are three specific causes of legal problems that can expose you and your employer to legal liability when you write negative messages? Give an example of each. (Obj. 1, pp. 326–327)

28. Name six possibilities to use in a buffer for a bad-news message. (Obj. 2, pp. 328–329)

29. List five thoughtful techniques for cushioning bad news. (Obj. 2, p. 330)

30. Discuss four ways to close a bad-news message. (Obj. 2, pp. 331–332)

31. In Asian cultures what are some signals that a request is being denied? (Obj. 7, p. 348)

Check your answers now!

CAREER TRACK SPELLING

In the spaces provided write the correct version of the words in parentheses. If a word is spelled correctly, write C.

 1. Fashions in car colors and clothes are equally (changible). _____
 2. Annual reports answer (legitimite) questions of stockholders. _____
 3. About 3 percent of stockholders (usully) attend meetings. _____
 4. Owners were (disatisfyed) with company managers' actions. _____
 5. A few hecklers tried to (harrass) company speakers. _____
 6. One (promminant) politician gave the keynote address. _____
 7. The president's address was (unneccessarily) technical. _____
 8. A feeling of optimism was (prevalent) among stockholders. _____
 9. Only those in attendance were (permited) to vote. _____
10. The current CEO was to be (exemp) from salary cutbacks. _____

My Spelling Monsters

List each word that you missed or had trouble with. Be sure to spell it correctly. Then, write it four or more times. Review this page often to help you vanquish these spelling demons.

_____

_____

_____

_____

_____

_____

CAREER TRACK VOCABULARY

Use your dictionary to define the words in Column A. Then select the best definition in Column B to match the word in Column A.

Column A	Column B
_____ 1. miscreant	a. hard, inflexible
_____ 2. mitigate	b. impertinent, pushy
_____ 3. notoriety	c. smooth, soften
_____ 4. obdurate	d. delinquent, criminal
_____ 5. obtrusive	e. concealed, unintelligible
_____ 6. obscure	f. shame, disfavor

Choose the best meaning for the following underlined words.

_____ 7. Art world critics were stunned by Warhol's paintings of <u>mundane</u> soup cans.

    a. ethereal   b. Campbell   c. commonplace

_____ 8. The <u>onus</u> of proving a product's safety rests with the manufacturer.

    a. burden   b. method   c. cost

_____ 9. In an <u>ominous</u> proposal, government officials discussed taxing the assets of pension plans.

    a. threatening   b. lengthy   c. liberal

_____ 10. The Duke and Duchess of Kent used to <u>officiate</u> at the Wimbledon trophy presentation.

    a. luxuriate   b. preside over   c. watch

_____ 11. To ensure privacy, Fred installed <u>opaque</u> plastic panels instead of glass.

    a. corrugated   b. flimsy   c. not transparent

_____ 12. A financial columnist <u>opines</u> that Microsoft should diversify its software business.

      a. demands   b. maintains   c. writes

_____ 13. Angered by the decline of Carl's Jr., founder Karcher threatened to <u>oust</u> the board of directors.

      a. control   b. eject   c. chastise

_____ 14. Investors, dissatisfied with <u>paltry</u> bond returns, have turned to stocks.

      a. insignificant   b. grandiose   c. average

Confusing Words

loose	not fastened	*patience*	calm perseverance
lose	to misplace	*patients*	people getting medical care

miner	person working in a mine
minor	a lesser item; underage person

15. Dr. Evans tries to give all his _____ at least 30 minutes each.

16. With parental permission a _____ may marry.

17. Please pick up all the _____ papers scattered about the desk.

18. Dr. Baker has the _____ necessary for delicate heart surgery.

19. If you don't want to _____ your computer work, save it often.

20. Every _____ dreams of striking a rich gold vein someday.

Look back over the 20 vocabulary words in this chapter. Select 5 new words that you would like to own. Remember, to "own" a word, you must be able to use it correctly in a sentence. Double-check the meanings of your selections in a dictionary. Then write a sentence for each of your words.

_____

_____

_____

_____

_____

COMPETENT LANGUAGE USAGE ESSENTIALS (C.L.U.E.)

Verb Tenses

Guide 4: Use present tense, past tense, and past participle verb forms correctly. The list below shows selected irregular verbs. To use these verbs correctly, practice them in the patterns shown. For example, *Today I begin, yesterday I began*, and *I have begun.*

Present Tense	Past Tense	Past Participle
Today I _____	*Yesterday I _____*	*I have _____*
am	was	been
begin	began	begun
break	broke	broken
bring	brought	brought
choose	chose	chosen
come	came	come
do	did	done
give	gave	given
go	went	gone
know	knew	known
pay	paid	paid
see	saw	seen
steal	stole	stolen
write	wrote	written

TIP. Probably the most frequent mistake in tenses results from substituting the past participle form for the past tense. Remember that the past participle tense requires auxiliary verbs such as *has, had, have, would have,* and *could have.*

Faulty: When he *come* over last night, he *brung* pizza.
Correct: When he *came* over last night, he *brought* pizza.

Faulty: If he *had came* earlier, we *could have saw* the video.
Correct: If he *had come* earlier, we *could have seen* the video.

Guide 5: Use the subjunctive mood to express hypothetical (untrue) ideas. The most frequent use of the subjunctive mood involves the use of *was* instead of *were* in clauses introduced by *if* and *as though* or containing *wish.*

If I *were* (not *was*) you, I would take a business writing course.

Sometimes I wish I *were* (not *was*) the manager of this department.

He acts as though he *were* (not *was*) in charge of this department.

TIP. If the statement could possibly be true, use *was.* For example, If I *was* to blame, I accept the consequences.

C.L.U.E. Checkpoint

Use proofreading marks to correct any errors. Mark *C* if correct.

21. If I was you, I would have gave the waitress a tip.

22. Mark must have knew the salary, or he would never have took the job.

23. When I seen Jan's letter, I immediately gave her a call.

24. I wish I was finished with my degree so that I could have went to work at LaserTech.

25. Many computer users wished they had choose a different printer.

Super C.L.U.E. Review

In this cumulative review, use proofreading marks to correct grammar, punctuation, number usage, capitalization, spelling, and confusing word use. Mark *C* if a sentence is correct.

1. If Jerry was manager I'm convinced he would have more patients with employees.

2. We payed every bill when it was due, however we still recieved late notices.

3. If the package had came earlier we could have made our deadline.

4. The Herald Post Dispatch our local newspaper suprised me with an article entitled How To Keep Employees Safe.

5. Unless he's more careful than he's been in the past, we are in danger of being sued for libel.

6. John should have knew that our competitors products would be featured at the Denver home and garden show.

7. If I was you I would schedule the conference for one of these cities Atlanta Memphis or Nashville.

8. We choose the Madison hotel because it can acommodate two hundred convention guests, and has parking facilities for one hundred cars.

9. The generals biography was wrote long before a publisher excepted it.

10. When she come to our office yesterday she brung a hole box of printer cartridges.

CAREER APPLICATION

Assume that you are Nelson R. Raymond, partner in the firm of Powell, Raymond, and Robbins Professional Accountancy Organization. Sherry A. Lopez, the daughter of one of your best clients, has asked you for a favor that you must refuse.

Sherry is president of Alpha Gamma Sigma, a student business honorary on the campus of Miami-Dade College. She wrote to you asking that you speak at a meeting February 17 on the topic of careers in public accounting. You are very pleased to learn that Sherry is studying business administration and that she is taking a leadership role in this organization. You're also flattered that she thought of you.

But you must refuse because you will be attending a seminar in Lake Worth, at which you will represent your accountancy organization. This seminar will focus on recent changes in tax laws as they relate to corporations. Your organization handles many corporate clients; therefore, it's something you don't feel that you can miss.

You start to write Sherry a letter saying that you can't make it, when you remember that your local CPA organization has a list of speakers. These accountants are prepared to make presentations on various topics, and you have a list of those topics somewhere. When you find the list, you discover that Paul Rosenberg, a Miami CPA with 14 years of experience, is the expert on careers in accountancy and preparation for the CPA examination. You can't decide whether to call him and ask him to speak to Alpha Gamma Sigma on February 17 or leave that decision up to Sherry. Perhaps Sherry would prefer to find another speaker herself.

Make a decision about what to do and write a refusal to Sherry A. Lopez, President, Alpha Gamma Sigma, 1150 Del Ray Avenue, Miami, FL 33178. But before you begin composing, answer the following questions.

Critical Thinking Questions

1. Should you use a direct or indirect approach in delivering this bad news? Why?

2. Of all the possible techniques for developing a buffer, what would be most appropriate for this letter?

3. What should follow the buffer in this letter to Sherry?

4. In delivering the bad news, is it necessary to state it directly? How could it be implied?

5. What compromise is available to you? When should you present the compromise?

6.   What should you strive to accomplish in the closing?

Check your responses with the solutions at the end of this chapter before writing your version. Then compare your letter with that shown in Appendix B.

SOLUTIONS

Chapter Review

1. a	7. d
2. d	8. b
3. d	9. c
4. c	10. b
5. c	11. b
6. b	12. a

13. F   Bad-news messages require more preparation than most other messages.

14. T

15. T

16. T

17. F   This is active voice; notice that the subject *we* is the actor.

18. T   Notice that the subject is being acted upon; attention is focused on the action rather than the person performing the action.

19. T   Passive-voice verbs focus on the action, rather than the actor.

20. F   Although explanations are helpful, apologies are unnecessary, since the writer has done nothing wrong.

21. F   The most important part is the discussion of reasons.

22. T   Naturally, you'll assess every situation individually, but in some instances resale information helps to regain the confidence of a customer.

23. T

24. T

25. F   British and German writers tend to be direct with bad news.

26. Four parts to the indirect pattern for revealing bad news:
   a. Buffer - a neutral or positive opening that does not reveal the bad news.
   b. Reasons - an explanation of the causes for the bad news, offered before disclosing it.
   c. Bad news - a clear but understated announcement of the bad news; it may include an alternative or a compromise.
   d. Closing - a personalized, forward-looking, pleasant statement.

27. Three causes of legal problems:
   a. Abusive language, such as, "You deadbeat, crook, or quack."
   b. Careless language, such as suggesting a workplace is dangerous or making a joking threat against a coworker.
   c. The good-guy syndrome, such as saying that poor work is satisfactory just to avoid confronting a person.

28. Six possibilities for buffers:
   a. Start with the best part of the news.
   b. Offer a sincere compliment regarding accomplishments or efforts.
   c. Show appreciation; offer thanks.
   d. Show agreement with the reader on some issue.
   e. Provide solid facts.
   f. Indicate that you understand the problem.

29. Five techniques for cushioning bad news:
    a. Position the bad news strategically. Sandwich it between other sentences. Avoid high visibility spots.
    b. Use the passive voice (*Parking is not permitted . . .*).
    c. Accentuate the positive. If possible, make positive statements (*Parking is permitted in . . .*).
    d. Imply the refusal (*Although our funds are tied up this year, perhaps next year . . .*).
    e. Suggest a compromise or an alternative (*Although my schedule is full, my colleague may be able to speak . . .*).

30. Four ways to close a bad-news message:
    a. Look forward to future relations or business.
    b. Offer your good wishes.
    c. Refer to free coupons, samples, or gifts.
    d. Employ resale or sales promotion.

31. To avoid saying "no," Asians might respond with silence or counter with a question. They might also change the subject or tell a white lie. Sometimes they might respond with a qualified "yes," which should be recognized as "no."

Career Track Spelling
1. changeable
2. legitimate
3. usually
4. dissatisfied
5. harass
6. prominent
7. unnecessarily
8. C
9. permitted
10. exempt

Career Track Vocabulary
1. d
2. c
3. f
4. a
5. b
6. e
7. c
8. a
9. a
10. b
11. c
12. b
13. b
14. a
15. patients
16. minor
17. loose
18. patience
19. lose
20. miner

C.L.U.E. Checkpoint
1. If I were you   given
2. must have known   have taken
3. I saw
4. I were   have gone
5. chosen

Super C.L.U.E. Review
1. If Jerry were manager,   pat<u>ie</u>nce
2. paid   due; however,   rec<u>ei</u>ved
3. had come earlier,
4. <u>Herald Post Dispatch</u>,   newspaper, su<u>rp</u>rised   "How <u>to</u> Keep Employees Safe."
5. C
6. have known   competitors'   Home and Garden Show.
7. I were you,   cities: Atlanta, Memphis,
8. ch<u>o</u>se   Hotel   ac<u>c</u>ommodate 200 convention guests [omit comma]   100 cars.
9. general's   was written   acc<u>e</u>pted
10. she came   yesterday, she brought a <u>wh</u>ole

Career Application - Critical Thinking Questions

1. Although this bad news is not earth-shattering, it still represents a disappointment to the reader. Therefore, the indirect approach would be worth the effort.

2. Your buffer might include both appreciation for being asked and perhaps acknowledgment of Sherry's role of leadership in this campus honorary organization. If you don't compliment her in the begining, you'll probably want to include praise later in the letter.

3. Following the buffer you should explain why you cannot accept the invitation on the date selected.

4. For this situation the bad news probably need not be stated bluntly ("I cannot accept your invitation"). The reader will doubtless infer the refusal because you are busy elsewhere on the same day.

5. The compromise, of course, is offering a substitute speaker. This compromise should be presented after the implied refusal.

6. The closing should end pleasantly without referring to the bad news or without an apology (you have done nothing for which you should apologize). This might be a good place to compliment Sherry for her success in this organization. You might volunteer for future programs.

Chapter 12

Preparing to Write Business Reports

CHAPTER REVIEW

Report Basics

analytical	focus	organizing	reports
component	letter	outline	schedule
factoring	limitations	persuasive	work plan

1. People in low-context cultures analyze the pros and cons of problems, study alternatives, and assess facts, figures and details. They pride themselves on being practical and logical. In business their values and attitudes prompt them to write _____, which are systematic attempts to answer questions and solve problems. (Obj. 1, pp. 365–366)

2. Reports that present data without analysis or recommendations are primarily informational. Reports that provide data, analyses, and conclusions are _____. The latter generally intend to persuade readers to act or to change their beliefs. (Obj. 1, p. 366)

3. The format of a report depends on its length, audience, topic, and purpose. Most reports are prepared in one of four formats: memo, manuscript, printed form, or _____ . (Obj. 1, pp. 367–369)

4. Because business reports are systematic attempts to answer questions and solve problems, the best reports are developed methodically. A report writer should analyze the problem and purpose; anticipate the audience and issues; prepare a _____; research the data; organize, analyze, interpret, and illustrate the data; compose the first draft; and revise, proofread, and evaluate. (Obj. 2, pp. 371–372)

5. Preparing a written purpose statement is always wise for a report writer because it defines the _____ of a report and provides a standard that keeps the project on target. (Obj. 2, p. 374)

6. Many report projects require an expanded statement of purpose in order to set boundaries on a project. This expanded statement of purpose should consider the project's scope, significance, and _____. (Obj. 2, p. 374)

Organizing and writing a business report can be frustrating unless its authors follow a solid work plan that outlines and guides the project.

7. A report writer must break the major investigative problem into subproblems. This process identifies issues to be investigated or possible solutions to the main problem. The process is called _____ . (Obj. 2, p. 374)

8. In breaking the major investigative problem into subproblems, you should prepare a(n) _____ showing the divisions. You should make sure that the divisions are consistent (don't mix issues), exclusive (don't overlap categories), and complete (don't skip significant issues). (Obj. 2, p. 374)

9. A good work plan for a report should include a statement of the problem; a statement of the purpose including scope, significance, and limitations; description of the sources and methods of collecting data; a tentative outline; and a work _____ . (Obj. 2, p. 375)

Gathering Report Information

accuracy	interview	primary	secondary
browser	observation	research	survey
FAQ	periodicals	resources	Web

10. One of the most important steps in the process of writing a report is that of _____. This is the process of gathering information. This information might consist of statistics, background data, expert opinions, group opinions, and organizational data. (Obj. 3, p. 375)

11. Data for reports fall into two categories. _____ data result from firsthand experience and observation. _____ data come from reading what others have experienced and observed. (Obj. 3, p. 377)

12. Although we're seeing a steady movement toward electronic sources, you will find that print sources can provide valuable historical, in-depth data on many subjects. Print sources are generally books and _____. The latter include magazines, pamphlets, and journals. (Obj. 3, pp. 378–379)

13. As a writer of business reports today, you will probably begin your secondary research with electronic _____. Many writers start with these cybersources because they are fast, cheap, and easy to use, even from remote locations. (Obj. 3, p. 379)

14. Unquestionably, one of the greatest sources of information now available to anyone needing facts quickly and inexpensively is the _____ . Unfortunately, finding that information can be frustrating and time-consuming. (Obj. 3, p. 380)

Most projects begin with secondary research.

15. Searching the Web requires a _____, such as Netscape Navigator or Microsoft Internet Explorer. In searching company Web sites, your goal should be finding the top-level Web page and locating the site index. (Obj. 3, p. 380)

16. In using search tools such as Google and AltaVista, you should generally prefer lowercase letters, use uncommon words, omit articles and prepositions, learn Boolean search strategies, and become familiar with the Help and _____ sections of your search tool. (Obj. 3, p. 383)

17. Although the Web provides a wealth of information, some of the sites are unreliable. Users must question any information found. In evaluating a Web source, you should ask questions about its currency, authority, content, and _____ . (Obj. 3, p. 385)

18. Nearly every business report assignment should begin with a search of secondary data. Some reports may also require primary, firsthand data. One way to collect primary data is through a mailed _____ . This source provides efficient and economical data, but response rates may be low. (Obj. 4, p. 385)

19. Another way to gather primary information is through a(n) _____ . You could talk to an in-house or outside expert on the topic of your report. This source is especially useful when little has been written about a topic. (Obj. 4, p. 388)

20. Some of the best report data come from firsthand _____ and investigation. Seeing for yourself produces rich data, but that information is especially prone to charges of subjectivity. You can become more objective by systematically collecting data and quantifying them. (Obj. 4, p. 388)

Illustrating and Documenting Data

Archiving	documentation	flow charts	pie charts
bar charts	emphasize	line charts	source
budget	factoring	organization charts	tables

21. Tables, charts, graphs, pictures, and other visuals perform important functions for report writers and readers. Visual aids clarify, condense, simplify, and _____ data. (Obj. 5, p. 389)

22. The most frequently used visual aids are _____ . They present quantitative or verbal information in systematic columns and rows and can clarify large quantities of data in small spaces. (Obj. 5, p. 389)

23. Although they lack the precision of tables, _____ enable readers to compare related items, see changes over time, and understand how parts relate to a whole. (Obj. 5, p. 391)

24. _____ are similar to bar charts, but their major advantage is that they emphasize changes in data over time, thus suggesting trends. (Obj. 5, p. 392)

25. _____ help readers visualize a whole and the proportion of its components. (Obj. 5, p. 392)

26. Procedures may be simplified and clarified by diagramming them in _____ . These visual aids generally use conventional symbols to illustrate the beginning and end of a process, decision points, or major activities. (Obj. 5, p. 393)

27. In selecting graphics, you will evaluate your audience, content, schedule, and _____ in determining how many visuals and what kind to use. (Obj. 5, p. 395)

28. Careful writers give credit to their sources of information. Citing sources serves three purposes: (a) strengthens an argument, (b) protects the writer, and (c) instructs the reader. The process of citing references is called _____. (Obj. 6, p. 397)

29. In the academic world, documentation is critical. In the work world, business communicators may find that business reports lack "proper" documentation. Yet, if facts are questioned, business writers must be able to produce their _____ materials. (Obj. 6, p. 397)

30. Manual notetaking involves recording precise quotations on cards. Electronic notetaking involves recording sources and data in folders on a hard drive or a floppy. Researchers should consider _____ on a zip disk those Web pages or articles used in research. (Obj. 6, p. 398)

31. What are the differences between formal and informal writing styles? (Obj. 1, p. 371)

32. How does primary information differ from secondary information? What are the principal sources of each? (Objs. 3 and 4, pp. 375–389)

33. Name four of the best Web search tools and describe each briefly. Which is your favorite? (Obj. 3, p. 382)

34. What is paraphrasing? (Obj. 6, p. 399)

35. When you write reports, especially in college, you are continually dealing with other people's ideas. You are expected to conduct research, synthesize ideas, and build on the work of others. But you are also expected to give credit for borrowed material. List four kinds of material that you should document. (Obj. 6, p. 398)

CAREER TRACK SPELLING

Underline misspelled words. Write correct forms in the spaces provided. Some sentences may have more than one misspelled word. If a sentence is correct, write *C*.

1. Our fiscal policy overlooked foriegn marketing efforts this year.   _____
2. It is a privilige to work with such pleasant employees.   _____
3. The consensus of the comittee is to investigate thorougly.   _____
4. Will it be sufficient to package the software separately?   _____
5. Our skedule calls for three restaurant openings in six months.   _____
6. Experts will analize sales and returns for February.   _____
7. In my judgment his services are totally indespensible.   _____
8. Some library expenditures are deductable as business expenses.   _____
9. Incidently, did you check the length of the guarantee?   _____
10. The manufacturer evidentally issues its own catalog.   _____

 **My Spelling Monsters**

List each word that you missed or had trouble with. Be sure to spell it correctly. Then, write it four or more times. Review this page often to help you vanquish these spelling demons.

_____

_____

_____

_____

_____

CAREER TRACK VOCABULARY

Use your dictionary to define the words in Column A. Then select the best definition in Column B to match the word in Column A.

<table>
<tr><td colspan="2">Column A</td><td>Column B</td></tr>
<tr><td>_____</td><td>1. passé</td><td>a. investments, documents</td></tr>
<tr><td>_____</td><td>2. paucity</td><td>b. drinkable, pure</td></tr>
<tr><td>_____</td><td>3. portfolio</td><td>c. scarcity, lack</td></tr>
<tr><td>_____</td><td>4. potable</td><td>d. quarrelsome, peevish</td></tr>
<tr><td>_____</td><td>5. procure</td><td>e. purchase, secure</td></tr>
<tr><td>_____</td><td>6. querulous</td><td>f. dated, old-fashioned</td></tr>
</table>

Choose the best meaning for the following underlined words.

_____ 7. Recently the word *basic* has become a pejorative term in the fashion industry.

      a. negative   b. commonplace   c. trendy

_____ 8. Several manufacturers relocated to the periphery of the city.

      a. suburbs   b. center   c. outskirts

_____ 9. To gain an edge in the perpetual videogame race, Nintendo and Silicon Graphics have merged.

      a. exciting   b. aggressive   c. constant

_____ 10. Small World Toys' perspicacious policy of selling to specialty stores helps it survive.

      a. shrewd   b. foolish   c. standard

_____ 11. His excuse for being late was too outrageous to be plausible.

      a. imaginary   b. unlikely   c. possible

_____ 12. The fate of the start-up athletic shoe company is precarious in the face of stiff competition.

      a. distinct   b. uncertain   c. prosperous

_____ 13. Ford's 450-horsepower Mustang Mach III drew profuse praise at the auto show.

      a. polite   b. lavish   c. restrained

_____ 14. Caught in the banking quagmire were top executives who acted unethically.

      a. swamp   b. fantasy   c. disaster

Confusing Words

personal   private, individual   *precede*   to go before
personnel employees   *proceed*   to continue

populous   adj. having a large population
populace   n. people, masses

15. Please do not read my _____ mail.

16. You will speak second; Victor will _____ you.

17. All _____ receive employment packets describing company benefits.

18. Tokyo is Japan's most _____ city.

19. After receiving identification passes, visitors may _____ inside.

20. Mexico City's _____ is approaching 10 million.

Look back over the 20 vocabulary words in this chapter. Select 5 new words that you would like to own. Remember, to "own" a word, you must be able to use it correctly in a sentence. Double-check the meanings of your selections in a dictionary. Then write a sentence for each of your words.

_____

_____

_____

_____

_____

_____

COMPETENT LANGUAGE USAGE ESSENTIALS (C.L.U.E.)

Verb Agreement

Guide 6: Make subjects agree with verbs despite intervening phrases and clauses. Become a real detective in locating *true* subjects. Don't be deceived by prepositional phrases and parenthetic words that often disguise the real subject of a sentence.

> The range of colors, models, and sizes *is* (not *are*) amazing. (The true subject is *range*.)

> One candidate from the hundreds of applicants *is* (not *are*) sure to meet our qualifications. (The true subject is *candidate*.)

> Lee's original plan, together with ideas from other employees, *is* best. (The true subject is *plan*.)

 TIP. Subjects are nouns or pronouns that control verbs. To find subjects, cross out prepositional phrases beginning with words like *about, at, by, for, from, of,* and *to.* Subjects of verbs are not found in prepositional phrases. Moreover, don't be tricked by expressions introduced by *together with, in addition to,* and *along with.*

Guide 7: Subjects joined by *and* require plural verbs. Watch for true subjects joined by the conjunction *and*. They require plural verbs.

> Our CEO and one vice president *have* (not *has*) accepted speaking invitations.

> Exercising in the gym and running every day *are* (not *is*) how he keeps fit.

> The letter that we sent and a memo that we received in return *are* (not *is*) missing.

> Considerable time and energy *were* (not *was*) spent in developing an acceptable alternative plan.

Guide 8: Subjects joined by *or* or *nor* may require singular or plural verbs. The verb should agree with the closer subject.

> Either the attorney or the judge *is* (not *are*) responsible for the delay.

> Neither the computer nor the printer *has* (not *have*) been working properly.

 TIP. In joining singular and plural subjects with *or* or *nor*, place the plural subject closer to the verb. Then, the plural verb sounds natural. For example, *Neither the president nor the faculty members favor the tuition increase.* Notice that the plural verb *favor* agrees with the plural subject *members*.

Guide 9: Use singular verbs for most indefinite pronouns. For example, *anyone, anybody, anything, each, either, every, everyone, everybody, everything, neither, nobody, nothing, someone, somebody*, and *something* all take singular verbs.

> Everybody in both classes *has* (not *have*) received the materials.

> Each of the printers *is* (not *are*) ready for replacement.

Guide 10: Use singular or plural verbs for collective nouns, depending on whether the members of the group are operating as a unit or individually. Words like *faculty, administration, class, crowd,* and *committee* are considered collective nouns. If the members of the collective are acting as a unit, treat them as singular subjects. If they are acting individually, it's usually better to add the word *members* and use a plural verb.

> The Admissions Committee *is* working harmoniously. (*Committee* is singular because its action is unified.)

> The Finance Committee *are* having difficulty agreeing. (*Committee* is plural because its members are acting individually. If the action is individual, the sentence will sound better if it's recast: *The Finance Committee members are having difficulty agreeing.*)

 TIP. Collective nouns in America are generally considered singular. In Britain these collective nouns are generally considered plural.

C.L.U.E. Checkpoint

Use proofreading marks to correct any errors in verb use. Mark *C* if a sentence is correct.

1. The Council on Consumer Prices have taken a firm position.

2. Either Ron or Lily have the door key.

3. The list of management objectives are filled with goals for employees.

4. Our president, along with the manager and three sales representatives, are flying to the meeting.

5. The tone and wording of the letter are difficult to improve.

6. A group of players, coaches, and fans are booking a charter flight.

7. Each of the class members are scheduled for a private conference.

8. One of your duties, in addition to the tasks already outlined, involve budgeting department expenses.

9. Considerable time and money was spent on publicizing the event.

10. Neither of the recalls was particularly costly to the car manufacturer.

Super C.L.U.E. Review

In this cumulative review, use proofreading marks to correct grammar, punctuation, number usage, capitalization, spelling, and confusing word use. Mark *C* if a sentence is correct.

1. An increase in our companies sales here at home have prompted us to insure our stockholders that we plan to expand overseas.

2. Research and development of course is essential. If we plan to have new products available for global expansion.

3. Although we called several bookstores neither of the dictionarys are available.

4. Either of the two applicants are satisfactory, however our personell department must check their references.

5. A set of guidelines to standardize input and output have allready been submitted to our document production department.

6. If stock prices has sank to their lowest point our broker will begin buying.

7. Something about these insurance claims appear questionable therefore I want the hole investigation reopened.

8. Anyone in the class action suit are eligible to make a personnal claim.

9. Mr. Wilson asked a clerk to help him select a tie and shirt that has complimentary colors.

10. Any one of the auditors are authorized to procede with an independant investigation.

CAREER APPLICATION

Your boss, Stew Beltz, vice president, Operations, asks you to help him research information leading to a decision about lighting in all offices where computers are used heavily. Your company, 21st Century Insurance, employs hundreds of administrative workers using computers. Within eight months the company will be remodeling many offices, and Stew is considering switching from standard lighting to indirect lighting.

As an administrative assistant, you are to find out all you can about both kinds of lighting. You will not be expected to conduct any primary research yet; Stew first wants you to search secondary sources. What has already been learned about lighting for computer working environments?

Immediately, you start to work. You learn that indirect lighting (uplighting) distributes the light across the ceiling and upper walls, lighting a room evenly and comfortably. Standard direct lighting (parabolic), on the other hand, shines directly onto the working environment, creating glare and harsh shadows.

Your research also shows that the use of indirect lighting is growing. The American Institute of Lighting collects data on the number of people working in computer environments where indirect lighting is installed. Here's what you found for 1988 through 2002.

1988	487,000 workers
1990	751,000
1992	1,012,000
1994	3,045,000
1996	3,441,000
1998	5,150,000
2000	6,033,000
2002	6,552,000

Even more interesting is a study done by Cornell University's Department of Design and Environmental Analysis. Researchers set out to learn the most effective lighting for computer working environments. They studied the performance, satisfaction, and visual health of 200 workers. Here are some specific results from the Cornell Study:

- Eleven percent of participants working under standard lighting reported losing time due to itching, watering eyes. Only 4 percent working under indirect light reported the same problem.

- Twenty-one percent had trouble focusing their eyes under standard lighting. Just 1 percent reported the problem with indirect lighting.

- Six percent complained of tired, lethargic eyes resulting from indirect lighting. Twenty-six percent had the same problem under standard lighting.

- Overall, more than 72 percent of the participants preferred indirect lighting over standard lighting, finding it to be more pleasant, more comfortable, and more likable.

- Indirect lighting produced production time losses estimated at 15 to 20 minutes per day.

Critical Thinking Questions

1. Who is the audience for your findings?

2. How could the data on use of indirect lighting from 1986 to 2000 be best presented? Table? Bar chart? Line chart? Pie chart? What influenced your choice?

3. You know that Stew will want you to interpret your findings. You think that he leans toward keeping the old direct, parabolic lighting because it is cheaper than installing indirect lighting. You, on the other hand, would like to see indirect lighting installed because it seems more attractive. When you draw conclusions from this set of data, should you emphasize the data that support indirect lighting? Why?

4. What did you learn that could be used against the installation of indirect lighting? How should you treat it? Forget it? Bury it? Emphasize it?

5. Based on the information you collected, would you recommend indirect lighting? Why?

6. To make the most readable line chart, what information should be plotted vertically, up the left side of the chart? What information should be plotted horizontally, across the bottom? In charting the number of workers, should you work with the numbers exactly as shown or round them off to even millions?

Check your responses with those shown in the solutions at the end of this chapter. Then, prepare a chart reflecting the worker figures from 1988 through 2002. Add appropriate legends and a title. Use a computer program to make your chart, or fill in the chart started below. You may wish to add vertical lines to divide the chart into squares. (Review the suggestions for making line charts on page 392 of Guffey's *Business Communication: Process and Product*.) On a separate sheet, write the Conclusions and Recommendations section of the report you will submit to your boss. When you finish, compare your chart and Conclusions/Recommendations with those shown in Appendix B.

```
8  ─────────────────────────────────────────────

7  ─────────────────────────────────────────────

6  ─────────────────────────────────────────────

5  ─────────────────────────────────────────────

4  ─────────────────────────────────────────────

3  ─────────────────────────────────────────────

2  ─────────────────────────────────────────────

1  ─────────────────────────────────────────────

0  ─────────────────────────────────────────────
    '88    '90    '92    '94    '96    '98    '00    '02
```

SOLUTIONS

1. reports
2. analytical
3. letter
4. work plan
5. focus
6. limitations
7. factoring
8. outline
9. schedule
10. research
11. Primary, Secondary
12. periodicals
13. resources
14. Web
15. browser
16. FAQ
17. accuracy
18. survey
19. interview
20. observation
21. emphasize
22. tables
23. bar charts
24. Line charts
25. Pie charts
26. flow charts
27. budget
28. documentation
29. source
30. archiving

31. A formal writing style is found in theses, research studies, and controversial or complex reports. It gives the impression of objectivity, accuracy, professionalism, and fairness. It generally creates a distance between the writer and reader. A formal style omits first-person pronouns, contractions, humor, figures of speech, and editorializing. It uses passive-voice verbs, complex sentences, and long words.

   An informal writing style is found in short, routine reports for familiar audiences. This style conveys a feeling of warmth, personal involvement, and closeness. This style uses first-person pronouns, contractions, active-voice verbs, shorter sentences, familiar words, occasional humor, and some editorializing.

32. Primary, firsthand information comes from surveys, interviews, observation, and experimentation. Secondary information results from reading what others have experienced and observed. Principal sources of secondary data are books, periodicals, newspapers, encyclopedias, dictionaries, handbooks, and electronic databases.

33. Some of the best Web search tools: Google, Yahoo!, HotBot, Northern Light, and LookSmart.

34. Paraphrasing involves restating an original passage in your own words and in your own style.

35. Four kinds of material to document:
    a. Another person's ideas, opinions, examples, or theory
    b. Any facts, statistics, graphs, and drawings that are not common knowledge
    c. Quotations of another person's actual spoken or written words
    d. Paraphrases of another person's spoken or written words

Career Track Spelling
1. foreign
2. privilege
3. committee, thoroughly
4. C
5. schedule
6. analyze
7. indispensable
8. deductible
9. Incidentally
10. evidently

Career Track Vocabulary
1. f
2. c
3. a
4. b
5. e
6. d
7. a
8. c
9. c
10. a
11. c
12. b
13. b
14. a
15. personal
16. precede
17. personnel
18. populous
19. proceed
20. populace

C.L.U.E. Checkpoint

1. has taken [*Council* is a collective noun; members of the Council seem unified.]
2. has [Make the verb agree with the closer subject, *Lily*.]
3. is filled [Make verb agree with the true subject, *list*.]
4. is flying [Make the verb agree with *president*.]
5. C [*Tone* and *wording* are plural subjects.]
6. is booking [The subject is *group*, a singular noun.]
7. is scheduled [Make the verb agree with the subject, *Each*.]
8. involves [The singular verb *involves* agrees with the singular subject *One*.]
9. were spent [The subjects are *time* and *money*.]
10. C

Super C.L.U.E. Review

1. company's   has prompted   to <u>ass</u>ure
2. development, of course, are essential if   [No punctuation should precede *if*.]
3. bookstores,   dictionaries is
4. is satisfactory; however, our Personnel Department
5. has a<u>l</u>ready   Document Production Department [Remember to capitalize departments within our organization.]
6. have sunk   point,
7. appears questionable; therefore,   whole
8. is eligible   perso<u>na</u>l
9. that have complementary
10. is authorized to proc<u>ee</u>d   independ<u>e</u>nt

Career Application - Critical Thinking Questions

1. The audience for this data will be your boss. The information may become part of a final report that your boss submits to management to support his recommendation about lighting in the remodeled offices.

2. The data for computer workers in environments with indirect lighting would be most readable in a line chart. Line charts are especially good for showing changes in data over time.

3. Although the thought crosses your mind to emphasize all the data that support indirect lighting, you realize immediately that your boss is depending on you to present *all* the data you collect, whether it supports your own personal view or not. Moreover, you think that the facts would be most credible if they showed both positive and negative effects of indirect lighting. Presenting only one side of a picture (or what appears to be only one side) could suggest that you didn't do a thorough job of researching.

4. Indirect lighting seemed to cause a loss in productivity of 15 to 20 minutes per day. This information should be presented objectively, without emphasis or deemphasis.

5. Based on this information, you will probably recommend the use of indirect lighting. Most of the information indicates that workers in a controlled research felt positive physical and mental effects as a result of indirect lighting.

6. Numbers of workers should be plotted vertically, perhaps in millions. Years from 1988 to 2002 should be plotted horizontally. The numbers should be rounded off to even millions or fractions thereof, such as .5 million, .75 million. For a half million, you would show a dot halfway up in the first box or increment.

Chapter 13

Organizing and Writing Typical Business Reports

CHAPTER REVIEW

Interpreting and Organizing Data

Answers	discussion/analysis	headings	recommendations
Conclusions	facts/findings	mean	schedule
Contract	grid	mode	tables

1. Data you've collected for a report often seems like a jumble of isolated facts. You must sort and analyze this information so that you can find meanings, relationships, and _____ to your research questions. (Obj. 1, p. 407)

2. Numerical data from questionnaires or interviews are usually summarized and simplified in _____, which use columns and rows to organize the data. (Obj. 1, p. 408)

3. Three statistical devices used to help researchers organize data are the three M's. When people say "average," they most frequently intend to indicate the _____, which is an arithmetic average. (Obj. 1, p. 409)

4. A technique that uses boxes to organize complex data is called a _____ . This device is particularly helpful in comparing verbal data. (Obj. 1, p. 411)

5. The most widely read portions of a report are the sections devoted to _____ and _____. Readers head straight for these sections to see what the report writer thinks about the data. (Obj. 2, p. 412)

6. Information reports are generally organized into three main sections: (a) introduction/background, (b) _____, and (c) summary/conclusion. (Obj. 2, p. 416)

7. Although the parts may be rearranged somewhat, analytical reports generally are organized into four sections: (a) introduction/problem, (b) facts/findings, (c) _____, and (d) conclusions/recommendations. (Obj. 2, p. 416)

8. Writers can guide readers through a report by providing the equivalent of a map and road signs. Cues that provide such direction include introductions, transitions, and _____. (Obj. 2, p. 418)

9. Good report introductions set up a _____ with the reader. The writer promises to cover certain topics in a specified order. Readers expect the writer to follow through on this agreement. (Obj. 2, p. 418)

Writing Reports

Action	direct	neutral	progress
Alternatives	equal	persuaded	solutions
Conclusions	feasibility	problems	yardstick

10. Informational reports generally describe periodic recurring activities, such as monthly sales or weekly customer calls, as well as nonrecurring events, such as trips, conferences, and progress. In these reports readers do not have to be _____; they are usually neutral or receptive. (Obj. 4, p. 421)

11. Periodic reports keep management informed of operations. They usually (a) summarize regular activities and events, (b) describe irregular events deserving the attention of management, and (c) highlight special needs and _____ . (Obj. 4, pp. 421–423)

12. Trip, convention, and conference reports generally (a) identify the event, (b) summarize three to five main points, (c) itemize expenses, and (d) express appreciation, synthesize the value of the event, and suggest any _____ to be taken. (Obj. 4, p. 423)

13. Continuing projects often require _____ or interim reports to describe their status. Such reports may go to customers, perhaps advising them of the headway of their projects, or to management, informing them of the status of some activity. (Obj. 4, p. 425)

14. Investigative or information reports deliver data for a specific situation. These nonrecurring reports are usually arranged in a direct pattern with three segments: introduction, body, and conclusions. What's important is dividing the topic into three to five areas that are roughly _____ and don't overlap. (Obj. 4, pp. 425–428)

15. Analytical reports seek to collect and present data clearly, but they also try to persuade the reader to accept the _____ and act on the recommendations presented. (Obj. 5, p. 429)

16. Organizing analytical reports with the conclusions and recommendations first is appropriate when the reader has confidence in the writer. This _____ pattern is also appropriate when the topic is familiar and the reader is supportive. (Obj. 5, p. 429)

17. Reports that examine the practicality and advisability of following a course of action are called _____ reports. They typically are internal reports written to advise on matters such as consolidating departments, offering a wellness program, or hiring an outside firm to handle some aspect of company operations. (Obj. 5, p. 433)

18. Some reports examine problems with two or more solutions. To evaluate the best solution, the writer establishes criteria by which to compare the alternatives. These reports are called _____ reports because of the measurement involved. (Obj. 5, p. 436)

19. The real advantage to such reports is that
_____ can be measured consistently
by using the same criteria. (Obj. 5, p. 436)

20. Reports that examine several alternatives or criteria
generally begin by describing the problem or need
and explaining possible _____ and alternatives. (Obj. 5, p. 436)

Indicate whether the following statements are true or
false by using T or F.

_____ 21. In the research phase of report writing, you
will begin by examining each item to see what
it means by itself and what it means when
connected with other data. (Obj. 1, p. 407)

_____ 22. Report writers should avoid the temptation to sensationalize or exaggerate their findings and conclusions. (Obj. 1, p. 414)

_____ 23. In reporting correlations, you must avoid suggesting that a cause-and-effect relationship
exists—unless it can be proved. (Obj. 1, p. 411)

_____ 24. It is difficult for a report writer to remain totally objective when drawing conclusions
from collected data. (Obj. 2, p. 413)

_____ 25. Recommendations explain a problem; conclusions offer specific suggestions for solving the problem. (Obj. 2, p. 415)

_____ 26. Because information reports generally have the same three parts, the method of organization of the facts will be the same in all reports. (Obj. 3, p. 416)

_____ 27. Transitional expressions (*on the contrary, however, first*) help reveal the logical flow of
report ideas. (Obj. 3, p. 418)

_____ 28. Most large businesses require periodic reports to keep management informed of operations. (Obj. 4, p. 421)

_____ 29. The average reader scans a page from left to right and from top to bottom in a Z pattern. (Obj. 4, p. 422)

_____ 30. If a writer announces the recommendations early in the report, a reader may think the
writer has oversimplified or overlooked something important. (Obj. 5, p. 429)

31. For this group of figures, calculate the mean, median, mode, and range: 2, 2, 3, 3, 3, 4, 5, 10.
(Obj. 1, p. 409)

32. Name five common methods for organizing the data sections of reports. Provide an original example of the kind of report where each could be used. (Obj. 3, pp. 416-418)

33. What are three techniques that prevent readers from getting lost in reports? (Obj. 3, p. 418)

34. Assume that you must write a report on the status of a company ride-sharing promotional drive (or some other activity that you name). Discuss the information that your progress report should contain. (Obj. 4, p. 425)

35. Give an original example of a business problem that could be solved by a yardstick report. Explain how the report would be organized using examples from your selected problem. (Obj. 5, p. 436)

CAREER TRACK SPELLING

For each group below identify misspelled words and write corrected versions in the spaces provided. Write *C* if all words are correct.

1. dominant	controversial	itinerery	conceive	_____
2. useable	accidentally	beginning	dropped	_____
3. transferred	until	simular	vegetable	_____
4. cylinder	apparent	shining	success	_____
5. defendent	mechanics	referring	peculiar	_____
6. shoulder	poison	huge	ninty	_____
7. laid	encourage	emphazise	knowledge	_____
8. existance	safety	rhythm	regard	_____
9. suspense	genuine	interupt	importance	_____
10. efficient	miscelanous	parallel	miniature	_____

My Spelling Monsters

List each word that you missed or had trouble with. Be sure to spell it correctly. Then, write it four or more times. Review this page often to help you vanquish these spelling demons.

_____

_____

_____

_____

_____

CAREER TRACK VOCABULARY

Use your dictionary to define the words in Column A. Then select the best definition in Column B to match the word in Column A.

Column A	Column B
_____ 1 quell	a. repetitious, superfluous
_____ 2. quiescent	b. deny, revoke
_____ 3. quixotic	c. imaginary, impractical
_____ 4. realm	d. still, latent
_____ 5. recant	e. subdue, suppress
_____ 6. redundant	f. region, field

Choose the best meaning for the following underlined words.

_____ 7. Five members constitute a <u>quorum</u>; therefore, we can't pass this motion.

      a. ratio   b. legal assembly   c. representation

_____ 8. Many new software programs have bugs that manufacturers must <u>rectify</u>.

      a. adulterate   b. acknowledge   c. fix

_____ 9. Evening air along the coast was <u>redolent</u> with seaweed and seaspray.

      a. fragrant   b. heavy   c. offensive

_____ 10. Mexico's president <u>reiterated</u> his plan to make Pemex an oil giant.

      a. abandoned   b. drafted   c. restated

_____ 11. An effective battery is the first <u>requisite</u> for a smog-free car.

      a. requirement   b. option   c. prototype

_____12. Despite pressure from manufacturers, the Air Quality Board refused to <u>rescind</u> its paint emission standards.

      a. increase   b. repeal   c. decrease

_____13. Enjoined against using his own name, Wally Amos <u>retaliated</u> with the Noname Cookie Co.

      a. reciprocated   b. protested   c. joined

_____14. The attorney general was <u>reticent</u> when asked about the antitrust case.

      a. smiling   b. silent   c. talkative

Confusing Words

precedence	priority	_persecute_	to oppress
precedents	events used as an example	_prosecute_	to sue

plaintiff	a party to a lawsuit
plaintive	mournful

15. Ahmad was a _____ who filed a claim against the asbestos manufacturer.

16. Who will _____ the antitrust case?

17. Although few _____ exist, our company decided to establish its own clean environment rules.

18. South Africans contend that their government continues to _____ them.

19. She was unable to resist the puppy's _____ cry.

20. Your health should take _____ over your job.

Look back over the 20 vocabulary words in this chapter. Select 5 new words that you would like to own. Remember, to "own" a word, you must be able to use it correctly in a sentence. Double-check the meanings of your selections in a dictionary. Then write a sentence for each of your words.

_____

_____

_____

_____

_____

_____

_____

_____

COMPETENT LANGUAGE USAGE ESSENTIALS (C.L.U.E.)

Pronouns

Guide 11: Learn the three cases of pronouns and how each is used. Pronouns are substitutes for nouns. Every business writer must know the following pronoun cases or categories:

Nominative or Subjective Case (Used for subjects of verbs and subject complements)	Objective Case (Used for objects of prepositions and objects of verbs)	Possessive Case (Used to show possession)
I	me	my, mine
we	us	our, ours
you	you	you, yours
he	him	his
she	her	her, hers
it	it	its
they	them	their, theirs
who, whoever	whom, whomever	whose

Guide 12: Use nominative case pronouns as subjects of verbs and as complements.
Complements are words that follow linking verbs (such as *am, is, are, was, were, be, being,* and *been*) and rename the words to which they refer.

> *He* and *I* (not *him* and *me*) are studying management. (Use nominative case pronouns as the subjects of the verb *are studying*.)

> We're convinced that *she* and *he* will win the election. (Use nominative case pronouns as the subjects of the verb *will win*.)

> It must have been *he* (not *him*) who left the package. (Use a nominative case pronoun as a subject complement following the linking verb *been*.)

 TIP. If you feel awkward using nominative pronouns after linking verbs, rephrase the sentence to avoid the dilemma. Instead of *It is he who is the manager*, say *He is the manager*.

Guide 13: Use objective case pronouns as objects of prepositions and verbs.

> Please send catalogs to *her* and *me* (not *she* and *I*). (The pronouns *her* and *me* are objects of the preposition *to*.)

> Professor James asked *me* (not *I*) to write a report. (The pronoun *me* is the object of the verb *asked*.)

TIP. When a pronoun appears in combination with a noun or another pronoun, ignore the extra noun or pronoun and its conjunction. Then, the case of the pronoun becomes more obvious. For example, *The CEO gave Derrick and* me (not *I*) *the assignment.* Ignoring *Derrick and* helps you see that the objective case, not the nominative case, is needed.

 TIP. Be especially alert to the following prepositions: *except, between, but,* and *like.* Be sure to use objective case pronouns as their objects. For example, *Just between you and* me (not *I*), *those shoes are made from recycled rubber. Everyone except Tom and* him *(*not *he*) received raises.*

Guide 14: Use possessive case pronouns to show ownership. Possessive pronouns (such as *hers, yours, whose, ours, theirs,* and *its*) require no apostrophes.

> My car is here. Where is *yours* (not *your's*)?

> Our cat licks *its* (not *it's*) fur.

 TIP. Don't confuse possessive pronouns and contractions. Contractions are shortened forms of subject-verb phrases (such as *it's* for *it is, there's* for *there is, who's* for *who is,* and *they're* for *they are*).

C.L.U.E. Checkpoint

Use proofreading marks to correct any errors in pronouns. Mark *C* if a sentence is correct.

1. Although my friend and me are interested in this printer, it's price seems high.

2. E-mail addressed to he and I was delivered to Thomas and she instead.

3. Just between you and I, the mail room and it's manager should be investigated.

4. All my packages were found, but your's and her's are still missing.

5. Do you think it was him who called this morning?

Super C.L.U.E. Review

In this cumulative review, use proofreading marks to correct grammar, punctuation, number usage, capitalization, spelling, and confusing word use. Mark *C* if a sentence is correct.

1. The CEO asked the Personnel Manager and I to council all newly hired employees about personnel hygiene.

2. Her knowledge of computing and her genuine interest in people is what appealed to the recruiter and I.

3. If anyone is dissapointed it will be me, however I do not anticipate bad news.

4. The body of the manuscript and it's footnotes are on seperate pages.

5. Because we have no precedents for problems like these Mr. Lopez and me will seek advice from a management consultant.

6. All class members except Kim and he knew the assignment, and were prepared with their reports when they were do.

7. Just between you and I, do you think it was him who complained?

8. If you will send the shipment to Tran or I; we will inspect its contents throughly.

9. The itinerary for Jason and he included these countrys holland france and germany.

10. The use of concrete nouns and active verbs are important. If you want to improve your writing.

CAREER APPLICATION

Your friend and fellow worker Rick Seid, assistant to the vice president for Human Resources, was asked by his boss to explore ways to begin training young managers for global assignments. Your company is already developing markets in Europe and Asia, but it has done little to prepare American managers to operate in these markets. The CEO and management council hope to begin training company employees to manage overseas production and marketing efforts, rather than relying on foreign nationals. Rick is to investigate ways to train our managers and to examine what other companies are doing. His boss expects a full report in two months and a progress report after one month.

Rick writes the following draft of his progress report, and he asks you to critique it. In evaluating this report, answer the questions below. Then prepare a progress report outline that might help Rick in revising his report.

Draft of Progress Report - To Be Revised

DATE: Current
TO: John R. Zurawski, Vice President, Human Resources
FROM: Rick Seid, Administrative Assistant
SUBJECT: Progress Report for International Training Programs

I am writing this progress report, as you requested, to inform you of the status of my research into developing training programs for young international managers. My research includes both secondary and primary sources. I have read lots of magazine, newspaper, and government articles on cross-cultural training and skills required of global managers. I have also talked with consultants and training schools. Because the topic is so broad, I have divided it into internal programs that could be conducted within our environment and external programs outside the company.

Let me describe what I have done thus far, John. Under internal training programs, I've learned that many companies are preparing employees for international assignments by using videotapes, in-house seminars, and intensive language and culture courses during work hours. Consultants and trainers conduct these short-term training sessions. Some companies are also improving their pool of young international managers by recruiting more globally oriented new employees who already possess many of the skills required.

In investigating external programs, I have found (primarily through reading tons of articles!) that at least six U.S. companies have developed extensive global management trainee programs. These companies are American Express, Colgate-Palmolive Company, General Electric aircraft-engine unit, PepsiCo international beverage division, and Raychem Corporation. Most of these companies use both short- and long-term assignments abroad as training for prospective international managers. They also send trainees to intensive training programs offered by specialized (and very expensive!) schools in this country.

Thus far, to investigate internal training programs, I have ordered some training videos, which I hope to evaluate in the next two weeks. I'm also talking with a training consultant who offers in-house seminars that can be individualized to our needs. For external training, I have ordered literature from some specialized schools, such as International Orientation Resources (Denver) and Business Services for Global Understanding (Chicago) to learn about their programs and costs. These intensive programs generally prepare prospective managers and their families for immediate transfer abroad, but I was assured that they will develop any program we want. I also plan to conduct telephone interviews with the six companies listed above to learn about their international training programs.

The biggest problem in gathering this information is the telephone interviewing of busy executives. I may not be able to reach representatives from all six companies. In that case, I hope you will forgive me for including in my report only as much information as I could gather by my deadline of November 15.

Critical Thinking Questions

1.   Who is the audience for Rick's report?

2.   Is the tone of the report, including its word choice and degree of formality, appropriate for its audiences? Cite specific examples. How could the tone be improved?

3.   Although his report may not appear so, Rick has already done considerable thinking to organize his research and findings. Why, then, is this report so hard to read? What three reader cues could Rick use to help readers comprehend his organization?

4.   Readers of progress reports expect to find what general categories? How could Rick make sure the organization is easier to comprehend?

5.   What critical data has Rick omitted from the closing of his report?

After comparing your responses to these questions with those in the solutions at the end of this chapter, prepare an outline here or on a separate page to guide Rick in improving this progress report. When you finish, look at the outline shown in Appendix B to see how yours compares.

SOLUTIONS

1. answers
2. tables
3. mean
4. grid
5. conclusions, recommendations
6. facts/findings
7. discussion/analysis
8. headings
9. contract
10. persuaded

11. problems
12. action
13. progress
14. equal
15. conclusions
16. direct
17. feasibility
18. yardstick
19. alternatives
20. solutions

21. T
22. T
23. T
24. T
25. F Conclusions explain a problem; recommendations offer specific suggestions for solving the problem.
26. F Many different organizational methods are possible.
27. T
28. T
29. T
30. T

31. Mean: 4   (The total, 32, divided by the total number of items, 8)
    Mode: 3   (The value most frequently represented)
    Median: 3   (The midpoint in the line of numbers)
    Range: 2 to 10

32. Five organizational methods:
    a. Time. Example: a trip report or a history of an organization.
    b. Component. Example: a sales report by company divisions.
    c. Importance. Example: a report analyzing reasons for customer complaints.
    d. Criteria. Example: a report comparing new printers.
    e. Convention. Example: a proposal offering a service, such as a telecommunications system, to a company.

33. Three techniques that prevent readers from getting lost in a report:
    a. Introductions
    b. Transitions
    c. Headings

34. A progress report about the status of a company ride-sharing program might contain this information:
    a. A concise description of the purpose and nature of the ride-sharing program
    b. Background information, if the audience is unfamiliar with the program
    c. Description of all ride-sharing efforts thus far
    d. Explanation of current activities, including names of people, methods, and results thus far
    e. Description of any anticipated problems, along with possible solutions
    f. Discussion of future activities and date for completion of program, if an end date has been established

35. Possible problem for a yardstick report: selection of new office printers. The organization of such a yardstick report is as follows:
    a. Begin by describing the need for new printers.
    b. Explain the kinds of new printers available and what each could do.
    c. Decide what criteria are most important for your printers (speed, quality print, pricing, or service, for example).
    d. Discuss each printer choice in terms of the criteria established.
    e. Draw conclusions and recommend one printer.

Career Track Spelling

1. itinerary
2. usable
3. similar
4. C
5. defendant
6. ninety
7. emphasize
8. existence
9. interrupt
10. miscellaneous

Career Track Vocabulary

1. e
2. d
3. c
4. f
5. b
6. a
7. b
8. c
9. a
10. c
11. a
12. b
13. a
14. b
15. plaintiff
16. prosecute
17. precedents
18. persecute
19. plaintive
20. precedence

C.L.U.E. Checkpoint

1. my friend and I   its price
2. to him and me   to Thomas and her
3. you and me   its manager
4. yours and hers
5. it was he

Super C.L.U.E. Review

1. personnel manager and me   counsel   personal hygiene
2. people are what appealed to the recruiter and me. [The two subjects, *knowledge* and *interest*, require a plural verb, *are*.]
3. di<u>s</u>app<u>o</u>inted, it will be I; however, [Use the nominative pronoun *I* as a complement following the linking verb *be*.]
4. its   sep<u>a</u>rate
5. precedence   these, Mr. Lopez and I
6. except Kim and him   assignment [omit comma]   d<u>ue</u>.
7. between you and me,   it was he
8. Tran or me,   th<u>o</u>roughly
9. for Jason and him   countries: Holland, France, and Germany.
10. verbs is important if [No punctuation is necessary in joining the fragment to the sentence.]

Career Application - Critical Thinking Questions

1. The primary audience for Rick's report is his boss, John Zurawski. However, the report could possibly be distributed to other executives who are interested in the project. Rick would be wise to look beyond the immediate audience.

2. The tone of the report is informal, including many *I*'s and addressing the receiver by his first name. The word choice and punctuation are also casual ("lots of," "tons of," and overuse of exclamation marks). The tone could be improved by less dependence on "I." In fact, Rick probably ought to check with his boss to learn how formal to be in both the progress and the final reports. Should his reports be written in first person ("I conducted research") or third person ("Research was conducted" or "Research reveals that")?

3. One reason the report is hard to read is its lack of headings. Moreover, the topic is broad and Rick was given little guidance. With many diverse items, a report is hard to organize. Yet, Rick has already partially ordered his findings. But he has given his readers few cues to help them see that organization. Three cues that help readers are (a) introductions that preview what is to follow, (b) transitional words, and (c) headings. Graphic highlighting (lists and bulleted items) might also improve readability.

4. Progress reports might contain categories such as Background, Work Completed, Work to Be Completed, and Anticipated Problems. By using these functional heads, Rick could make the report much easier to read.

5. Rick forgets to indicate whether he is on schedule and when the final report will be completed.

Now prepare an outline to guide Rick in revising his progress report.

Chapter 14

Proposals and Formal Reports

CHAPTER REVIEW

Formal and Informal Proposals

Use the listed words to complete the following sentences. Each word is used but once.

budget	feedback	problem	request for proposal
contracts	format	proposal	sales
executive summary	online	qualifications	timetable

1. A written offer to solve a problem, provide services, or sell equipment is referred to as a(n) _____. (Obj. 1, p. 452)

2. Government agencies and large companies often prepare a(n) _____ to announce their specifications for a project and to solicit competitive bids. (Obj. 1, p. 452)

3. An important point to remember about proposals, whether solicited or unsolicited, is that they are _____ presentations. They must be persuasive, not mere mechanical descriptions of what can be done. (Obj. 1, p. 453)

4. Most proposals begin by explaining the reasons for the proposal and by highlighting the writer's _____. (Obj. 1, p. 454)

5. After the introduction, the next section of a proposal discusses the goals or purposes of the project. For unsolicited proposals the writer might have to convince the reader that a(n) _____ exists. (Obj. 1, p. 454)

6. Formal proposals differ from informal proposals in size and _____. Formal proposals may range from 5 to 200 or more pages and contain many more parts than informal proposals. (Obj. 2, p. 457)

7. Proposals in the past were always paper-based and delivered by mail or special messenger. Companies today, however, increasingly prefer _____ proposals. (Obj. 2, p. 458)

8. An important part of a formal proposal is an abstract or _____. This section summarizes the proposal's highlights. (Obj. 2, p. 457)

9. Well-written proposals win _____ and business for companies. Many companies depend entirely on proposals to generate their income, so proposal writing becomes crucial. (Obj. 2, p. 458)

Formal Reports

audiences	first	outline	second
bibliography	formatting	recommendations	timetable
body	investigation	redundancy	transmittal

10. Formal reports are similar to formal proposals in length, organization, and serious tone. Instead of making an offer, however, formal reports represent the end product of thorough _____ and analysis. (Objs. 3 & 4, p. 461)

11. Many front and end items lengthen formal reports but enhance their professional tone and serve their multiple _____. Formal reports may be read by many levels of managers, technical specialists, financial consultants, and others. (Obj. 3, p. 461)

12. A letter or memorandum of _____ introduces a formal report. This message announces the topic, describes the project, highlights the findings, and closes with appreciation for the assignment or instructions for follow-up actions. (Obj. 3, p. 462)

13. Because they contain many parts serving different purposes, formal reports have a degree of _____. The same information may be repeated in several places. (Obj. 4, p. 463)

14. The principal section in any formal report is the _____. It discusses, analyzes, interprets, and evaluates the research findings or solution to the initial problem. (Obj. 5, p. 464)

15. When requested, you should submit _____ that make precise suggestions for actions that are practical and reasonable in solving the report problem. (Obj. 5, p. 465)

16. An alphabetic list of references on a topic is called a _____. Arranged by author, it may include all the works consulted as well as those actually cited in the report. (Obj. 5, p. 465)

17. The main reason that writers are disappointed with their reports is that they run out of time. To avoid this problem, develop a realistic _____ and stick to it. (Obj. 6, p. 466)

18. A big project like a formal report needs the order and direction provided by a clear _____ , even if its parts have to be revised as the project unfolds. (Obj. 6, p. 466)

19. To make formal reports as objective and credible as possible, most writers omit _____-person pronouns. (Obj. 6, p. 466)

20. The best way to proofread a formal report is to read a printed copy slowly for word meanings and content. Then read it again for spelling, punctuation, grammar, and other mechanical errors. Finally, scan the entire report for _____ and consistency. (Obj. 6, p. 467)

21. How do informal and formal proposals differ? (Objs. 1 & 2, pp. 452–458)

22. What are some techniques for capturing the interest of the reader in the introduction to a proposal? (Obj. 1, p. 454)

23. In a solicited proposal responding to an RFP, what is your aim? (Obj. 1, p. 454)

24. What should the staffing section of a proposal include? (Obj. 1, p. 456)

25. Why is the budget section of a proposal so important? (Obj. 1, p. 457)

26. To whom should you address a letter of transmittal for a formal proposal? (Obj. 2, p. 457)

27. Why are online proposals increasingly popular? (Obj. 4, p. 458)

28. How does the executive summary of a formal report differ from its introduction? (Obj. 3, p. 462)

29. What is a "quick-and-dirty" first draft? What are the advantages and disadvantages of such a method? (Obj. 6, p. 466)

30. How many times should a formal report be proofread? Why? (Obj. 6, p. 467)

Check your answers now!

CAREER TRACK SPELLING

In the spaces provided write the correct version of the words in parentheses. If a word is spelled correctly, write *C*.

1. Every language has a (grammer) or system of rules for use.   _____
2. Your (conscince) often tells you what is right and wrong.   _____
3. The office is located in a (dezireable) business section.   _____
4. Is it (fezable) to convert these three rooms into four offices?   _____
5. The board of directors and the CEO had (opposete) views.   _____
6. What (milage) do you expect from your new truck?   _____
7. (Congradulations) on your recent promotion!   _____
8. We are solidly (commited) to service and quality.   _____
9. The business made an (encredable) recovery last year.   _____
10. You must pass (threw) the outer office to enter the showroom.   _____

My Spelling Monsters

List each word that you missed or had trouble with. Be sure to spell it correctly. Then, write it four or more times. Review this page often to help you vanquish these spelling demons.

_____

_____

_____

_____

_____

CAREER TRACK VOCABULARY

Use your dictionary to define the words in Column A. Then select the best definition in Column B to match the word in Column A.

Column A	Column B
_____ 1. schism	a. examination, review
_____ 2. scrutiny	b. discord, split
_____ 3. sequester	c. terse, concise
_____ 4. succinct	d. chain, restrain
_____ 5. teem	e. abound, overflow
_____ 6. tether	f. separate, seclude

Choose the best meaning for the following underlined words.

_____ 7. The board of directors <u>sanctioned</u> the stock split.

      a. prevented   b. authorized   c. forbid

_____ 8. When interest rates are down, <u>savvy</u> homeowners refinance.

      a. wealthy   b. complacent   c. shrewd

_____ 9. Our accountant gave <u>scrupulous</u> attention to the totals.

      a. casual   b. careful   c. fleeting

_____ 10. Federal investigators destroyed the <u>sham</u> Rolex watches.

      a. fake   b. reliable   c. colorful

_____ 11. A series of scandals left the company's finances in <u>shambles</u>.

      a. debt   b. prosperity   c. disorder

_____ 12. At the end of the seventh inning, the pitcher had a <u>tally</u> of 11 strikeouts.

      a.   list   b. performance   c. showing

_____13. Japan collects a stiff <u>tariff</u> on rice imports.

        a. stipend   b. penalty   c. tax

_____14. Chinese student demonstrators threw <u>taunts</u> at the police.

        a. ridicule   b. stones   c. projectiles

Confusing Words

principal	n.: capital sum; school official	_reality_	that which is real
	adj.: chief, primary	_realty_	real estate
principle	rule of action		
stationary	immovable		
stationery	writing material		

15. After our area code was changed, we had to order new office _____.

16. Critics complain that the _____ goal of taxes is the redistribution of wealth.

17. After earning a broker's license, Ruth opened her own _____ office specializing in commercial buildings.

18. Justin was a man of high _____ and refused to back down in the confrontation.

19. Although two wooden counters in the office are _____, the desk can be relocated.

20. Few people have experienced the _____ of an earthquake at its epicenter.

Look over the vocabulary words in this chapter. Select five or more new words that you would like to add to your vocabulary. Double-check the meanings of your selections in a dictionary. Then write a sentence for each of your words.

_____

_____

_____

_____

_____

_____

_____

_____

COMPETENT LANGUAGE USAGE ESSENTIALS (C.L.U.E.)

Pronouns (cont.)

Guide 11: Use *self*-ending pronouns only when they refer to previously mentioned nouns or pronouns.

> The manager *herself* signed all purchase orders.

> Send the check to Michael or *me* (not *myself*).

> **TIP.** Trying to sound less egocentric, some radio and TV announcers incorrectly substitute *myself* when they should use *I*. For example, "Robin and *myself* (should be *I*) will be jetting to Acapulco." Remember that a *self*-ending pronoun can be used only when it refers to a previously mentioned antecedent.

Guide 16: Use *who* or *whoever* for nominative case constructions and *whom* or *whomever* for objective case constructions. In determining the correct choice, it's helpful to substitute *he* for *who* or *whoever* and *him* for *whom* or *whomever*.

> To *whom* did he address the letter? (The letter was addressed to *him*?)

> *Who* did you say left the message? (You did say *he* left the message?)

> Give the award to *whoever* deserves it. (In this sentence the clause *whoever deserves it* functions as the object of the preposition *to*. Within the clause *whoever* is the subject of the verb *deserves*. Again, try substituting *he*: *he deserves it.)*

C.L.U.E. Checkpoint 1

Use proofreading marks to correct all errors in *self*-ending pronouns and *who/whoever, whom/whomever*.

1. The president himself is willing to nominate whoever we recommend for the job.

2. Send all contributions to Mr. Rather or myself.

3. Who would you prefer to see elected president?

4. When the printer ribbons arrived, we distributed them to whomever ordered them.

5. The CEO and myself plan to attend the morning session of the seminar.

Guide 17: Make pronouns agree in number and gender with the words to which they refer (their antecedents). When the gender of the antecedent is obvious, pronoun references are simple.

> One of the men left *his* (not *their*) lights on. (The singular pronoun *his* refers to the singular antecedent *One*.)

Each of the women received *her* (not *their*) license. (The singular pronoun *her* agrees with the singular antecedent *Each*.)

When the gender of the antecedent could be male or female, sensitive writers today have a number of options—some acceptable and others not.

Faulty: Any subscriber may cancel *their* subscription. (The plural pronoun *their* does not agree with its singular antecedent *subscriber*.)

Improved: All subscribers may cancel their subscriptions. (Make the subject plural so that the plural pronoun *their* is acceptable. This option is preferred by many writers today.)

All subscribers may cancel subscriptions. (Omit the possessive pronoun entirely.)

Any subscriber may cancel a subscription. (Substitute *a* for a pronoun.)

Every subscriber may cancel *his or her* subscription. (Use the combination *his or her*. However, this option is wordy and should be avoided.)

Guide 18: Be sure that pronouns like *it, which, this,* and *that* refer to clear antecedents. Vague pronouns are confusing when they have no clear single antecedents. Replace vague pronouns with concrete words, or provide these pronouns with clear antecedents.

Faulty: Homeowners responded enthusiastically to separating their trash and recycling newspaper, but *it* caused more problems than solutions. [To what does *it* refer?]

Improved: Homeowners responded enthusiastically to separating their trash and recycling newspaper, but *these efforts* caused more problems than solutions. [Replace the vague pronoun *it* with more concrete words.]

Faulty: Stocks fell, the bond market slipped, and interest rates rose, *which* caused distress on Wall Street. [To what does *which* refer?]

Improved: Stocks fell, the bond market slipped, and interest rates rose. This combination of circumstances caused distress on Wall Street. [Remove the vague pronoun *which* and use a concrete reference.]

Faulty: We collected newsletters, brochures, announcements, and other printed samples. *This* helped us design our first newsletter. [To what does *This* refer?]

Improved: We collected newsletters, brochures, announcements, and other printed samples. *This sample collection* helped us design our first newsletter. [Add specific words to the pronoun to clarify its reference.]

TIP. Whenever you use the words *this, that, these,* and *those* by themselves, a red flag should pop up. These words are dangerous when they stand alone. Inexperienced writers often use them to refer to an entire previous idea, rather than to a specific antecedent, as shown in the preceding example. You can often solve the problem by adding another idea to the pronoun (*this sample collection*).

C.L.U.E. Checkpoint 2

Use proofreading marks to correct poor pronoun references.

1. In creating a successful business plan, you must define your overall company goals, identify customer characteristics, and project potential sales. This is what most beginning entrepreneurs fail to do.

2. Every employee should receive their parking assignment by Friday.

3. Connecticut provides tax credits, customized job training, and fast-track permitting, which is why many companies are moving there.

4. Our new business had cash-flow problems, partnership squabbles, and a leaky roof; however, we didn't let it get us down.

5. Anybody who opens a new business is sure to have their own start-up problems.

Super C.L.U.E. Review

In this cumulative review, use proofreading marks to correct grammar, punctuation, number usage, capitalization, spelling, and confusing word use. Mark *C* if a sentence is correct.

1. Please send the software to myself or whomever submitted the order.

2. Research and development of course is essential. If we plan to expand into the following key markets; pacific rim countries, the european community, and south america.

3. Exports from small companys has increased; but it is still insufficient to effect the balance of trade.

4. Our's is the only country with a sizable middle class and they are hungry for consumer goods.

5. First federal promised complementary checks to all new customers but it attracted only fifty-seven new accounts.

6. Every new employee must apply to recieve his permit to park in lot 5-A.

7. Jeffrey and myself was preparing a 4-page newsletter; each page consisting of 3 vertical columes.

8. Poor ventilation, inadequate lighting and hazardous working conditions were sighted in the complaint. This must be improved before negotiations may continue.

9. We reccommend therefore that a committee study our working conditions for a 3-week period, and submit a report of it's findings.

10. The rules of business etiquette is based primarily on the principals of good manners, everyone should exercise them in the workplace.

CAREER APPLICATION

Ramon Prentice is founder and president of Prentice Consultants, a national research group. Together with his staff, he is putting together a proposal that would test consumer satisfaction for a growing airline based in the Southeast. The airline solicited this proposal, as it plans to expand along the Eastern Seaboard and into Midwest markets. Before doing so, it wants to test its image and current levels of customer satisfaction. What is the airline doing right and what is it doing wrong?

Ramon assigns you the task of coordinating the final proposal. Here's what has been done thus far:

- Sally has worked out a plan of focus groups and survey research (questionnaires) that should provide excellent data about customer feelings. She has also worked out a schedule showing when the focus groups would meet and when and how the questionnaires would be administered.

- Tom looked over Sally's plan and prepared a budget showing how much time would be required and how much the total project would cost. The budget includes the costs of collecting and interpreting the data, plus preparing a final report with recommendations.

- Ramon wants you to look in the files and find samples of satisfaction surveys that the company has done for other customers. He would also like you to include a partial list of "satisfied" customers. Incidentally, Ramon usually writes the introduction and background sections for proposals.

- Amanda is the personnel expert. She has current résumés of the principal investigators who would work on this project. Amanda insists on submitting each person's complete résumé with the proposal because "these investigators have impressive qualifications and experience."

Ramon asks you to prepare a list showing all parts of the proposal package, in the proper order, along with the name of the person who is responsible for preparing that part. He'd also like you to include a brief description or reminder of what goes in each part.

Before preparing your list, answer the critical thinking questions on the next page.

Critical Thinking Questions

1. Who is the audience for your list?

2. Would you classify this proposal as "formal" or "informal"? Does it make any difference for your project?

3. What proposal parts have been accounted for?

4. What parts have been omitted that you think would improve this proposal? How should you treat these omissions?

5. Ramon didn't mention the company's new computer software that facilitates factor and cluster analysis. All your data processing is now done in-house, unlike many other research firms. You know he would want this information included. Where does it go?

6. Who should establish a deadline for the budget submitted with the proposal? Where should it be listed?

Check your responses to these questions against those at the end of this chapter before preparing your list. Then write your list and compare it with the one shown in Appendix B.

SOLUTIONS

Chapter Review

1. proposal
2. request for proposal
3. sales
4. qualifications
5. problem
6. format
7. online
8. executive summary
9. contracts
10. investigation
11. audiences
12. transmittal
13. redundancy
14. body
15. recommendations
16. bibliography
17. timetable
18. outline
19. first
20. formatting

21. Informal proposals may be short (two to four pages) and may use a letter format. They concentrate on six principal components: (a) introduction, (b) background, problem, and purpose, (c) proposal, plan, and schedule, (d) staffing, (e) budget, and (f) authorization. Formal proposals may have these additional parts: (a) copy of RFP, (b) letter of transmittal, (c) abstract or executive summary, (d) title page, (e) table of contents, (f) list of figures, and (g) appendix.

22. To capture interest in the introduction to a proposal,
    a. hint at extraordinary results with details to be revealed shortly.
    b. promise low costs or speedy results.
    c. mention a remarkable resource available exclusively to you.
    d. identify a serious problem (worry item) and promise a solution.
    e. specify a key issue or benefit that you believe is the heart of the proposal.

23. Your chief aim in a solicited proposal is to convince the reader that you understand the problem completely.

24. The staffing section should describe the credentials and expertise of the project leaders. It may also identify the size and qualifications of the support staff, along with other resources such as computer facilities and special programs for analyzing statistics. In longer proposals, résumés of key people may be provided.

25. The budget is especially important because it represents a contract; you can't change its figures later.

26. The letter of transmittal for a proposal should be addressed to the person who is designated to receive the proposal or to the person who will make the final decision.

27. Online proposals are increasingly popular because they can be transmitted to all levels of management without printing a page, thus appealing to environmentally conscious organizations.

28. The executive summary of a formal report summarizes report findings, conclusions, and recommendations. The introduction covers these elements: background, problem or purpose, significance, scope, and organization. The introduction may also include identification of the person authorizing the report, a literature review, sources and methods, and definitions of key terms.

29. A "quick-and-dirty" first draft means that the writer works quickly without revision. This method avoids wasted effort spent in polishing sentences that may be cut later. It also encourages fluency and creativity. The disadvantage is that the writer has a great deal of revision to do. Not everyone is cut out for rapid writing.

30. A formal report should be proofread at least three times. Read once slowly for word meanings and content. Read a second time for spelling, punctuation, grammar, and other mechanical errors. Read a third time for formatting and consistency.

Career Track Spelling

1. grammar
2. conscience
3. desirable
4. feasible
5. opposite
6. mileage
7. Congratulations
8. committed
9. incredible
10. through

Career Track Vocabulary

1. b
2. a
3. f
4. c
5. e
6. d
7. b
8. c
9. b
10. a
11. c
12. a
13. c
14. a
15. stationery
16. principal
17. realty
18. principle
19. stationary
20. reality

C.L.U.E. Checkpoint 1

1. whomever [*We recommend him/whomever for the job.*]
2. to Mr. Rather or me.
3. Whom [*Would you prefer to see him/whom elected president?*]
4. whoever [*he/whoever ordered them. Whoever* functions as the subject of the verb *ordered.*]
5. The CEO and I

C.L.U.E. Checkpoint 2

1. sales.   These actions [Replace the vague pronoun *This.*]
2. receive <u>a</u> parking [Or use a plural subject: *All employees should receive their parking assignments. A less acceptable alternative: Every employee should receive his or her . . .*]
3. permitting.   These incentives explain why many [Replace the vague pronoun *which.*]
4. didn't let these problems get us down. [Replace the vague pronoun *it.*]
5. People who open new businesses are [Make the sentence plural. Or keep the sentence singular and omit *their own.*]

Super C.L.U.E. Review

1. to me or whoever

2. development, of course, are essential if   markets: Pacific Rim countries, the European Community, and South America. [Note that no comma is used before *if.*]

3. compan<u>ie</u>s have increased, but they are still insuffic<u>ie</u>nt to <u>a</u>ffect

4. Our<u>s</u>   class, and it is [Note that *it* replaces *they* to agree with its antecedent, *class.*]

5. First Federal   complimentary   customers, but this offer attracted only 57 [Replace the vague pronoun *it* with something more specific.]

6. rec<u>ei</u>ve a permit   Lot 5-A. [The sentence could also be made plural, *All new employees must apply to receive their permits. . . .*]

7. Jeffrey and I were   four-page newsletter,   three vertical colum<u>n</u>s.

8. lighting,   were cited in the complaint. These conditions [Replace the vague pronoun *This* with more specific words.]

9. re<u>c</u>ommend, therefore,   three-week period [omit comma]   it<u>s</u>

10. are based   princip<u>le</u>s   manners. Everyone should exercise these principles [Note that the last clause may also be joined with a semicolon to the first clause.]

Career Application - Critical Thinking Questions

1. The audience for the list is Ramon, president of Prentice Consultants. However, the list will probably also be read by all the members of the proposal team.

2. Since no RFP has been submitted, this proposal is less formal than those with specific requirements. However, it makes little difference whether it is classified as formal or informal. What's important is submitting a persuasive, complete proposal.

3. These proposal parts have been mentioned:
   Introduction
   Background/problem
   Proposal/plan/schedule
   Staffing
   Budget
   Appendix

4. These proposal parts have not been included and perhaps should be:
   Authorization section
   Letter of transmittal
   Abstract or executive summary

   You could ask Ramon whether these should be included. Ramon is out of the office, though, and you decide to include those sections on your list with the word "optional" after each and the name of a possible person to write that section.

I knew I should have backed up that report!

5. Information about the new computer software should be included in the Staffing section.

6. The deadline should be established by Ramon or by consensus of the team. The deadline will then become part of the Budget section.

Chapter 15

Speaking Skills

CHAPTER REVIEW

_____ 1. The opening of an oral presentation should do all but which of the following?
   a. Capture listeners' attention and get them involved.
   b. Identify the speaker and establish credibility.
   c. Develop the main point with adequate explanation and details.
   d. Preview the main points of the presentation. (Obj. 2, p. 492)

_____ 2. Speakers establish credibility by describing their
   a. qualifications.
   b. knowledge.
   c. experience.
   d. all of the above. (Obj. 2, p. 492)

_____ 3. All but which of the following are effective ways to gain attention when giving an oral presentation?
   a. Show the audience what's in it for them.
   b. Stand behind the lectern throughout the presentation.
   c. Use rhetorical questions to get each listener thinking.
   d. Introduce the topic by telling an emotionally moving story or by describing a serious problem that involves the audience. (Obj. 2, p. 493)

_____ 4. Many business speakers are using electronic presentation software because
   a. speakers have nothing to fear in making such presentations.
   b. such presentations are economical, flexible, and easy to prepare.
   c. the software takes care of outlining and organizing the presentation.
   d. the equipment is more dependable than overhead projectors. (Obj. 4, p. 498)

_____ 5. When using PowerPoint slides or transparencies during an oral presentation,
   a. be sure to outline the entire presentation on the visual aids.
   b. include a visual for each point covered in the presentation.
   c. read each visual word for word so the audience will not miss anything important.
   d. talk to the audience, not to the slide. (Obj. 4, p. 503)

_____ 6. Probably the most effective strategy for reducing stage fright is to
  a. memorize the presentation.
  b. know the subject thoroughly.
  c. have a complete "script" of the presentation handy for reference.
  d. none of the above. (Obj. 5, p. 507)

_____ 7. Reading an oral presentation does all but which of the following?
  a. Prevents eye contact with the audience.
  b. Suggests to the audience that the speaker is unfamiliar with the topic.
  c. Allows feedback to be used to advantage.
  d. Causes the audience to lose confidence in the speaker's expertise. (Obj. 5, p. 505)

_____ 8. In adapting to international and cross-cultural audiences, speakers should
  a. avoid wasting time and get to the main point immediately.
  b. use flip charts and speak off the cuff to show their command of the topic.
  c. speak slowly, enunciate clearly, and use more volume than normal.
  d. develop topics separately, encouraging discussion periods after each topic.
     (Obj. 6, p. 509)

_____ 9. When placing a telephone call, you should immediately
  a. name the person you are calling, identify yourself, and briefly explain why you are calling.
  b. ask for the person you wish to speak to but, to save time, say nothing else.
  c. frontload with an explanation of why you are calling.
  d. greet the person who answers with a cheerful thought, such as "Good morning! How are you?" (Obj. 7, p. 512)

_____10. Which statement does *not* accurately describe voice mail?
  a. Most people feel that voice mail systems are a warm and personal method of leaving messages.
  b. Voice mail eliminates telephone tag.
  c. Voice mail saves companies large sums of money.
  d. Voice mail eliminates time-zone barriers. (Obj. 7, p. 514)

Use T or F to indicate whether the following statements are true or false.

_____11. Preparing for an oral presentation is much like preparing to write a report; both activities begin with analysis of purpose and audience. (Obj. 1, p. 490)

_____12. Writing the introduction should always be the first step taken when preparing for an oral presentation. (Obj. 2, p. 492)

_____13. Good speakers reveal something of themselves and identify themselves with the audience. (Obj. 2, p. 492)

_____14. Most short presentations of 20 minutes or less can easily focus on five to eight main points. (Obj. 2, p. 492)

_____15. A knowledgeable speaker prepares only the material that will definitely be needed for an oral presentation. (Obj. 2, p. 495)

_____16. Do not be repetitious by repeating important ideas in the conclusion of an oral presentation. (Obj. 2, p. 495)

_____ 17. You will lose your audience quickly if your talk is filled with abstractions, generalities, and dry facts. (Obj. 3, p. 496)

_____ 18. Memorizing the opening sentence of an oral presentation allows a speaker to quickly establish rapport with the audience through eye contact. (Obj. 5, p. 506)

19. In preparing an effective oral presentation, what two key elements should a speaker think seriously about in advance? (Obj. 1, p. 490)

20. What should the introduction of an oral presentation do? (Obj. 2, p. 492)

21. How can the ideas in an oral presentation be organized? (Obj. 2, pp. 493–495)

22. What are verbal signposts in a speech, and why are they important? (Obj. 3, p. 497)

23. Name seven kinds of visual aids and handouts that can enhance a presentation. Give an original example of how each could be used in a talk you might give in your profession. (Obj. 3, p. 499)

24. What is the best method for delivering an oral presentation? Why? (Obj. 5, p. 505)

25. Name six tips for preparing and using electronic presentation slides. (Obj. 4, p. 503)

Check your answers now!

CAREER TRACK SPELLING

Underline misspelled words. Write correct forms in the spaces provided. Some sentences may have more than one misspelled word. If a sentence is correct, write *C*.

1. In international correspondents we carefully control our language. _____

2. All headings throughout the report must be consistant. _____

3. Efficient employees in the electronics division won a prize. _____

4. They were suprised and graiteful regarding the development. _____

5. The pamphlet said that applicants qualify for valueable prizes. _____

6. We're genuinely hoping that every supervisor will succede. _____

7. Some questionaire items produced irelevant information. _____

8. It is desirable that the defendant be courteous in court. _____

9. We emphasize excelent service for truely incredible profits. _____

10. You have undoubtlessly checked your maintenance agreement. _____

My Spelling Monsters

List each word that you missed or had trouble with. Be sure to spell it correctly. Then, write it four or more times. Review this page often to help you vanquish these spelling demons.

_____

_____

_____

_____

_____

_____

_____

_____

CAREER TRACK VOCABULARY

Use your dictionary to define the words in Column A. Then select the best definition in Column B to match the word in Column A.

Column A	Column B
_____ 1. tenable	a. overused, banal
_____ 2. tepid	b. belligerent, cruel
_____ 3. transgression	c. transparent
_____ 4. translucent	d. lukewarm
_____ 5. trite	e. sin, indiscretion
_____ 6. truculent	f. reasonable, defensible

Choose the best meaning for the following underlined words.

_____ 7. United Nations leaders issued an <u>ultimatum</u> to the warring countries.

        a. retaliation   b. demand   c. reward

_____ 8. Secretaries may take <u>umbrage</u> at the president's remarks.

        a. offense   b. heart   c. fancy

_____ 9. Fans at the international soccer match were <u>uncouth</u>.

        a. unshaved   b. vehement   c. vulgar

_____ 10. Some oil companies seemed <u>unfettered</u> by regulations.

        a. unaffected   b. unrestrained   c. unchanged

_____ 11. Israel made a <u>unilateral</u> decision about its borders.

        a. dictatorial   b. forceful   c. one-sided

_____ 12. Students and faculty rarely acted in <u>unison</u>.

        a. agreement   b. retaliation   c. compliance

_____ 13. Not only was the package late, but it was <u>unwieldy</u>.

        a. heavy   b. ominous   c. cumbersome

_____ 14. If you continue to <u>vacillate</u>, we'll never choose a movie.

        a. argue   b. waver   c. dissent

Confusing Words

than	conjunction showing comparison	*to*	a preposition; the sign of the infinitive
then	adv.: at that time	*too*	adv.: also, to an excessive extent
		two	a number
their	possessive form of they		
there	at that place or point		
they're	contraction of they are		

15. Florida is nice in the winter, but it is _____ warm in the summer.

16. Have you been _____ in the winter?

17. Most groups schedule _____ meetings in the winter rather _____ face the summer heat.

18. A favorite time _____ visit Florida is January; _____ it is pleasantly warm.

19. We're considering Tampa and St. Petersburg, _____ cities near the beach.

20. Richard and Whitney said that _____ visiting Tampa in February.

Look over the vocabulary words in this chapter. Select five to add to your working vocabulary. Double-check the meanings of your selections in a dictionary. Then write a sentence for each of your words.

_____

_____

_____

_____

_____

_____

COMPETENT LANGUAGE USAGE ESSENTIALS (C.L.U.E.)

Adjectives and Adverbs

Guide 19: Use adverbs, not adjectives, to describe or limit the action of verbs.

> Coach Willis said the team had done *well* (not *good*) in the game.

> How *quickly* (not *quick*) can you finish that photocopying?

> The engine runs *smoothly* (not *smooth*) after its tune-up.

Guide 20: Hyphenate two or more adjectives that are joined to create a compound modifier before a noun.

> A *once-in-a-lifetime* opportunity presented itself.

> We made *last-minute* preparations before leaving on a *two-week* vacation.

 TIP. Don't confuse adverbs ending in *ly* with compound adjectives. For example, *recently elected* official and *highly regarded* president would not be hyphenated. Almost never is a word ending in *ly* hyphenated.

C.L.U.E. Checkpoint

Use proofreading marks to make all necessary corrections.

1. Our technician performed a point by point checkup of the newly installed equipment.

2. Only the four year old printer was retained, and it will be inspected year by year.

3. Please don't take this comment personal.

4. We moved into the newly remodeled offices over the three day weekend.

5. Ron felt that he had completed the two hour aptitude test satisfactory.

Super C.L.U.E. Review

In this cumulative review, use proofreading marks to correct grammar, punctuation, number usage, capitalization, spelling, and confusing word use. Mark *C* if a sentence is correct.

1. Was any of the supervisers absent on the monday following the 4 day weekend.

2. Their going to visit there relatives in Flint Michigan following they're coast to coast trip.

3. The three Cs of credit is the following; character, capacity and capitol.

4. All branches except the Pear Valley Office is now using state of the art equipment.

5. After you have checked the matter farther please report to the CEO and I.

6. Laura thought she had done good on the employment exam but she heard nothing.

7. Some trucks acceded the 5,000 pound weight limit, others were under it.

8. To attract people to our convention exhibit we rented a popcorn machine and hired a magician. This was very successful.

9. Each of the beautifully-printed art books have been priced at one hundred fifty dollars.

10. James Roosevelt said that his Father gave him this advice on making speeches "Be sincere, be brief; and be seated.

CAREER APPLICATION

Your friend and fellow employee Kevin must give his first oral presentation next week, and he asks you to look over his outline. He knows that you have recently studied business communications, and he hopes you can make constructive suggestions. You both work on the staff of a large construction company. Kevin is assistant safety officer.

As part of STOP (Safety Training Observation Program), Kevin must address new construction workers. His major goal is convincing employees that safety begins with the way they act. *The cause of over 96 percent of all workplace injuries is unsafe acts by workers.*

Kevin has worked out the first two sections of his talk, and he wants you to critique and revise them. Read over his draft, and then answer the questions following it.

First Draft of Kevin's Safety Talk

First section: Tools

   1. Hand tools
      a. You should use tools only for their designed purposes.
      b. Keep hand tools in peak condition. You want them to be sharp, clean, oiled, and dressed.
      c. Don't use "cheaters" to force tools beyond their capacity.
      d. Don't abuse tools, such as using a wrench as a pry bar.
   2. Portable power tools
      a. You must not operate power tools unless you are trained and authorized to do so.
      b. Proper eye protection is important.
      c. Moving parts must be kept directed away from your body.
      d. Never touch a part unless its power source is disconnected.

Second section: Equipment

   1. Some general suggestions
      a. You must inspect all equipment before using.
      b. Know the limitations of the equipment you use; do not exceed them.
      c. Equipment from other contractors must not be interchanged without permission.
   2. Safety belts/harnesses
      a. Wear belts when working on sloping roofs, flat roofs without handrails, any suspended platform or stage, any scaffold, ladders near roof edges, and all elevated work.
      b. Demonstrate how to wear belts.
   3. Welding and burning equipment. Contact your supervisor before performing these tasks.

4. Compressed air
   a. Hoses and couplings must be checked daily before use.
   b. Never crimp, couple, or uncouple a pressurized hose. Shut off valve and bleed down hose.
   c. Do not allow pressure to exceed 30 psi when cleaning workbenches and machinery.
   d. Hoses must be kept off the ground or floor whenever they interfere with walkways, roads, and so forth.

Critical Thinking Questions

1. You know the importance of good planning before a talk. You are especially concerned about audience analysis. What should Kevin know about his audience? Why? How can he learn more?

2. Did Kevin follow a standard outlining format? Should he?

3. Are Kevin's first two sections well organized? What suggestions would you make about the wording of his outline?

4. Should Kevin have an introduction? If so, what should it include?

5. Does this talk need visual aids? What would you suggest?

6. Kevin also wants to talk about flammable and corrosive liquids, but much of the information is available in a good brochure. How would you advise him to treat these two topics?

7. Should Kevin include transitions? If so, where? Give him one specific example of an effective transition.

8.   What would you advise Kevin about using concrete examples in his talk?

9.   What advice can you give about the conclusion?

After answering these questions, check your responses with those in the Solutions. Then revise Kevin's outline using the format shown in Activity 15.5 on page 447 of the textbook. Include a title and purpose. Also include, in outline form only, an introduction and conclusion. Revise the two sections he has written. When you finish, compare your solution with that shown in Appendix B.

SOLUTIONS

Chapter Review

1. c
2. d
3. b
4. b
5. d
6. b
7. c
8. d
9. a
10. a

11. T
12. F   It's better to write the introduction after you have established the main ideas.
13. T
14. F   Short presentations should focus on three to five major points.
15. F   Good speakers always prepare extra material in case it's needed.
16. F   Listeners need repetition to be able to remember primary ideas.
17. T
18. T

19. Two key elements a speaker should give serious thought to are (a) determining the purpose or what is to be accomplished in the talk and (b) knowing the audience and anticipating its reactions to the topic.

20. The opening of an oral presentation should (a) capture listeners' attention and get them involved, (b) identify the speaker and establish credibility, and (c) preview the main points.

21. The ideas in an oral presentation can be organized by (a) time, (b) component, (c) importance, (d) criteria, or (e) conventional groupings.

22. Verbal signposts are previews, summaries, and transitions that help listeners recognize the organization and main points in a presentation. They are important because the audience gets lost easily; they have no pages to flip back through.

23. Seven kinds of visual aids or handouts and examples of each:
    a. An overhead projector might be used by an accountant to show transparencies of financial statements.
    b. A flipchart might be used by an administrative assistant to show budget projections.
    c. A write-and-wipe board might show how to calculate interest.
    d. A slide projector could be used by a realtor to show pictures of new listings.
    e. A video monitor could be used by a furniture designer to show a new line.
    f. Computer slides could be used by an engineer to show auto systems.
    g. Handouts can include summaries, outlines, additional material, and so forth.

24. The best method for delivering a talk is the "notes" method. Note cards contain key sentences and major ideas. Such cards keep you on track, prompt your memory, and help you sound natural.

25. Tips for preparing and using electronic presentation slides:
    a. Keep all visuals simple; spotlight major points only.
    b. Use the same font size and style for similar headings.
    c. Apply the Rule of Seven: No more than seven words on a line, seven total lines, and 7 x 7 or 49 total words.
    d. Be sure that everyone in the audience can see the slides.
    e. Show a slide, allow audience to read it, then paraphrase it. Do not read from a slide.
    f. Rehearse by practicing talking to the audience, not to the slides.
    g. Bring back-up transparencies in case of equipment failure.

Career Track Spelling
1. correspondence
2. consistent
3. C
4. surprised, grateful
5. valuable
6. succeed
7. questionnaire, irrelevant
8. C
9. excellent, truly
10. undoubtedly

Career Track Vocabulary
1. f
2. d
3. e
4. c
5. a
6. b
7. b
8. a
9. c
10. b
11. c
12. a
13. c
14. b
15. too
16. there
17. their, than
18. to, then
19. two
20. they're

C.L.U.E. Checkpoint
1. point-by-point   [Don't hyphenate *newly installed*.]
2. four-year-old   [Don't be tempted to hyphenate *year by year*. Notice that no noun follows it; therefore, it's not a compound modifier.]
3. personally
4. three-day
5. two-hour   satisfactorily

Super C.L.U.E. Review
1. Were   supervis<u>o</u>rs   Monday   four-day weekend?
2. They're going to visit their   Flint, Michigan,   their coast-to-coast
3. are the following: character, capacity, and capit<u>a</u>l.
4. office are   state-of-the-art
5. f<u>u</u>rther,   CEO and me.
6. done well   exam,
7. exceeded   5,000-pound   limit;
8. exhibit,   These attractions were   [Replace the vague pronoun *This* with specific ideas.]
9. beautifully printed [omit hyphen]   has been $150.
10. father   speeches: brief,   seated."

Career Application - Critical Thinking Questions

1. Kevin should know how many people will be in his audience, as well as their ages, gender, knowledge of the topic, experience, and perhaps educational levels. He must know this kind of information to be able to choose appropriate words and examples. For instance, his present talk has some jargon ("psi," "dressed," "cheaters," and "bleed the hose"). Will his listeners know what he means? He could learn more about his listeners by checking their employment applications in Human Resources. He could also talk with other employees about what the audience will be like. He might also ask how former groups of new employees received this kind of talk.

2. No, Kevin's first two sections do not follow standard outlining format. However, they could easily be converted into the Roman numeral format, with main points identified by I and II.

3. Actually, his two sections are well organized. He has grouped major ideas into two headings, and items are appropriately subdivided. His wording, though, is inconsistent. Good outlines use parallel phrasing. Some of his items are commands, while others are statements in either active or passive voice. Probably the best wording uses commands. Each statement should begin with a verb ("Use tools only for their designed purposes; operate power tools only if you are trained and authorized to do so.")

4. Yes, Kevin needs a good introduction. It should gain the attention of the audience, try to get them involved, and establish his credibility. Why or how is he an expert on this topic? He also needs to preview his main points and lay the foundation for his primary goal: convincing workers that safety begins with the way they act.

5. Kevin's talk would be much improved with visual aids. He could demonstrate many of the techniques he's discussing and show tools. He could show pictures of sloping roofs and other

dangerous places requiring safety belts. He should also demonstrate how to wear a safety belt. Kevin might use a flipchart, overhead projector, or PowerPoint slides to summarize his key safety techniques.

6. To cover flammable and corrosive liquids, Kevin should probably briefly discuss these topics and then distribute literature about them after his talk.

7. Good speakers move gracefully from one major topic to another with transitions, such as "Now that we've learned about safety techniques in using hand and portable power tools, I'd like to talk with you next about other kinds of equipment. First, I have some some general suggestions, and then I'll speak specifically about safety belts, welding equipment, and compressed air."

8. Kevin's talk has many general references, and these references are natural in an outline. You might encourage him to flesh out the references with specific examples. For example, he should be prepared to give several examples of "cheaters" used to force tools beyond their capacity.

9. The conclusion should summarize the main points and provide a final focus. That focus, of course, is convincing workers that their actions are critical to safety on the job. Kevin should also encourage questions.

"A talk is a voyage with a purpose, and it must be charted. The man who starts out going nowhere usually gets there."
—Dale Carnegie

Chapter 16

Employment Communication

CHAPTER REVIEW

Writing a Résumé

Use the listed words to complete the following sentences. Each word is used but once.

chronological	experience	heading	networking	qualifications
employment	functional	internship	objective	scan

1. You can't expect to find the position of your dreams without first (a) knowing yourself, (b) knowing the job market, and (c) knowing the _____ process. (Obj. 1, p. 522)

2. Preparing for employment often means identifying your interests and evaluating your _____. Employers want to know what assets you have to offer them. (Obj. 1, p. 524)

3. Before choosing a career path, gather career information at your career center or library. Another excellent way to learn about your field is to take a summer job, _____, or part-time position so that you can try out your career. (Obj. 1, p. 525)

4. Some job openings are advertised in classified ads. Many, however, are found in the "hidden" job market, and these positions are best located through _____. This process involves developing a group of contacts and referrals who all know that you are looking for a job. (Obj. 1, p. 527)

5. Résumés that list work history job by job, starting with the most recent position, are classified as _____ résumés. Most recruiters favor this résumé style. (Obj. 2, p. 529)

6. Résumés that emphasize skill categories and deemphasize work history are classified as _____ résumés. This résumé can be used to focus on accomplishments and to hide a negative employment history. (Obj. 2, p. 529)

7. A résumé should always begin with a main _____ that includes name, address, and telephone number. (Obj. 3, p. 533)

8. Opinion is divided on whether to include a career _____ on a résumé. Although this statement makes

the recruiter's life easier, it can limit a candidate's opportunities. (Obj. 3, p. 533)

9. One of the most important sections of a résumé is devoted to work _____. List
    your most recent employment first and work backward. (Obj. 3, p. 534)

10. Many large companies today use computers to _____ incoming résumés into
    applicant-tracking programs. (Obj. 4, p. 537)

Writing Letters of Application and Other Employment Messages

| confidence | evidence | needs | outcomes | source |
| direct | interview | negotiable | resistance | thanks |

11. A letter of application has three purposes: (a) introducing the résumé, (b) highlighting
    strengths, and (c) gaining a(n) _____. (Obj. 5, p. 549)

12. If an employment position has been announced and applicants are being solicited, you can use
    a(n) _____ approach in writing your letter. For letters that are prospecting for
    jobs, your approach may have to be more imaginative. (Obj. 5, p. 549)

13. The opening of a letter applying for an advertised opening may begin with a reference to the
    _____ of information, such as the advertisement or job description.
    (Obj. 5, p. 550)

14. Once you have captured the attention of the reader, use the body of a cover letter to build in-
    terest and reduce _____. (Obj. 5, p. 551)

15. A good letter of application emphasizes a candidate's strong points in relation to the
    _____ of the employer. Recruiters want to know what candidates can do for them.
    (Obj. 5, p. 552)

16. In writing and revising your letter, beware of overusing "I." One way to reduce its use is to
    make activities and _____, not yourself, the subjects of sentences.
    (Obj. 5, p. 554)

17. Before listing a person as a reference, a candidate must
    always get that person's permission. To get good let-
    ters of recommendation, a candidate should also pro-
    vide _____ that could be used to support
    generalizations. (Obj. 6, p. 555)

18. After a job interview a candidate should always send a
    letter of _____. This letter should convey
    enthusiasm and confidence as well as appreciation.
    (Obj. 6, p. 556)

Long résumés and long
letters of application
tend to annoy recruiters

19. If you've been rejected for a job, writing a follow-up letter is a good idea. This letter should emphasize your continuing interest and express _____ in meeting the job requirements. (Obj. 6, p. 557)

20. In filling out job applications, you may find that the best strategy in responding to salary questions is to write *Open* or _____. (Obj. 6, p. 558)

Multiple Choice

_____21. Which of the following statements accurately describes the changing nature of jobs?
   a. Employers are less willing to hire people into jobs with narrow descriptions.
   b. Employees can expect to work for the same employer for a lifetime.
   c. People are increasingly working in stable positions for larger companies.
   d. Employees feel more secure because more jobs are outsourced. (Obj. 1, p. 524)

_____22. The average employee can expect to
   a. work at 5 to 10 jobs over the course of a career.
   b. work at 12 to 15 jobs over the course of a career.
   c. find one terrific job and stick with it through a working career.
   d. find a job at a Web job site. (Obj. 1, p. 525)

_____23. Some of the best online job listings can be found at
   a. company Web sites.
   b. www.hoovers.com.
   c. the Monster Board.
   d. the U.S. Post Office. (Obj. 1, p. 528)

_____24. Landing a job today depends largely on
   a. reading many newspaper ads.
   b. knowing the right keywords to include in your résumé.
   c. personal contacts.
   d. visiting all of the Web sites that post jobs. (Obj. 1, p. 529)

_____25. In preparing a résumé that will be scanned, you should
   a. include as many relevant keywords as possible.
   b. emphasize active verbs and colorful adjectives.
   c. demonstrate your computer skills with fancy formatting and graphics.
   d. include 25 interpersonal traits most requested by employers. (Obj. 4, p. 539)

_____26. An online, hypertext résumé
   a. suggests that you have exceptional technical savvy.
   b. serves as an electronic portfolio with links to examples of your work.
   c. is impressive, but you should prepare a traditional résumé as well.
   d. all of the above (Obj. 4, p. 540)

_____ 27. The *best* opening for a solicited letter of application is
   a. *I happened to be reading the* Gazette *and saw your ad for a management trainee in retail sales.*
   b. *Please consider me an applicant for the position of financial analyst.*
   c. *If you are in need of a staff accountant, please consider my qualifications.*
   d. *William Vanderer of your Advertising Department suggested that I apply for the brand manager position that is currently vacant.* (Obj. 5, pp. 549–550)

28. In identifying your career interests, you first must understand your dreams. Take a few moments to describe here or on another sheet what you consider to be the perfect job, boss, and coworkers. (Obj. 1, p. 523)

29. Examine the advice beginning on page 525 of the textbook describing career path data. From this list name five activities that seem most appropriate for you in starting your job search. (Obj. 1)

30. From the candidate's view, what are the advantages of chronological résumés? Of functional résumés? (Obj. 2, p. 529)

31. How do traditional job search techniques differ from electronic job search techniques? (Obj. 1, pp. 526–527)

32. Name five Web sites listing job openings. Which one seems best for you? (Obj. 1, p. 528)

33. When should you include a career objective on your résumé? When should you avoid one? (Obj. 3, p. 533)

A résumé is a balance sheet without liabilities.

34. Should you include references on your résumé? Why or why not? (Obj. 3, p. 535)

35. Provide two examples of "puffing" a résumé. Why is this dangerous? (Obj. 7, p. 546)

CAREER TRACK SPELLING

For each group below identify misspelled words and write corrected versions in the spaces provided. Write *C* if all words are correct.

1. intelligence	luxury	useing	jealous	_____
2. efficent	involve	explanation	sacrifice	_____
3. niece	automaticly	simply	hungry	_____
4. generally	exaggerate	suspense	yield	_____
5. noticeable	original	independant	secretaries	_____
6. sincerly	exercise	dominant	beautiful	_____
7. admitted	imediate	colume	define	_____
8. discipline	vacuum	technique	biggest	_____
9. certain	represenative	dissatisfied	repetition	_____
10. seperate	requirement	opinion	happiness	_____

My Spelling Monsters

List each word that you missed or had trouble with. Be sure to spell it correctly. Then, write it four or more times. Review this page often to help you vanquish these spelling demons.

_____

_____

_____

_____

_____

CAREER TRACK VOCABULARY

Use your dictionary to define the words in Column A. Then select the best definition in Column B to match the word in Column A.

	Column A		Column B
_____	1. vacuous	a.	word for word
_____	2. vagary	b.	empty, lacking content
_____	3. vapid	c.	truthfulness, accuracy
_____	4. vendor	d.	impulse, whim
_____	5. veracity	e.	seller
_____	6. verbatim	f.	insipid, uninteresting

Choose the best meaning for the following underlined words.

_____ 7. Our newly elected mayor is certainly <u>verbose</u>.

      a. portly   b. exuberant   c. wordy

_____ 8. Even in New York City, Central Park is <u>verdant</u> in the summer.

      a. dangerous   b. green   c. cheerful

_____ 9. TV commercials are often full of <u>vernacular</u> expressions.

      a. informal   b. offensive   c. pushy

_____ 10. Despite declaring Chapter 11, Globex maintained <u>viable</u> relationships with many long-time customers.

      a. sincere   b. working   c. adversarial

_____ 11. Tim was <u>voracious</u> when he returned from jogging.

      a. very hungry   b. exhausted   c. talkative

_____ 12. Corporate profits began to <u>wane</u> when the old-timers were replaced.

      a. multiply   b. waver   c. diminish

_____ 13. Police had difficulty finding the person who perpetrated the <u>wanton</u> act.

      a. bloody   b. mischievous   c. beneficial

_____ 14. A cartoonist created the <u>whimsical</u> picture of President Smith that appeared in the annual report.

      a. diminutive   b. lively   c. fanciful

Confusing Words

vary	to change	*weather*	n.: the state of the atmosphere
very	extremely		v.: to bear up against
		whether	an introduction to alternatives
waiver	abandonment of a claim		
waver	to shake or fluctuate		

15. We're unsure _____ to fly or to drive to the conference.

16. If the _____ is good, attendance at the conference workshops may suffer.

17. Colors in the paint finishes may _____ slightly from batch to batch.

18. Only when you are _____ certain of the cost can we proceed with our plan.

19. Developers requested a _____ on local restrictions before proceeding with the office complex.

20. Mitchell did not _____ in his decision to prosecute.

Look back over the 20 vocabulary words in this chapter. Select 5 new words that you would like to own. Remember, to "own" a word, you must be able to use it correctly in a sentence. Double-check the meanings of your selections in a dictionary. Then write a sentence for each of your words.

_____

_____

_____

_____

_____

_____

_____

_____

COMPETENT LANGUAGE USAGE ESSENTIALS (C.L.U.E.)

Review

This chapter introduces no new language guidelines. Instead, it gives you a chance to reinforce the 50 guidelines from previous chapters.

In the following two cumulative reviews, use proofreading marks to correct grammar, punctuation, number usage, capitalization, spelling, and confusing word use. Mark *C* if a sentence is correct.

Super C.L.U.E. Review 1

1. City officials begged the two corporations board of directors not to dessert they're locations and not to abandon local employees.

2. One store listed it's Timex Watch at forty dollars; while its competitor listed the same watch at thirty-five dollars.

3. China the worlds fastest growing economy, will be snapping up personal computers at a 22% rate by 2,005.

4. The registration of employees cars for parking permits had went smooth; until we run out of stickers.

5. If we are to remain freinds this personal information must be kept strictly between you and I.

6. The quality of the letters, memos, and reports in this organization need to be improved.

7. Although its usually difficult to illicit contributions I think you will find this charity drive incredibely fruitful.

8. Roy Waters who was recently appointed Sales Manager submitted 6 different suggestions for boosting sales, which everyone hopes will turn around our sales decline.

9. Stored on open shelves in room 15, is a group of office supplies and at least 7 reams of stationary.

10. The additional premium you were charged which amounted to fifty-five dollars and 40 cents, was issued because of you're recent accident.

Super C.L.U.E. Review 2

1. A letter sent to customers, must have a professional appearance, otherwise it's message may be disregarded.

2. Here are a group of participating manufactures, who you may wish to contact regarding there products.

3. As soon as the merger is completed we will inform the entire staff, until then its business as usual.

4. The entire team of thirty-five managers were willing to procede with the proposal for asian expansion.

5. Several copys of the sales' report was sent to the CEO and I immediatley after we requested it.

6. The miami river is such a narrow and congested waterway, that tugboat captains joke about needing vaseline to slip freighters through.

7. Companys such as Amway and Avon, discovered that there unique door to door selling method was very successful in japan.

8. Locating foriegn markets and developing it requires aggressive efforts, however many companies dont know where to begin.

9. Many companies sell better at home then abroad; because they lack experience.

10. Smart organizations can boost profits almost one hundred percent by retaining just 5% more of there customers.

CAREER APPLICATION

You are a recruiting specialist in the Human Resources Development Department of International Life Insurance Company. The business club from a nearby campus asks your boss to send a representative to tell club members about writing résumés, and you were selected to go. As you consider what you can say to these soon-to-be-graduated business majors, you decide to take two résumés as examples—a good one and a poor one.

Look over the two résumés shown on pages 209 and 210. You should see some real differences.

Now answer the following questions in preparation for drawing conclusions about these two résumés.

Critical Thinking Questions

1. You know something about your audience, but should you know more? What specific information should you have? How can you learn more?

2. Rather than speak in generalities, you want to show *real* résumés that have been submitted to your company. Should you feel any ethical conflict about showing these examples? What are some actions you can take to resolve this conflict in your mind? Should you speak to your boss?

3. In preparing your discussion of these two résumés, you try to decide how to use the samples. Should you make copies of the résumés and distribute them as handouts? Or should you project them as transparencies? Why?

4. Should you talk about the poor one first and then talk about the better one next? Or should you discuss major points—such as appearance, use of headings, description of experience—and flip back and forth from one résumé to the other as you discuss each point? Why?

5. What are some specific weaknesses of résumé No. 1?

6. What are specific strengths of résumé No. 2?

When you complete your responses, read over those provided at the end of this chapter. Then prepare a list of conclusions that could be drawn from your analysis of these two résumés. You should have six to ten conclusions. They may include advice to student writers. Finally, compare your conclusions with those shown in Appendix B.

Résumé No. 1
(Poor Example)

JOSEPH J. RADER
5402 Ferndale Avenue
Brockton, MA 02402
(215) 419-4421

CAREER OBJECTIVE

I'm looking for a challenging entry-level position in accounting with a progressive firm. Desire opportunity for advancement into management.

EDUCATION

Degree in Business Administration, Accounting and Management Information Systems, Mid-State University, 2003. Relevant courses completed:

    Accounting I and II
    Computer Applications in Business
    Income Tax I
    Cost Accounting
    Auditing Principles
    Senior Seminar in Accounting Theory and Practice

EXPERIENCE

V.I.T.A. campus program. Was responsible for helping local individuals fill out their tax returns; two years as a volunteer. 2002–2003.

Part-time bookkeeper, 2001–2003. Commonwealth International.
Completed various functions demanding accounting and computer expertise. Assisted owner; helped prepare financial statements.

Counter person, assistant manager, Pizza Bob's, Westmoreland, 1999–2001. Responsibility for all managerial duties when manager was gone.

ACTIVITIES AND OTHER

Computer Lab assistant, work study program 1998–1999. Responsible for overseeing students in campus lab.

Familiar with personal computer, mainframe, and Macintosh environments.

Counselor/manager, Mid-State University. Summer, 1999.

Enjoy outdoor sports. Active in Big Brothers, Westland County.

REFERENCES

Available on request.

Résumé No. 2
(Better Example)

DAVID M. GROSS
330 Water Street
Augusta, ME 04330
(405) 344-2109

OBJECTIVE
Position as underwriter with International Life Insurance Company.

EXPERIENCE
Atlantic Federal Bank, Boston, MA
Courier - Corporate Distribution Services - 2000 to present

- Contribute to Atlantic Federal's efficiency and productivity by expediting information throughout its ten-building complex, providing courier service for internal distribution
- Maintain consistent and timely delivery schedule

J. C. Penney, Greenfield, MA
Management Trainee Intern - Summer, 2002

- Successfully met department quotas by targeting customer's needs, setting goals for sales associates, and providing incentives through recognition and reward
- Developed marketing management skills in purchase of seasonable merchandise through direct broadcast satellite systems
- Systemized department inventory and visual displays
- Prepared detailed computerized reports to senior management
- Developed customer service and communication skills through training and experience with retail customers

Mid-Atlantic University, Boston, MA
Language Lab Assistant - Work Study - 1999–2001

- Reproduced over 500 master and student tapes; maintained tape inventory
- Instructed and monitored over 200 students a semester in use of lab equipment

Mid-Atlantic University, Boston, MA
Summer Resident Manager - 2001

- Managed logistics of summer conferences and seminars; prepared function rooms, processed registrations, administered front desk management
- Supervised 140 student residents; coordinated student orientation, peer counseling, and academic and social activities

EDUCATION
Mid-Atlantic University, Boston, MA
B.S., Business Administration, 2003. GPA in major: 3.2
Concentration: Business Finance, Investment Management, and Commercial Banking

COMPUTER SKILLS
Languages: COBOL, BASIC
Software Packages: d-Base IV, Lotus 1-2-3, Excelerator, WordPerfect, Minitab, PowerPoint

SOLUTIONS

Chapter Review
1. employment
2. qualifications
3. internship
4. networking
5. chronological
6. functional
7. heading
8. objective
9. experience
10. scan

11. interview
12. direct
13. source
14. resistance
15. needs
16. outcome
17. evidence
18. thanks
19. confidence
20. negotiable

21. a
22. b
23. a
24. c
25. a
26. d
27. d

28. Evaluate what you have written to describe the perfect job, boss, and coworkers. Are your expectations realistic? What will you have to do to achieve your dream? What steps can you be taking now to help you reach your goals?

29. Activities to get you started in your job search:
    a. Visit your school or campus career center.
    b. Search the Web.
    c. Use your library to look up government publications.
    d. Take a summer job, internship, or part-time position in your field.
    e. Contact companies in which you're interested, even if no opening exists.
    f. Sign up for campus interviews with company representatives.
    g. Ask for advice from your professors.
    h. Interview someone in your field.
    i. Monitor the classified ads.
    j. Join professional organizations in your field.

30. The advantages of chronological résumés:
    a. Recruiters expect and favor them.
    b. They quickly reveal steady career growth, if you have such growth.
    c. They're easier to write than functional résumés.

    The advantages of functional résumés:
    a. They can help deemphasize a negative employment history.
    b. They are useful for people with little employment experience or for those who are changing career areas.
    c. Employers can quickly see skill areas.

31. Traditional job search techniques include checking classified ads in newspapers, looking at announcements in publications of professional organizations, and contacting companies in which you are interested. You should also sign up for campus interviews, ask for advice from professors, and, especially, develop your own network of contacts. Electronic job search techniques include using your computer to visit many of the special Web sites that list jobs. You can learn a great deal about the job market from these sites.

32. Web sites to visit:
    a. America's Job Bank
    b. CareerBuilder
    c. CareerCity
    d. College Grad Job Hunter
    e. Wet Feet
    f. Monster Board

    What's best for you depends on what you want and where you wish to locate.

33. A career objective on a résumé should be included when it can be targeted to a specific job. It should probably be omitted when the résumé is general and will be submitted to many employers.

34. References may be listed on a résumé if you know that the employer expects them. However, the trend is away from listing them on résumés. They take up space and are not normally useful in securing an interview.

35. Two examples of "puffing up" a résumé: (a) using a more impressive job title, such as "manager," than one really held, and (b) increasing your grade-point average. Résumé inflation is dangerous because any falsehood on a résumé is grounds for dismissal in most organizations.

Career Track Spelling
1. using
2. efficient
3. automatically
4. C
5. independent
6. sincerely
7. immediate, column
8. C
9. representative
10. separate

Career Track Vocabulary

1. b
2. d
3. f
4. e
5. c
6. a
7. c
8. b
9. a
10. b
11. a
12. c
13. b
14. c
15. whether
16. weather
17. vary
18. very
19. waiver
20. waver

Super C.L.U.E. Review 1

1. corporations' boards desert their
2. its Timex watch at $40, $35. [Note that a comma, not a semicolon, joins the dependent clause.]
3. China, the world's   22 percent   2005. [Note the lack of comma in *2005*.]
4. employees'   had gone smoothly, until we ran
5. friends,   you and me.
6. needs
7. it's usually difficult to elicit contributions,   incredibly
8. Waters, who   sales manager, submitted six   sales. Everyone hopes that his suggestions [The best way to remedy the vague pronoun *which* is to start a new sentence without a pronoun.]
9. Stored on open shelves in Room 15 [omit comma] are   seven   stationery. [Note that the plural verb *are* is necessary because of the plural subjects *group* and *seven reams*.]
10. charged, which $55.40,   your

Super C.L.U.E. Review 2

1. customers [omit comma]   appearance; otherwise, its
2. Here is   manufacturers, [optional comma] whom   their
3. completed,   staff; until then, it's
4. 35 managers was   proceed   Asian
5. copies   sales [omit apostrophe] report were   CEO and me   requested them (replaces *it*)
6. Miami River   waterway [omit comma]   Vaseline
7. Companies   Avon [omit comma]   their   door-to-door   Japan.
8. foreign   developing them [replaced *it*]   require   efforts; however,   don't
9. than abroad [omit semicolon]
10. 100 percent   5 percent   their

Career Application - Critical Thinking Questions

1. Yes, more information would be helpful. Specifically, you need some of the following data: age and gender make-up of the audience, approximate size of the audience, major areas of study, and employment goals. You could obtain most of this information by speaking to the program chair for the campus organization.

2. Showing real résumés presents ethical and perhaps legal complications. These résumés have been submitted in confidence; their writers might charge invasion of privacy if their résumés were used as examples. However, by removing the names and addresses, you could eliminate this barrier. It would still be a good idea, though, to discuss your concerns with your supervisor. [When you do this, she thinks it's a good idea to use the real résumés, *if* the identity of the writer can be totally concealed.]

3. If you distribute these résumés as handouts, you will lose the audience. As they study the résumés, you will no longer have their attention. A better plan is to enlarge the résumés and show them as transparencies. If you do use them as hand-outs, pass them out after you finish.

4. The audience will be less bewildered if you talk about one résumé first and then talk about the other. Switching back and forth between them would be confusing and frustrating for the audience.

5. Weaknesses of résumé No. 1:
    a. Fails to specify a specific career objective. Either target the objective for a specific job or omit it.
    b. Uses personal pronoun "I." Rephrase to avoid.
    c. Lists college courses. Makes boring reading.
    d. Fails to keep items in Experience section consistent.
    e. Makes Experience section difficult to read. Skills do not stand out. Fails to give details on what he can do for future employer.
    f. Must reorganize and rename Activities and Other section.
    g. Fails to give enough details. No effort to sell or promote his talents.
    h. Makes résumé look skimpy. Seems that the candidate has little to offer, but in reality, he has considerable experience. But it is poorly described and presented.

6. Strengths of résumé No. 2:
    a. Targets specific job in objective. Reader becomes interested immediately.
    b. Develops each item in Experience section consistently. Promotes readability and comprehension by underscoring job titles and dates of employment.
    c. Uses action words to highlight transferable skills achieved.
    d. Describes specific skills from each job that might be transferable to the position for which he is applying.
    e. Organizes Education section for instant recognition of important facts.
    f. Emphasizes computer skills with special section.
    g. Overall, this résumé sells the candidate.
    h. Fills only one page!

Although this résumé is good, it's not perfect. Some of the writer's statements sound a little inflated, such as the description of his duties as a courier.

Chapter 16

Employment Interview Kit

Should you be nervous about an upcoming job interview? Of course! Everyone is uneasy about being scrutinized, judged, and possibly rejected. But think of how much *more* nervous you would be if you had no idea what to expect in the interview and if you were unprepared.

This interview kit supplements the suggestions provided in Chapter 16. It helps you get ready for an interview by introducing the kinds of interviews and showing you how to learn about the employer. It will help you reduce your nervousness by teaching you to practice for the interview, check your body language, and fight fear. You'll pick up tips for responding to recruiters' favorite questions, as well as coping with illegal questions and salary matters. Moreover, you'll receive pointers on questions you can ask. Finally, you'll learn what you should do to successfully follow up an interview.

Yes, you can expect to be nervous. But you can also expect to ace an interview when you know what's coming and when you prepare thoroughly.

SUCCEEDING IN TWO KINDS OF EMPLOYMENT INTERVIEWS

Job applicants generally face two kinds of interviews: (a) screening interviews and (b) hiring/placement interviews. You must succeed in the first to proceed to the second.

Screening Interviews. Screening interviews do just that—they screen candidates to eliminate those who fail to meet minimum requirements. Telephone conversations, sometimes as short as five minutes, are often used for screening interviews. The important thing to remember about screening interviews is being prepared!

- Keep a list near the telephone of positions for which you have applied.

- Have your résumé, references, a calendar, and a note pad handy.

- If caught off guard, defer your response: "I was just going out the door," or "We just sat down to dinner. May I call you back in ten minutes from the telephone in my office?"

- Sell your qualifications and sound enthusiastic.

Hiring/placement interviews. These interviews are the real thing. Conducted in depth, hiring/placement interviews may take many forms.

- *One-to-one interviews* are most common. You can expect to sit down with a company representative and talk about the job and your qualifications. If the representative is the hiring manager, questions will be specific and job-related. If the representative is from human resources, the questions will probably be more general.

- *Sequential and group interviews* are common with companies that rule by consensus. You may face many interviewers in sequence, all of whom you must listen to carefully and respond to positively. In group interviews, the employer may be looking for signs of leadership. Strive to stay focused, summarize important points, and ask good questions.

- *Stress interviews* are meant to test your reactions. If asked rapid-fire questions from many directions, take the time to slow things down. For example, "I would be happy to answer your question Ms. X, but first I must finish responding to Mr. Z." If greeted with silence, another stress technique, you might say, "Would you like me to begin the interview?" "Let me tell you about myself." Or ask a question such as "Can you give me more information about the position?"

INVESTIGATING THE TARGET

The more you know about a prospective employer, the better you'll be able to tailor your responses to the organization's needs. Moreover, companies are impressed by candidates who have done their homework. For companies that are publicly held, you can generally learn a great deal from annual reports and financial disclosure reports. Company information is available at many Web sites, including Hoovers Online (www.hoovers.com), Annual Reports Library (www.zpub.com/sf/arl), and Corporate Financials Online (www.cfonews.com). If these URLs don't work, use your favorite search tool to locate the sites. Another way to get information is to call the receptionist or the interviewer directly. Ask what you can read to prepare you for the interview. Here are some specifics for which to look:

- Find out all you can about company leaders. Their goals, ambitions, and values often are adopted by the entire organization—including your interviewer.

- Investigate the business philosophy of the leaders, involving their priorities, strategies, and managerial approach. Are you a good match with your target employer? If so, be sure to let the employer know that there is a correlation between their needs and your qualifications.

- Learn about the company's accomplishments and setbacks. This information should help you determine where you might make your best contribution.

- Study the company's finances. Are they so shaky that a takeover is imminent?

- Examine its products and customers. What excites you about this company?

For smaller companies and those that are not publicly owned, you'll probably have to do a little more footwork.

- Start by searching for a company site on the Web.

- Try your local library. Ask the reference librarian to help you locate information. Newspapers might contain stories or press releases with news of an organization.

- Visit the Better Business Bureau to discover if the company has had any difficulties with other companies or consumers.

- Check out the competition. What are its products, strengths, and weaknesses?

- Investigate the chamber of commerce to see what you can learn about the target company.

- Analyze the company's advertising. How does it promote its products or service?

- Talk with company employees. They are probably the best source of inside information. Try to get introduced to someone who is currently employed—but not working in the immediate area where you wish to be hired. Seek someone who is discreet.

PREPARING AND PRACTICING

After you have learned about the target organization,

- Study the job description. It not only helps you write a focused résumé but also helps you prepare to match your education, experience, and interests with the employer's position. Finding out the duties and responsibilities of the position will enable you to practice your best response strategies.

- Itemize your (a) most strategic skills, (b) greatest areas of knowledge, (c) strongest personality traits, and (d) key accomplishments. Be ready to relate these items to the kinds of questions frequently asked in interviews.

- Practice giving responses in a mock interview with a friend. Remember to be concise. You might wish to videotape or tape record a practice session to see and hear how you really come across.

- Be ready to answer questions about alcohol and drug use.

- Expect to explain problem areas on your résumé. For example, if you have little or no experience, you might emphasize your recent training and up-to-date skills. If you have gaps in your résumé, be prepared to answer questions about them positively and truthfully.

- Try to build interviewing experience with less important jobs first. You will become more confident and better able to sell your strengths with repeated interviewing exposure.

SENDING POSITIVE NONVERBAL MESSAGES

What comes out of your mouth and what's written on your résumé are not the only messages an interviewer receives about you. Nonverbal messages also create powerful impressions on people. Here are suggestions that will help you send the right nonverbal messages during interviews.

- Arrive on time or a little early. If necessary, find the location on a trial run a few days before the interview so that you know where to park and how much time the drive takes.

- Be courteous and congenial to everyone. Remember that you are being judged not only by the interviewer but by the receptionist and anyone else who sees you before and after the interview. They will notice how you sit, what you read, and how you look. Introduce yourself to the receptionist and wait to be invited to sit.

- Dress professionally. Even if some employees in the organization dress casually, you should look qualified, competent, and successful. Dress the part!

- Greet the interviewer confidently. Extend your hand, look him or her directly in the eye, and say, "I'm pleased to meet you Mr. X. I am Z." In this culture a firm, not crushing, handshake sends a nonverbal message of poise and assurance.

- Wait for the interviewer to offer you a chair. Make small talk with upbeat comments, such as "This is a beautiful headquarters. How many employees work here?" Don't immediately begin rummaging in your briefcase for your résumé. Being at ease and unrushed suggest that you are self-confident.

- Control your body. Keep your hands, arms, and elbows to yourself. Don't lean on a desk. Sit erect, leaning forward slightly. Keep your feet on the floor.

- Make eye contact frequently but don't get into a staring contest. In this culture a direct eye gaze suggests interest and trustworthiness.

- Smile enough to convey a positive attitude. Have a friend give you honest feedback on whether you generally smile too much or not enough.

- Sound enthusiastic and interested—but sincere.

FIGHTING FEAR

Expect to be nervous. It's natural! Other than public speaking, employment interviews are the most dreaded events in people's lives. You can, however, reduce your fears by focusing on a few suggestions.

- Practice interviewing as much as you can—especially with real companies. The more times you experience the interview situation, the less nervous you will be.

- Prepare 110 percent! Know how you will answer the most frequently asked questions. Be ready with success stories. Rehearse your closing statement. One of the best ways to reduce butterflies is to know that you have done all you can to be ready for the interview.

- Take deep breaths, particularly if you feel anxious while waiting for the interviewer. Deep breathing makes you concentrate on something other than the interview and also provides much-needed oxygen.

- Remember that the interviewer isn't the only one who is gleaning information. You have come to learn about the job and the company. In fact, during some parts of the interview, you will be in charge. This should give you courage.

ANSWERING QUESTIONS

The way you answer questions can be almost as important as what you say. The following tips will help you make the best impression.

- Use the interviewer's name and title from time to time when you answer. "Ms. Lyon, I would be pleased to tell you about ..." People like to hear their own names. But be sure you are pronouncing the name correctly!

- Refocus and clarify vague questions. Some interviewers are inexperienced and ill at ease in the role. Occasionally, you may have to ask your own question to understand what was asked, "By ____ do you mean ____?"

- Aim your answers at the key characteristics interviewers seek: expertise and competence, motivation, interpersonal skills, decision-making skills, enthusiasm for the job, and a pleasing personality. Employers are looking for these skills and traits.

- Stay focused on your strengths. Don't reveal weaknesses, even if you think they make you look human. You won't be hired for your weaknesses, only for your strengths.

- Use good English and enunciate clearly. Remember, you will be judged by how you communicate. Avoid slurred words like "gonna" and "din't," as well as slangy expressions like "yeah" and overuse of "like."

- Eliminate verbal static ("ah," "and ah," "uhm"). Make a tape recording as you practice answering expected interview questions. Is it filled with verbal static?

- Consider closing out some of your responses with "Does that answer your question?" or "Would you like me to elaborate on any particular experience?"

ALL-TIME FAVORITE QUESTIONS WITH SELECTED ANSWERS

The following questions represent those frequently asked of recent graduates and other job seekers. You'll also find a section of questions for you to ask when it is your turn. The interview questions are divided into groups. In each group the first question is answered. As you read the remaining questions, think about how you could respond most effectively.

Questions to Get Acquainted

1. Tell me about yourself.

   Experts agree that you must keep this answer short (1 to 2 minutes tops) but on target. Try practicing this formula:
   "My name is _____. I have completed a _____ degree with a major in _____. Recently I worked for _____ as a _____. Before that I worked for _____ as a _____. My strengths are _____ (interpersonal) and _____ (technical)." Try rehearsing your response in 30-second segments devoted to your education, your work experience, and your qualities/skills. Some candidates end with, "Now that I've told you about myself, can you tell me a little more about the position?"
2. What was your college major and why did you choose it?
3. If you had it to do over again, would you choose the same major? Why?
4. Tell me about your college and why you chose it.
5. Do you prefer to work by yourself or with others? Why?
6. What are your key strengths?
7. What are some things you do in your spare time? Hobbies? Sports?
8. Were you active in any extra-curricular activities in college?
9. What college professors did you like the most? The least? Why?
10. Have you changed your major in college? Why?
11. Are you willing to travel?
12. How did you happen to apply for this job?
13. What particular qualifications do you have for this job?
14. What courses prepared you for this job?
15. Do you consider yourself a team player? Describe your style as a team player.

Questions About Your Experience and Accomplishments

16. Why should we hire you when we have applicants with more experience or better credentials?

   In answering this question, remember that employers often hire people who present themselves well instead of others with better credentials. Emphasize your personal strengths that could be an advantage with this employer. Are you a hard worker? How can you demonstrate it? Have you had recent training? Some people have had more years of experience but actually have less knowledge because they have done the same thing over and over. Stress your experience using the latest methods and equipment. Emphasize that you are open to new ideas and learn quickly.

17. Tell me about your part-time jobs, internships, or other experience.
18. What were your major accomplishments in each of your past jobs?
19. Why did you change jobs?
20. What was a typical work day like?
21. What were your responsibilities at _____?
22. What job functions did you enjoy most? Least? Why?
23. Who was the toughest boss you ever worked for and why?
24. What were your major achievements in college?
25. What was your overall grade-point average? In your major?

Crystal Ball Gazing and Questions About the Future

26. Where do you expect to be five years from now?

It's a sure kiss of death to respond that you'd like to have the interviewer's job! Instead, show an interest in the current job and in making a contribution to the organization. Talk about the levels of responsibility you'd like to achieve. One employment counselor suggests showing ambition but not committing to a specific job title. Suggest that you will have learned enough to have progressed to a position where you will continue to grow.

27. If you got this position, what would you do to be sure you fit in?
28. What if your supervisor gave you an assignment and then left town for two weeks. What would you do?
29. This is a large (or small) organization. Do you think that you'd like that environment?
30. You are aware that a coworker is falsifying data. What would you do?
31. Your supervisor is dissatisfied with your work. You think it is acceptable. How would you resolve the conflict?
32. After completing a job, how would you evaluate it?
33. What does dependability mean to you?
34. Describe someone whom you consider to be an excellent communicator. Explain your choice.
35. Do you plan to continue your education?

Questions to Make You Squirm

36. What are your key weaknesses?

It's amazing how many candidates knock themselves out of the competition by answering this question poorly. Actually, you have many choices. You can present a strength as a weakness ("Some people complain that I'm a workaholic or too attentive to details"). You can mention a corrected weakness ("I found that I really needed to learn about the Internet, so I took a course. . ."). You could cite an unrelated skill ("I really need to brush up my Spanish"). You can cite a learning objective ("One of my long-term goals is to learn more about international management. Does your company have any plans to expand overseas?") Another possibility is to reaffirm your qualifications ("I have no weaknesses that affect my ability to do this job").

37. If you could change one thing about your personality, what would it be and why?
38. If I met some of your college chums, what do you think they would say about you?
39. What would your former boss say about you?
40. What do you want the most from your job? Money? Security? Power?
41. How do you handle authority? Criticism?
42. How did you prepare for this interview?
43. Do you feel you achieved the best grade-point average of which you were capable in college?
44. Do you ever lose your temper?
45. To what extent do you use liquor?
46. Have you ever used drugs?
47. Relate an incident when you faced an ethical dilemma. How did you react? How did you feel?
48. How long do you think this position will be challenging to you?
49. If your supervisor told you to do something a certain way, and you knew that way was dead wrong, what would you do?
50. When you are supervising people, how do you motivate them?

Questions About Money

51. How much money are you looking for?

One way to handle salary questions is to ask politely to defer the discussion until it's clear that a job will be offered to you. ("I'm sure when the time comes, we'll be able to work out a fair compensation package. Right now, I'd rather focus on whether we have a match.") Another possible response is to reply candidly that you can't know what to ask until you know more about the position and the company. If you continue to be pressed for a dollar figure, give a salary range. Be sure to do research before the interview so that you know what similar jobs are paying. For example, check salary information on the Web at <www.salary.com>.

52. How much are you presently earning?
53. How did you finance your education?
54. Have you saved any money?
55. How much money do you expect to earn at age ____?

Questions for You to Ask

At some point in the interview, you will be asked if you have any questions. Your questions should not only help you gain information, but they should impress the interviewer with your thoughtfulness and interest in the position. Remember, though, that this interview is a two-way street. You must be happy with the prospect of working for this organization. You want a position for which your skills and personality are matched. Use this opportunity to find out whether this job is right for you.

1. What will my duties be (if not already discussed)?
2. Tell me what it's like working here in terms of the people, management practices, work loads, expected performance, and rewards.
3. Why is this position open? Did the person who held it previously leave?
4. What training programs are available from this organization? What specific training will be given for this position?
5. What are the possibilities for promotion from this position?
6. Who would be my immediate supervisor?
7. What is the organizational structure, and where does this position fit in?
8. Is travel required in this position?
9. What are housing conditions in the surrounding area?
10. Assuming my work is excellent, where do you see me in five years?
11. How long do employees generally stay with this organization?
12. What are the major challenges for a person in this position?
13. What can I do to make myself more employable to you?
14. What is the salary for this position?
15. When will I hear from you regarding further action on my application?

FIELDING ILLEGAL QUESTIONS

Because federal laws prohibit discrimination, interviewers may not ask questions like those in the following list. Nevertheless, you may face an inexperienced or unscrupulous interviewer who does ask some of these questions. How should you react? If you find the question harmless and if you want the job, go ahead and answer it. If you think that answering it would damage your chance to be hired, try to deflect the question tactfully with a response such as, "Could you tell me how my marital status relates to the responsibilities of this position?" Another option, of course, is to respond to any illegal question by confronting the interviewer and threatening a lawsuit. However, you could not expect to be hired under these circumstances. You might wish to reconsider working for an organization that sanctions such procedures.

Here are some illegal questions that you may or may not wish to answer.

1. Are you married, divorced, separated, or single?
2. Do you have any disabilities that would prevent you from doing this job? (But it is legal to ask "Can you carry a 50-pound sack up a 10-foot ladder five times daily?")
3. What is your corrected vision? (But it is legal to ask "Do you have 20/20 corrected vision?")
4. Does stress ever affect your ability to be productive? (But it is legal to ask "How well can you handle stress?")
5. How much alcohol do you drink per week? (But it is legal to ask "Do you drink alcohol?")

6. Have you ever been arrested? (But it is legal to ask "Have you ever been convicted of a crime?")

7. How old are you? What is your date of birth? (But it is legal to ask "Are you 18 years old or older?")

8. Of what country are you a citizen? (But it is legal to ask "Are you a citizen of the U.S.?")

9. What is your maiden name? (But it is legal to ask "What is your full name?")

10. What is your religious preference?

11. Do you have children?

12. Are you practicing birth control?

13. Are you living with anyone?

14. Do you own or rent your home?

15. How much do you weigh? How tall are you?

INTERVIEW DON'TS

No one is perfect in an interview. You can, however, avert sure disaster by avoiding certain topics and behaviors such as the following.

- Don't ask for the job. It's naive, undignified, and unprofessional. Wait to see how the interview develops.

- Don't trash your previous employer, supervisors, or colleagues. The tendency is for interviewers to wonder whether you would speak about their companies similarly.

- Don't be a threat to the interviewer. Avoid suggesting directly or indirectly that your goal is to become head honcho, a path that might include the interviewer's job.

- Don't try to memorize question answers. Your responses will sound "canned."

- Don't be late or too early for your appointment.

- Don't discuss controversial subjects, and don't use profanity.

- Don't smoke unless the interviewer smokes.

- Don't emphasize salary or benefits. If the interview goes well and these subjects have not been addressed, you may mention them toward the end of the interview.

- Don't be negative about yourself or others. Never dwell on your liabilities.

- Don't interrupt.

- Don't accept a job immediately after getting an offer.

- Don't accept an offer until you have completed all your interviews.

CAREER APPLICATION

1. Assume you have sent out your résumé to many companies. What information should you keep near your telephone and why?

2. Your first interview is with a small local company. What kind of information should you seek about this company and where could you expect to find it?

3. Name at least two ways in which you can practice for the interview and receive feedback on your performance.

4. What nonverbal messages do you think your appearance and demeanor send? How could you make sure your nonverbal messages are working for you?

5. Why is it important to make frequent eye contact with an interviewer?

6. What is your greatest fear of what you might do or what might happen to you during an employment interview? How can you overcome your fears?

7. Should you be candid with an interviewer when asked about your weaknesses?

8. How can you clarify vague questions?

9. Select three get-acquainted questions. Write each question on a separate sheet and then write an answer to it.

10. Select three crystal-ball and future questions. Write each question on a separate sheet and then answer it.

11. Select three squirm questions. Write each question on a separate sheet and then answer it.

12. Select two money questions. Write each question on a separate sheet and answer it.

13. Select three questions for you to ask. Write each on a separate sheet and answer it.

14. Select three illegal questions. Write each question on a separate sheet and then answer it.

15. Why is it important not to accept a job immediately after getting an offer?

SOLUTIONS

Career Application

1. Keep near the telephone a list of all the positions for which you have applied. You should also keep a copy of your résumé, references, a calendar, and a note pad. Many companies use telephone screening interviews to select those individuals whom they wish to interview in person.

2. For a small local company, you can probably find information in the local library. The reference librarian and newspapers might be helpful. The Better Business Bureau and the chamber of commerce could also provide information. Checking out the company's advertising as well as its competition will tell you about its current focus. Best of all would be talks with current or previous employees.

3. You could conduct a mock interview with a friend. Recording the interview with a video recorder or a tape recorder will provide feedback. If no friend is available, practice responding to typical questions and record your answers.

4. Do you think you send nonverbal messages that suggest confidence and success? To gain feedback, you could ask a friend or relative to be candid with you about your appearance and demeanor.

5. In this culture frequent eye contact suggests than an individual is interested and is trustworthy.

6. Some students fear that they will choke and start a coughing fit. Others fear drawing a blank and not being able to answer a question at all. Some worry that they will drop something or stumble over a rug or perspire profusely. Your fears may be different. You can overcome most fears by preparing thoroughly for the interview. Conduct mock interviews. Rehearse answers to all the favorite questions generally asked at interviews. Practice deep breathing.

7. Never be candid about your weaknesses! No one was ever hired for a job because of his or her weaknesses. If pressed to name a weakness, name a strength disguised as weakness, identify a corrected weakness, cite an unrelated skill or a learning objective, or simply state that you have no weaknesses that would affect your ability to perform this job.

8. If asked vague questions, you can respond, "Would you please clarify what you mean by _____." Or say, "By _____, do you mean _____?"

9–14. Questions and answers will vary.

15. You'll want to consider a job offer carefully. Every opportunity has pluses and minuses. You may have additional questions or concerns that must be resolved before accepting the position. Give yourself time to think about this big decision. No reasonable company would deny you a chance to think it over.

Appendix A

160 FREQUENTLY MISSPELLED WORDS

absence	desirable	independent	prominent
accommodate	destroy	interrupt	qualify
acknowledgment	development	indispensable	quantity
achieve	disappoint	irrelevant	questionnaire
across	dissatisfied	itinerary	receipt
adequate	division	judgment	receive
advisable	efficient	knowledgeable	recognize
analyze	embarrass	legitimate	recommendation
annually	emphasis	library	referred
appointment	emphasize	license	regarding
argument	employee	maintenance	remittance
automatically	envelope	manageable	representative
bankruptcy	equipped	manufacturer	restaurant
becoming	especially	mileage	schedule
beneficial	evidently	miscellaneous	secretary
budget	exaggerate	mortgage	separate
business	excellent	necessary	similar
calendar	exempt	nevertheless	sincerely
canceled	existence	ninety	software
catalog	extraordinary	ninth	succeed
changeable	familiar	noticeable	sufficient
column	fascinate	occasionally	supervisor
committee	feasible	occurred	surprise
congratulate	February	offered	tenant
conscience	fiscal	omission	therefore
conscious	foreign	omitted	thorough
consecutive	forty	opportunity	though
consensus	fourth	opposite	through
consistent	friend	ordinarily	truly
control	genuine	paid	undoubtedly
convenient	government	pamphlet	unnecessarily
correspondence	grammar	permanent	usable
courteous	grateful	permitted	usage
criticize	guarantee	pleasant	using
decision	harass	practical	usually
deductible	height	prevalent	valuable
defendant	hoping	privilege	volume
definitely	immediate	probably	weekday
dependent	incidentally	procedure	writing
describe	incredible	profited	yield

CONFUSING WORDS

accede: to agree or consent

exceed: over a limit

accept: to receive

except: to exclude; (prep) but

adverse: unfavorable, antagonistic

averse: unwilling, opposed to

advice: suggestion, opinion

advise: to counsel or recommend

affect: to influence

effect: (n) outcome, result; (v) to bring about, to create

all ready: prepared

already: by this time

all right: satisfactory

alright: [unacceptable variant spelling]

altar: structure for worship

alter: to change

appraise: to estimate

apprise: to inform

ascent: (n) rising or going up

assent: (v) to agree or consent

assure: to promise

ensure: to make certain

insure: to protect from loss

ascent: rising, going up

assent: agree or consent

capital: (n) city that is seat of government; wealth of an individual; (adj) foremost in importance; punishable by death

capitol: building used by state lawmakers

cereal: breakfast food

serial: arranged in sequence

cite: to quote; to summon

site: location

sight: (n) a view; (v) to see

coarse: rough texture

course: a route; part of a meal; a unit of learning

complement: that which completes

compliment: to praise or flatter

conscience: regard for fairness

conscious: aware

council: governing body

counsel: to give advice; advice

credible: believable

creditable good enough for praise or esteem; reliable

desert: (n) arid land; (v) to abandon

dessert: sweet food

device: invention or mechanism

devise: to design or arrange

disburse: to pay out

disperse: to scatter widely

elicit: to draw out

illicit: unlawful

envelop: (v) to wrap, surround, or conceal

envelope: (n) a container for a written message

every day: each single day

everyday: ordinary

farther: a greater distance

further: additional

flair: natural talent, aptitude

flare: to blaze up or spread out

formally: in a formal manner

formerly: in the past

grate: (v) to reduce to small particles; to cause irritation; (n) a frame of crossed bars blocking a passage

great: (adj) large in size; numerous; eminent or distinguished

hole: an opening

whole: complete

imply: to suggest indirectly

infer: to reach a conclusion

lean: (v) to rest against; to incline toward; (adj) not fat

lien: (n) a legal right or claim to property

liable: legally responsible

libel: damaging written statement

loose: not fastened

lose: to misplace

miner: person working in a mine

minor: a lesser item; person under age

patience: calm perseverance

patients: people receiving medical treatment

persecute: to oppress

prosecute: to sue

personal:	private, individual	*than:*	conjunction showing comparison
personnel:	employees	*then:*	adverb meaning "at that time"
plaintiff:	a party to a lawsuit	*their:*	possessive form of they
plaintive:	mournful	*there:*	at that place or point
populace:	(n) the masses; population of a place	*they're:*	contraction of they are
populous:	(adj) densely populated	*to:*	a preposition; the sign of the infinitive
precede:	to go before	*too:*	an adverb meaning "also" or "to an excessive extent"
proceed:	to continue		
precedence:	priority	*two:*	a number
precedents:	events used as an example	*vary:*	to change
principal:	(n) capital sum; school official; (adj) chief	*very:*	extremely
		waiver:	abandonment of a claim
principle:	rule of action	*waver:*	to shake or fluctuate
reality:	that which is real	*weather:*	(n) the state of the atmosphere; (v) to bear up against
realty:	real estate		
stationary:	immovable	*whether:*	an introduction to alternatives
stationery:	writing material		

Appendix B

SOLUTIONS TO CAREER APPLICATION CASES

Chapter 7

Current date

Ms. Sharon Taylor
Title Guaranty Company
3401 Providence Avenue
Anchorage, AK, 99508

Dear Sharon:

Two agents' packages will be sent to you October 6. Because you need these immediately, we are using Federal Express.

We are able to offer new agents a 60/40 commission split. Two new agreement forms show this commission ratio. When you sign new agents, have them fill in both forms.

When you send me an executed agency agreement, please tell me what agency package was assigned to the agent. We need this information to distribute commissions promptly.

Call if you have any questions.

Very truly yours,

*All solutions illustrate one way the problem could be solved. Other good solutions are also possible.

Chapter 8

TO: Staff Members   DATE: Current

FROM: Pauline M. Wu, Director
            Human Resources

SUBJECT: OPEN ENROLLMENT FOR BENEFIT PROGRAMS

Please examine the enclosed open enrollment package so that you may make any changes before November 29.

Your decisions about coverage are very important because they affect your well-being and that of your family. You'll want to study the choices carefully, since your decisions will remain in effect until the next open enrollment period one year from now.

Although most of the program is unchanged, we have made the following improvements:

- Dental coverage has been expanded; you now have two carriers from which to choose.

- Life insurance options increase coverage for family members.

- Medical coverage now includes a basic plan and a prudent buyer plan.

Representatives from Human Resources will be available to answer your questions in the East Lounge at the following times:

Tuesday, November 19   3 p.m. to 5 p.m.
Wednesday, November 20   7 a.m. to 9 a.m.
Friday, November 22   11 a.m. to 1 p.m.

Remember, this is the only time you may make changes in your benefits package, other than a qualified change in family status.

For employees making changes, complete the enclosed form and return it to Human Resources by November 29.

Enclosure

Chapter 9

Current date

Mrs. Thomas Dobbin
2950 King Street
Alexandria, VA 22313

Dear Mrs. Dobbin:

You're right! Instead of starting a new subscription, Mrs. Dobbin, we should have extended your current subscription to *Home Computing.* Beginning in January, you will receive issues for 14 additional months—a bonus of two free months.

Apparently, when you ordered magazines through your son's school program, your name was recorded as Patricia R. Dobbin. Your current subscription is listed under Mrs. Thomas Dobbin. Therefore, our computers started a new account for you. That's why you are receiving two issues each month.

You may receive one or two more double issues, but you're not being charged for them. Please share these magazines with your friends or neighbors. Although you ordered 12 months of *Home Computing,* we're giving you 14 months—just to let you know how important your satisfaction is to us.

Sincerely,

Roger W. Hobart
Circulation Manager

Chapter 10

Current date

Mr. James Ferraro
Vice President, Sales
Copy World
2510 East Pine Street
Tulsa, OK 74160-2510

Dear Mr. Ferraro:

The four CopyMaster Model S-5 photocopiers that we purchased three months ago are inadequate for our volume of copying.

Although we told your salesperson, Kevin Woo, that we averaged 3,000 copies a day, he recommended the Model S-5. This model appears to be the wrong choice for our heavy use, and we're disappointed in its performance. Therefore, we'd like to trade in our four S-5 copiers (about $2,500 each as shown on the enclosed invoice) on the purchase of two Model S-55 copiers (about $13,500 each).

When I discussed this possibility with your district manager, Keith Sumner, he said that we would be charged 50 percent depreciation if we traded in the four S-5 copiers. That amounts to $5,000, a considerable sum for three months of copier use. We think a depreciation rate of 20 percent is more reasonable. Your company would profit in three ways:

1. The S-5 machines were used a short time, and they can be resold easily.
2. You'll be making a sizable profit when we purchase two Model S-55 copiers.
3. Your service technicians will save time by making fewer trips to repair our overworked S-5 machines.

We purchased the Model S-5 copiers in good faith on the recommendation of your salesperson. It is your responsibility to help us secure the proper model for our needs.

Please approve my request to trade in four CopyMaster Model S-5s for a value of $8,000 (allowing for 20 percent depreciation) toward the purchase of two CopyMaster Model S-5s. Just initial this letter showing your approval, and return it to me in the enclosed envelope. I'll work out the details of the new purchase with your salesperson.

Sincerely yours,

Tracy W. Quincy or Your Name
Manager

Enclosure

Chapter 11

Current date

Ms. Sherry A. Lopez
President, Alpha Gamma Sigma
1150 Del Ray Avenue
Miami, FL 33178

Dear Sherry:

It's good to learn that Miami-Dade has an active student business honorary, and I appreciate your invitation to speak at its February meeting on the topic of careers in public accounting.

On February 17, the day of your meeting, I will be in Lake Worth representing our firm at a three-day seminar about recent changes in tax laws related to corporations. Since many of our clients file corporate tax returns, this seminar is particularly important to my organization and my clients.

Our local Miami CPA organization has a list of speakers who are prepared to make presentations on various topics. In consulting this list, I found that Paul Rosenberg, a Miami CPA with 14 years of experience, is our expert on careers in accountancy and preparation for the CPA examination. I checked with him and found that he could address your organization if you will call him before January 28. His telephone number is 390-1930.

I'm very pleased that you have taken a leadership role in your campus business honorary, Sherry, and you may be sure that you can call on me for any future assistance in developing appropriate programs.

Sincerely,

Nelson R. Raymond

Chapter 12

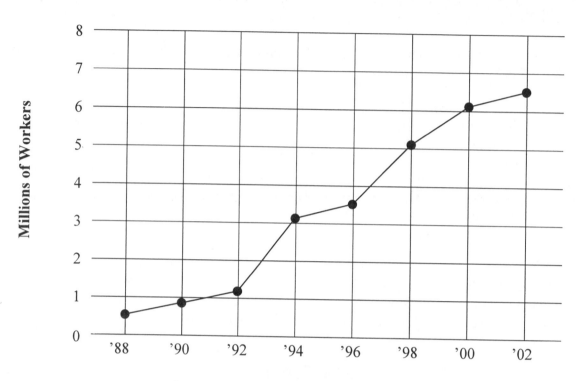

**Computer Workers in Environments With
Indirect Lighting, 1988 through 2002**

Conclusions

Based on the research I have conducted, the following conclusions may be drawn about direct and indirect lighting for workers in computer environments:

1. Management and workers must think that indirect lighting is better than direct lighting, since the number of computer workers in indirect lighting environments has grown steadily from fewer than a half million workers to over 6.5 million in the past 14 years.

2. In a study of 200 computer workers conducted by Cornell University, indirect lighting had a positive effect on the performance, satisfaction, and visual health of participants.

3. Overall, 72 percent of the participants preferred indirect lighting to standard lighting, finding it more pleasant, more comfortable, and more likable.

4. Although workers in the study preferred indirect lighting, the lighting seemed to produce loss in production of 15 to 20 minutes per day. Apparently, indirect lighting causes workers to slow down or to make mistakes that reduce their overall productivity somewhat.

Recommendations

As a result of my research and analysis, I submit the following recommendations in regard to the installation of indirect lighting in computer environments:

1. The company, 21st Century Insurance, should install indirect lighting when it remodels offices where computers are used extensively.

2. Because we can expect slightly reduced productivity to accompany indirect lighting, I recommend that we treat this reduced productivity as a small price to pay for improving the health and happiness of our computer workers.

3. If reduced productivity as a result of indirect lighting seems significant, I recommend that we ask computer workers to search for ways to maintain or improve their productivity after indirect lighting is installed.

Chapter 13 - Outline Revision

Outline for Progress Report

I.   Introduction
   A. Identify report specifically
   B. Describe purpose
   C. Preview how report is organized

II. Background
   A. Tell why report is necessary
   B. Describe methods for collecting data

III. Work completed
   A. Internal programs and recruitment
      1. Videotapes
      2. In-house seminars
      3. Intensive language and culture courses
      4. Emphasis on recruiting globally oriented young employees
   B. External programs
      1. Short- and long-term assignments abroad offered by six model companies
      2. Intensive programs at specialized schools

IV. Work to be completed
   A. Internal programs
      1. Evaluate training videos
      2. Interview consultant for in-house seminar
   B. External programs
      1. Evaluate literature from specialized schools
      2. Conduct telephone interviews with U.S. companies about their programs

V.   Problems
   A. Not being able to reach busy executives for interviews
   B. Report will include only the data collected before deadline

VI. Completion
   A. Cutoff date for collection of data
   B. Date when final report will be submitted

Chapter 14

1. Letter of transmittal - optional - Ramon?

2. Abstract or executive summary - optional - Ramon?

3. Introduction - Ramon
   Brief discussion of proposal and benefits of research

4. Background, problem - Ramon
   Description of problem and how this research can solve it

5. Proposal, plan, schedule - Sally
   Research methods (focus groups, questionnaires)
   Description of how the data will be gathered, tabulated, and interpreted
   Monitoring methods
   Timetable

6. Staffing - Amanda
   Credentials (résumés) of project leaders
   Staff description
   Discussion of new computer software

7. Budget - Tom
   Hourly or total cost figures
   Deadline for costs submitted

8. Authorization - optional - Ramon?
   Request for approval

9. Appendix - your name
   Samples of other customer satisfaction surveys
   List of satisfied customers

Chapter 15 - Outline Revision

Title: Using Tools and Equipment Safely

Purpose: To convince new construction workers that safety begins with them.

I. Introduction
  A. Gain attention of audience.
  B. Get audience involved.
  C. Establish your credibility.
  D. Preview the main points.
TRANSITION

II. Tools
  A. Hand tools
    1. Use every tool for its designed purpose only.
    2. Keep hand tools in peak condition: sharp, clean, oiled, and dressed.
    3. Don't use "cheaters" to force tools beyond their capacity.
    4. Don't abuse tools, such as using a wrench as a pry bar.
  B. Portable power tools
    1. Don't operate unless you are trained and authorized to do so.
    2. Use proper eye protection.
    3. Keep all moving parts directed away from your body.
    4. Never touch a part unless its power source is disconnected.
TRANSITION

III. Equipment
  A. General suggestions
    1. Inspect all equipment before using.
    2. Know the limitations of the equipment you use; do not exceed them.
    3. Do not interchange equipment with other contractors without permission.
  B. Safety belts/harnesses
    1. Wear belts when working on sloping roofs, flat roofs without handrails, any suspended platform or stage, any scaffold, ladders near edge of roofs, and all elevated work. [All the examples here could be lettered and listed vertically.]
    2. Wear belts correctly. (Demonstrate.)
  C. Welding and burning. Contact our supervisor before performing these tasks.
  D. Compressed air
    1. Check hoses and couplings daily before use.
    2. Never crimp, couple, or uncouple a pressurized hose. Shut off valve and bleed down the hose.
    3. Do not allow pressure to exceed 30 psi when cleaning workbenches and machinery.
    4. Keep hoses off the ground or floor wherever they interfere with walkways, roads, and so forth.
TRANSITION

IV. Conclusion
  A. Summarize the main points.
  B. Provide a final focus.
  C. Encourage questions.

Chapter 16 - Conclusions

Possible Conclusions to Be Drawn From Analysis of Two Résumés

1.   Résumés of recent graduates should fill one page and be arranged attractively.

2.   Consistency in headings and graphic highlighting—bullets, underlines, indenting, capital letters, white space—will enhance readability and comprehension.

3.   Some résumé formats look more professional than others. Look at many model résumés. Experiment with different designs.

4.   First-person pronouns are not used. Use concise wording that avoids "I."

5.   The best résumés sell candidates' talents; they don't just list job duties. Use action verbs in specific statements to describe achievements.

6.   Recruiters are most interested in seeing job skills that relate to the jobs they have to fill. Candidates should emphasize the skills and traits that will be useful for a targeted job.